The State and Politics in Japan

D1264941

The State and Politics in Japan

Ian Neary

polity

Copyright © Ian Neary 2002

The right of Ian Neary to be identified as author of this work has been asserted in accordance with the Copyright, Designs and Patents Act 1988.

First published in 2002 by Polity Press in association with Blackwell Publishers Ltd

Reprinted 2005

Polity Press
65 Bridge Street
Cambridge CB2 1UR, UK

Polity Press
350 Main Street
Maldon, MA 02148, USA

All rights reserved. Except for the quotation of short passages for the purposes of criticism and review, no part of this publication may be reproduced, stored in a retrieval system, or transmitted, in any form or by any means, electronic, mechanical, photocopying, recording or otherwise, without the prior permission of the publisher.

Except in the United States of America, this book is sold subject to the condition that it shall not, by way of trade or otherwise, be lent, re-sold, hired out, or otherwise circulated without the publisher's prior consent in any form of binding or cover other than that in which it is published and without a similar condition including this condition being imposed on the subsequent purchaser.

A catalogue record for this book is available from the British Library.

Library of Congress Cataloging-in-Publication Data

Neary, Ian.
    The state and politics in Japan / Ian Neary.
        p.   cm.
    Includes bibliographical references and index.
        ISBN 0-7456-2133-3 – ISBN 0-7456-2134-1 (pbk.)
        1. Japan – Politics and government – 1868–   I. Title.
    DS881.9 .N43 2002
                                            2002001671

Typeset in 10.5 on 12 pt Times New Roman
by SNP Best-set Typesetter Ltd., Hong Kong
Printed and bound in Great Britain by Marston Book Services Limited, Oxford

This book is printed on acid-free paper.

For further information on Polity, visit our website: www.polity.co.uk

Contents

Acknowledgements

Recently, I moved rooms within the university and decided to use the opportunity to throw away some of the papers that had accumulated over the years. I was surprised and somewhat alarmed to discover among the files many well-known articles ordered through inter-library loan which I had carefully annotated but which I could not remember reading. Many of the ideas that turned up in the lectures and seminars I have given while teaching in Huddersfield, Newcastle and Essex universities had originated in these articles, which I had read and then squirrelled away. This book is a product of reading all those articles and many other books over the last twenty years in preparation for classes on Japanese politics. As such, it owes an enormous amount to previous writers. As far as possible I have acknowledged my sources in the text, but, as I discovered when I moved rooms, there are many sources of ideas of which I am not fully aware. I apologize in advance to those whose ideas I have appropriated without acknowledgement.

Though often overshadowed by its American counterpart, there is a thriving academic community working on Japan in the UK. Since 1975 they have met annually as the British Association of Japanese Studies, and this conference has provided us with an arena for the exchange of ideas about Japanese history and politics. Since 1991 a Japanese Politics Colloquium has convened each September, bringing together academics and others to reflect on recent trends and research in Japanese politics. These meetings have been an important source of new perspectives on political life in Japan, and have influenced how and what I think about politics there.

Institutions have been important too. As mentioned above, I have worked in three British universities, in Huddersfield, Newcastle and Essex, where successive cohorts of students have made me think more carefully about what I say about Japan. Numerous colleagues in these places have supported or challenged my ideas, forcing my thinking to evolve. In Japan I have developed a close association with colleagues in the Department of Law, Kyushu University, and numerous visits there have given me the, possibly illusory, feeling that I was getting closer to Japanese political life as I heard papers and overheard conversations about the practice of politics. I am grateful to all those in these institutions who have inadvertently contributed to the development of this book.

So far I have avoided thanking specific individuals for their contribution to the work that follows on the grounds that the list would be either too long or unfairly omit those who have been important. However, two people – Robert Jones and Oishi Yutaka – read the manuscript in its final draft and made numerous suggestions that both improved readability and eliminated errors. None of the above has been directly involved in the process of writing anything that follows and they are not responsible for any of the facts or opinions. However, Suzuko, Rose and Tomas have accompanied me on my expeditions to Japan and played a key role in influencing if not the content then the timing of the writing of what follows. Despite that, I am grateful to them. They supported and interrupted in equal proportions.

St Osyth, Essex

The author and publishers would like to thank all those who have granted permission to reproduce copyright material. Every effort has been made to trace the copyright holders, but if any have been inadvertently overlooked, the publishers will be pleased to make the necessary arrangements at the first opportunity.

Glossary of Abbreviations and Japanese Terms

amakudari 'descent from heaven'; practice of senior bureaucrats to take up posts in industry following retirement in their mid-50s, often in companies they used to supervise

AMPO abbreviation of Nichibei Anzen Hoshō Jōyaku, US–Japan Security Treaty

APEC Asia Pacific Economic Cooperation, formed in 1989, now consisting of 21 countries and regions from North and South America, East Asia (including Russia) and Australasia

ASEAN Association of South East Asian Nations formed in 1975 by Indonesia, the Philippines, Thailand, Singapore and Malaysia, later joined by Brunei, Vietnam, Laos, Myanmar and Cambodia

ASEM Asia Europe Meeting, 7 countries from ASEAN plus the 15 EU countries and Japan, South Korea and China

Aum Shinrikyō new new-religion based on a mix of Buddhism, Hinduism, Christianity and Nostradamus. Followers launched an attack on the Tokyo metro on 20 March 1995 which killed 12 and injured thousands of people

BLL Buraku Liberation League, formed 1955

CCPR United Nations International Covenant on Civil and Political Rights

CEDAW United Nations Convention on the Ending of Discrimination Against Women

CERD United Nations Convention on the Elimination of all forms of Racial Discrimination

CGP Clean Government Party, Kōmeitō

chō   town, local government unit with more than 10,000 but fewer than 50,000 residents

Chongryun   abbreviation for Chaeilbon Chosonin Ryonhaphoe, the North Korean-oriented General Association for Korean Residents in Japan

Chōshū   south of the main island of Japan, produced many leaders of the Meiji restoration. Now part of Yamaguchi prefecture

Chūritsurōren   centrist labour union federation allied with no party, joined with Dōmei in 1987 to form Rengō

daimyō   feudal lords who dominated during the Tokugawa period

Dōmei   abbreviation for Zennihon Rōdō Sōdōmei, Japan Confederation of Labor, the centre-left union federation

Dōmei Yuai Kaigi   organization created to support the DSP when Dōmei merged into Rengō

DPJ   Democratic Party of Japan (Minshutō), formed just before the lower house election of 1996, composed of remnants of the JSP, DSP and some defectors from the LDP Takeshita faction

Edo   political capital of Tokugawa shogun rule, renamed Tokyo in 1869

EEOL   Equal Employment Opportunities Law, 1985 and 1997

EHI   Employers' Health Insurance

ESCR   United Nations International Covenant on Economic, Social and Cultural Rights

FDI   Foreign Direct Investment

FILP   Fiscal Investment and Loan Programme

G7   seven major industrial countries which have held an annual summit meeting since 1975

GDP   Gross Domestic Product

genrō   small group of senior statesmen from Satsuma and Chōshu who played a critical role in politics between 1890 and 1940, acting as a link between the emperor and government. They intervened in all major political decisions but especially on the choice of a new prime minister

gyōsei shidō   administrative guidance

gyūho shinjutsu   cow walk tactic: stalling strategy used by opposition parties to delay parliamentary procedure

habatsu   faction

han   semi-autonomous domains ruled over by *daimyō*

HC   House of Councillors, upper house, Sangiin

Heisei   'Achieving Peace': reign name of emperor Akihito which began in 1989

Hinomaru   the rising sun flag: though widely used from the 1880s, it was only formally adopted amid great controversy as the national flag in summer 1999

Hizen   domain in the north of Kyushu, one of the four which produced leaders of the Meiji restoration

HR   House of Representatives, lower house, Shūgiin

IMF   International Monetary Fund

IMRA   Imperial Military Reserve Association, formed in 1910 to encourage military spirit among former conscript soldiers, later organized youth and women's branches and an important pro-war pressure group in the 1930s

ippanshoku   'general work': the clerical career track in Japanese corporations

IRAA   Imperial Rule Assistance Association founded in 1940 to incorporate all political groups and form a 'new political structure'. It never succeeded in becoming a mass political party although it did operate as an instrument of political control for most of the Pacific War

JCCI   Japan Chamber of Commerce and Industry, Nisshō

JCP   Japan Communist Party

JDB   Japan Development Bank

JETRO   Japan External Trade Organization

JFBA   Japan Federation of Bar Associations

Jichirō   abbreviation for Zennihon Jichidantai Rōdōkumiai, All Japan Prefectural and Municipal Workers Union, the local government workers' union

Jiyūtō   Liberal Party

JNP   Japan New Party

JNR   Japan National Railways, from 1987 JR

JSP   Japanese Socialist Party

JTU   Japan Teachers' Union, Nikkyōso

kaishin   reform

Kantō   Area around and including Tokyo

Kasumigaseki   Area in Central Tokyo where all the ministries are located

Keidanren   Abbreviation of Keizai Dantai Rengōkai, Federation of Economic Associations

Keizai Dōyūkai   Committee for Economic Development, business organization which represents both big business and small and medium-size enterprises

Kenseikai   constitutional association, formed in October 1916; it was one of the two main parliamentary parties (along with the Seiyūkai) in the era of Taishō democracy. It reconstituted itself as the Minseitō in October 1927

Kimigayo   song widely adopted in schools and elsewhere from the 1890s as a national anthem, but not formally adopted as such until summer 1999

KMT   Kuomintang (Chinese) National Party. Fought the Chinese communists until forced to withdraw to Taiwan in 1949

kōenkai   support group for local or national politician which is separate from the party office

kokkai   parliament

Kokuhonsha   founded in 1924 it claimed 200,000 members and 170 branches at its peak, strongly right wing, led by Hiranuma Kiichirō, it was disbanded in 1936

Kokurō   abbreviation of Kokutetsu Rōdō Kumiai, the railway workers' union

Kokusuikai   National Essence Association, right-wing group active in the 1920s and 1930s

kokutai   national polity, term used particularly in period 1890–1945 to denote the mystical essence of the imperial Japanese state

Kōmeitō   Clean Government Party, constituted in 1964 as the political arm of Sōka Gakkai. In the early 1970s it ended its formal link but still relies on it for most of its electoral support

ku   ward, local government electoral district

LDP   Liberal Democratic Party, formed 1955

MAFF   Ministry of Agriculture, Forestry and Fisheries

MCA   Management and Coordination Agency

Meiji   'Enlightened Rule': posthumous name of the emperor who ruled Japan from 1867 until his death in 1912, also the name for the period 1868–1912

MFA   Ministry of Foreign Affairs

MHA   Ministry of Home Affairs, in 2001 incorporated into the Ministry of Public Management, Home Affairs, Posts and Telecommunications

MHW   Ministry of Health and Welfare, from 2001 part of the Ministry of Health, Labour and Welfare

Mindan   Abbreviation of Zainihon Daikanminkoku-mindan, the South Korean-oriented Korean Residents' Union in Japan

minponshugi   theory developed in 1910–30 that the welfare of the people was, or should be, the basic concern of government even though sovereignty resided in the emperor

minseiiin   welfare officers, semi-official volunteers who are the front-line of welfare administration

Minseitō   one of the two main parties in the period 1900–45

Minshutō   Democratic Party of Japan

MITI   Ministry of International Trade and Industry

MoC   Ministry of Construction

MoE   Ministry of Education

MoF   Ministry of Finance

MoL   Ministry of Labour, from 2001 part of the Ministry of Health, Labour and Welfare

MOSS   Market-Oriented Sector Specific, series of talks held between the US and Japanese governments to eliminate non-tariff barriers to trade in 1986

MoT   Ministry of Transport, from 2001 part of the Ministry of Land, Infrastructure and Transport

MPT   Ministry of Posts and Telecommunications, from 2001 incorporated into the Ministry of Public Management, Home Affairs, Posts and Telecommunications

Naimushō   Ministry of the Interior, formed in 1873 with a broad remit to control most aspects of the lives of citizens; dismantled in 1947

NCP   New Conservative Party, formed in summer 2000 when Ozawa and the Liberal Party left the coalition with the LDP

NFP   New Frontier Party, Shinshintō

NGO   non-government organization

NHI   National Health Insurance

NHRI   National Human Rights Institution

nihonjinron   genre of pseudo-social scientific writing which emphasizes Japan's supposed cultural uniqueness

Nikkeiren   abbreviation for Nihon Keieisha Dantai Renmei, Japan Federation of Employers' Associations

NLC   New Liberal Club

Nōkyō   abbreviation for Nōgyō Kyōdō Kumiai, the Agricultural Cooperatives' Association

NTT   Nippon Telephone and Telegraph

ODA   Overseas Development Aid

OECD Organization for Economic Cooperation and Development

Okurashō Ministry of Finance, from 2001 known as Zaimushō

PAB Pharmaceutical Affairs Bureau

PARC Policy Affairs Research Council, main arena for debate on policy matters within the LDP

PLO Palestine Liberation Organization

PMO Prime Minister's Office

PR Proportional Representation

PRC People's Republic of China

DSP Democratic Socialist Party

Rengō Japanese Trade Union Council, the national centre for unions formed in November 1989

RoC Republic of China (Taiwan)

RoK Republic of Korea (South)

samurai elite social group during the Tokugawa era, officially dissolved as a class in the 1870s

Sangiin House of Councillors

Satsuma region in south Kyushu, now part of Kagoshima; one of the four regions which produced the leaders of the Meiji restoration

SCAP Supreme Commander of the Allied Powers, term used both for General MacArthur and General Headquarters during the occupation

SDF Self Defence Forces

SDP Social Democratic Party, name adopted by JSP from January 1996

seimu jikan Parliamentary Vice-Minister

Seiyūkai one of the two main political parties, founded in 1900 and active until it dissolved into the IRAA in 1940

Shaminren abbreviation of Shakai Minshu Rengō, Social Democratic League, formed in 1977; it never had more than 4 HR members and took part in the coalition arrangements of the 1990s; its members joined the DPJ in 1996

shi city, local government unit with more than 50,000 residents

shingikai Advisory Council

Shinseitō Japan Renewal Party, party formed by defectors from LDP in June 1993, later merged along with DSP, Kōmeitō and JNP to form Shinshintō in December 1994

Shinshintō   New Frontier Party, formed in December 1994, split into six parties in December 1997 several of which ended up joining the DPJ in April 1998, with the notable exception of Ozawa's Liberal Party

Shintō Heiwa   New Party Peace, name adopted by former Kōmeitō members of HR when Shinshintō collapsed in 1997

Shintō   Pantheistic religion with roots deep in Japanese tradition

(Shintō) Sakigake   (New Party) Harbinger, formed in June 1993 by Takemura Masayoshi from LDP members, most of whom joined the DPJ in September 1996 (though not Takemura)

Shogun   Military rulers of Japan from the twelfth to nineteenth centuries

Shōwa   'Illustrious Peace': posthumous name of the emperor who ruled Japan 1926–89

Shūgiin   House of Representatives

Shuntō   Annual Spring Offensive, in which unions coordinate their demands on employers

SII   Special Impediments Initiative, discussion held in 1989 between the US and Japanese governments to eliminate non-tariff barriers to trade

SMD   Single Member District

SME   Small and Medium-sized Enterprises

sōgōshoku   comprehensive work, the managerial career track in Japanese corporations

Sōhyō   left-leaning union federation, merged with Rengō in 1989

Sōka Gakkai   major new religion with strong Buddhist connections, the parent body to Kōmeitō

son   village, local government unit of fewer than 10,000 residents

STA   Science and Technology Agency

Taishō   'Great Justice': posthumous name of the emperor who ruled 1912–26

Taiyōtō   Sun Party, party led by Hata from December 1996, most of whose members joined the DPJ the following April

Tanrō   abbreviation for Nihon Tankō Rōdō Kumiai, the Japan Miners' Union

tarento   entertainer/celebrity who enters politics

Tosa   domain in the south of Shikoku, now part of Kōchi, which generated leaders who played a prominent part in the Meiji restoration and subsequent politics

USSR   Union of Soviet Socialist Republics

Yasukuni   Shintō shrine in Tokyo dedicated to Japan's military war dead

zaibatsu   major business conglomerations – Mitsui, Mitsubishi, Sumitomo, Yasuda – which acquired massive influence in the 1930s; attempts to dissolve them during the occupation were only partially successful

Zaimushō   Ministry of Finance

Zenkoku Kakushinkon   National Reform Group, organization of supporters (not members) of the JCP

Zenrōren   National Labour Federation (of JCP-supporting unions)

minister in 1947–8. During the 1950s he was on the right wing of the party and founded the DSP in 1960, which he chaired until his retirement in 1967.

Nosaka Sanzō (1892–1993)   Union activist who visited London to study, where he joined the Communist Party. He played key roles in the JCP in the 1920s until he fled to Moscow in 1931 where he played an important role in the Comintern. From 1940 to 1945 he was based in China and returned to Japan in 1946 where he was a moderate within the reformed JCP. He was purged in 1950. He remained Chairman Emeritus of the JCP until 1990 when he was expelled from the party for activities in the 1930s.

Obuchi Keizō (1937–2000)   Member of HR from 1968 and member of the Tanaka/Takeshita faction. Served in a number of senior positions in the party and government until he succeeded Hashimoto as prime minister in August 1998. Died suddenly in April 2000.

Ogi Chikage (aka Hayashi Hiroko, 1933–)   Following an early career as a dancer in the Takarazuka, she entered the HC in 1980. During the 1990s she left the LDP and moved through Shinseitō, Shinshintō and then Ozawa's Liberal Party. When this split in summer 2000, she became head of the New Conservative Party. She was minister for Land, Infrastructure and Transport in Koizumi's cabinet.

Ohira Masayoshi (1910–80)   After working in the MoF he was elected to HR in 1952 and served as foreign minister 1962–4 and at MITI 1968–70. In 1971 he took over the Ikeda faction and stood for leader of the LDP in 1972, 1973 and 1976 before success in 1978. His position was weakened by factional rivalry which resulted in two elections within twelve months; during the latter campaign he died.

Ozawa Ichirō (1941–)   Member of the HR from 1969, when he 'inherited' his father's seat. A leading member of the Tanaka/Takeshita faction and rival of Hashimoto. His split from the LDP caused its fall from power in 1993 and the formation of the Shinseitō and Shinshintō. His attempts to create a broad church conservative rival to the LDP broke down in late 1996, since when he has been leader of the Liberal Party.

Park Chung-hee (1917–79)   Leader of a military coup in South Korea in 1961 which put the army at the centre of government until the 1990s. Party leader from 1961, he was assassinated by army colleagues in 1979.

Saionji Kimmochi (1849–1940)   Prime minister twice in the 1900s; longest-lived member of the *genrō*.

Satō Eisaku (1901–75)   Brother of Kishi, he entered the bureaucracy in 1924 and the HR in 1948. Held several key party posts and was minister at the MoF 1958–60 and MITI 1961–2. Served as prime minister from November 1964 to June 1972. Awarded Nobel Peace Prize in 1974 for his anti-nuclear diplomacy amid considerable controversy.

Shidehara Kijūrō (1872–1951)   Bureaucrat in MFA from 1896, but critical of wartime policy, which made him acceptable to SCAP and he served as prime minister from October 1945 to April 1946. Elected to the HR in 1947, he was speaker of the HR until his death.

Shii Kazuo (1954–)   Chairperson of the Executive Committee of the JCP, elected to the HR in 1993. He has pioneered a more moderate line and created a more voter-friendly image for the party.

Suzuki Zenko (1911–)   Worked in the fishing industry until elected to the HR in 1947 as a JSP candidate. In the 1950s he switched to the LDP and served in several cabinet posts in the 1960s and '70s. He took over as party leader and prime minister after Ohira died in July 1980 and served until 1982.

Takemura Masayoshi (1934–)   Elected to the HR in July 1986 as a member of the LDP, he left the party in June 1993 to found the Sakigake and played a key role in the coalition governments of 1993–8.

Takeshita Noboru (1934–2000)   Became a member of HR in 1948 and was chief lieutenant to Tanaka before taking over the faction in 1986, when it was clear he would not recover from a stroke. Served as prime minister 1987–9 when he was forced to resign because of links with the Recruit company. Remained an influential figure throughout the 1990s.

Tanaka Kakuei (1918–93)   Made a personal fortune from his transport and construction companies while pursuing a political career from 1947. Served in various cabinet posts in the 1950s and '60s before beating Fukuda for the post of prime minister in 1972, largely by dint of money. His time at the top was short, as he was forced to resign in 1974 following criticism of his financial dealings. He was also charged with corrupt practices relating to the Lockheed scandal, but he never gave up his ambition to regain the post of prime minister and he created a huge faction. He had a serious stroke in 1985 and died in 1993.

Tanaka Makiko (1944–)   Daughter of Kakuei, first elected to the HR in 1993. An outspoken member of the LDP, she supported Koizumi during his election campaign in 2001 and was rewarded with the post of minister of foreign affairs.

Tokugawa Ieyasu (1543–1616)   From his power base around Edo (Tokyo) he took over on Toyotomi's death as undisputed leader of Japan. After the emperor granted him the title of Shogun in 1603, he created an administrative structure that would ensure his descendants would rule until 1867.

Toyotomi Hideyoshi (1536–98)   From lowly origins he rose swiftly in the service of Oda Nobunaga and defeated all rivals to succeed him. Having united Japan under his wing, he embarked on a campaign to conquer Korea, causing massive destruction and loss of Japanese and Korean lives.

Uno Sōsuke (1922–)   Member of the Nakasone faction since his election to the HR in 1960, he had been Takeshita's foreign minister and took over as prime minister when he resigned. A much publicized sex scandal damaged an already weak LDP in the HC election campaign of July 1989. Uno took responsibility for the party's disastrous performance and resigned in August.

Yoshida Shigeru (1878–1967)   Joined the MFA in 1906 and served in Europe during the 1930s. His criticism of wartime policy made him acceptable to SCAP, which allowed him to take over as prime minister in April 1947. He remained in power until 1954 apart from May 1947–October 1948. He was a powerful force in politics until his death, and his foreign policy line dominated mainstream thinking until the 1990s.

Map 1: East Asia

Map 2: Japan

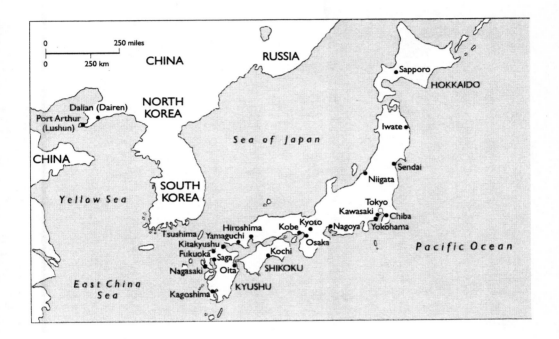

Introduction

In the late 1980s and early 1990s the study of Japan needed no justification. The economy was booming. Not only was there money to be made from knowing about Japan, but it was thought to be necessary to learn from Japan. At the start of the twenty-first century, when the Japanese economy has experienced little to no growth for nearly ten years and bureaucrats, businessmen and politicians are seemingly unable to do anything about it, no one talks about learning from Japan. So one might ask why anyone should need to know about Japanese politics. Given that anyone reading this Introduction has already bought the book or enrolled for the course, further discussion of this point may be redundant, but in case the reader is undecided, and as a way of discussing the approach taken in this book, let us start by trying to answer that question.

First, Japan is and will continue to be important because of its size. With more than 126 million people, it is the eighth most populous country in the world and, as of 1998, had a GDP of $32,370 billion, second only to that of the USA and said to be bigger than the rest of Asia put together. Japan's years of miraculous growth are over. Its economy may have lost some, perhaps all, of its dynamism. It is practically certain that China's GDP will exceed that of Japan at some stage during the twenty-first century, and will possibly overshadow it. But, for the foreseeable future and at least for the next ten years, Japan will still be the dominant Asian economy. What Japanese politicians do with that economic power will continue to be important both regionally and globally.

Secondly, Japan is important as the first non-western power to be accepted in the international order in 1919 and the first non-western economy to 'develop'. There are some excellent texts on Japan's economic development (for example, Francks 1999) and we will make only passing reference to it. More significantly for our purposes, not only did Japan develop economically but it did so at the same time as adopting democratic forms of government. Questions were asked about the extent to which the pre-war government was committed to democratic norms of behaviour and doubts persisted throughout the rest of the twentieth century. At the end of the 1990s, when the idea that 'Asian values' might not be compatible with western democratic practice acquired a degree of respectability, Japan became an important test case for the transferability of such 'democratic' ideas as human rights, equality of opportunity and rule of law.

Thus far, analyses of the Japanese polity have mainly been conducted by those in the mainstream of American scholarship whose vision has been bounded by the parameters of the Cold War. Often they seem to have been keen to locate in Japan evidence of the kind of political behaviour they were familiar with at home or which their political science training had made them sensitive to. They usually found what they were looking for and were able to demonstrate that Japan was one of 'us'. Post-Cold War, there has been a growing plurality of views about Japan. The debate about the nature of politics there has opened up as more detailed studies have been produced by scholars from Japan, western Europe and North America, using a variety of methodologies. Doubts have been raised about how similar Japan really is to other industrial democracies. Concepts such as the developmental state, various forms of neo-pluralism and corporatism, ideas about private interest government and, most recently and controversially, studies based on rational choice approaches have competed with each other as ways to explain policy-making in Japan. While not always compatible with each other, they are complementary to the extent that they insist on a nuanced approach to policy-making that takes the Japanese context seriously. (For an overview of approaches to Japanese politics in the 1990s, see Wright 1999.) Japan has emerged as an important test case for theories of governance developed largely in western Europe and North America.

Finally, Japan is important because it is about to confront issues that will soon test other industrial democracies. I will mention only two.

Japan's population will peak in 2005. For the next twenty years it will decline very slowly, but the proportion of elderly people will grow until 2025. Meanwhile, the number of children born per woman is likely to continue to fall from an already very low 1.39. Where will industry find its workforce? How will society be able to afford long-term care for its old people when there are so few in work? Migration of foreign workers into Japan could solve the industrial recruitment problem and their taxes would help to pay for the care of the elderly. But what if the immigrants do not want to return to their own countries? What happens when they get old? What about the social cost of absorbing non-Japanese citizens into a society that has always taken pride in its homogeneity?

In 2001 Japan officially entered an era of deflation – two consecutive years of falls in consumer prices – which made it rational for citizens to put off any major purchase until prices fell still further and to save money under the mattress rather than place it in banks which could offer practically no interest and which could not guarantee to stay solvent. Keynesian solutions

– trying to stimulate the economy by massive government spending – have not worked. It is not clear what will. When Koizumi Junichirō became prime minister in May 2001, he won massive approval ratings by promising two years of recession, higher unemployment and more bankruptcies as the price of restructuring the economy. Both the politics and the economics of the approach are unusual and will reward careful observation. Japanese politics is worth studying because it is getting interesting, at last.

The chapters that follow address some of these broad issues. We start from the premise that politics in Japan is no more difficult, or easy, for the non-native to understand than the politics of, say, Italy or Australia. Secondly, that it is crucial to have a firm grasp of the historical context which has generated the political institutions. We begin, therefore, in Part I with three chapters that summarize key features of political history up to the 1950s.

However, most readers will be primarily concerned to understand what is going on in Japanese politics today. All politics textbooks are necessarily out of date by the time they are published, but there are any number of sources available now that can provide instant access to news as it breaks. What an introductory text such as this can provide is the contextual information that will enable the reader to make sense of the breaking news. The central chapters, in Parts II and III, describe the parties and structures within which Japanese politics unfolds and the principal actors who play roles in these events. During the 1990s some quite fundamental changes were made in the electoral system and governmental structure which have affected both party politics and policy-making. Chapters 6, 7 and 8 consider those reforms and their intended and unforeseen consequences.

However, as the main concern of political acts is with resource allocation, it is not enough to describe the structures and actors. We need to see the system in action. For this reason, in Part IV we focus on four policy areas in a way that highlights the dynamic interplay of actors, structures and arenas – policies concerned with foreign policy and defence, industry, social welfare and human rights. This is not enough to provide a picture of the full range of political activity; several others could, and probably should, have been included had space been available. Nevertheless, these four case studies indicate the richness and complexity of policy-making which is often missed by the more basic descriptions of politics in Japan.

The chapters have been written to provide a coherent text. But, in the knowledge that few people will start at page 1 and read through to the end, most chapters can be read as self-contained units. This means that there is an element of repetition, but not too much, I hope, to be tedious for the determined reader.

Debate about Japan intensified during the 1990s at home and abroad. Japanese responses to recent crises range from a quiet confidence that 'We are doomed' to frantic shouts of 'Don't panic'. Meanwhile, more seasoned observers both home and away either have faith in the basic strength of the Japanese manufacturing base and Japanese culture to see them through, or are convinced that the financial structure is deeply flawed and most of Japanese tradition has been undermined. This book will not take sides in this debate, but will instead seek to provide sufficient information to enable readers to draw their own conclusions about where Japan is going.

Part I
History

I

Restoration and Reform in Meiji Japan

Discussion about Japanese politics in the twentieth century has often focused on the topic of continuity and change. Did defeat in 1945 set Japan on a completely new trajectory? Or did important parts of the political infrastructure survive through into the 1950s? There is less disagreement about the revolutionary nature of the changes made in Japan's political, economic and social structures during the 1870s and 1880s following the Meiji restoration of 1868. Most of these changes were a clean break with the past, as statesmen consciously sought to create a nation-state capable of resisting the threats facing Japan. Both the structures created by these reforms and the ideas that supported them had acquired an air of permanency by the start of the twentieth century. Nevertheless, political practices and political theory evolved rapidly over succeeding decades – the theme of chapter 2. The American occupation of 1945–52 purported to have as its main aim the injection of democratic practice into Japanese life, and we will discuss that in some detail in chapter 3. However, in order to evaluate the extent of the changes experienced by the state in the twentieth century, it is necessary to begin with a description of the circumstances which surrounded and conditioned the re-creation of the Japanese state in the late nineteenth century. What follows in this chapter seeks to locate this process in the context of Japanese political tradition and developments in the wider world. In the next chapter we will consider how these structures and actors reacted to the economic and political storms of the early twentieth century.

Japan in the middle of the nineteenth century was facing a series of crises generated both from within the country and from outside. Ultimately unable to devise effective policies to deal with its problems, the decentralized government structured around the Tokugawa family was replaced by a new government led, in theory at least, by the sixteen-year-old emperor Mutsuhito whose reign in 1868 was designated Meiji, 'enlightened rule'. This process, which put the emperor back at the centre of the political system, is known as the Meiji restoration.

Throughout the rest of the nineteenth century, the main task of government was the very basic one of all states: to protect the country from foreign invasion. This was not straightforward. As the leaders of the new Meiji state well understood, ensuring independence required social, political and economic reform if the country was to resist the menace posed by the imperialist powers encircling Japan. However, let us begin by describing the problems that these reforms sought to solve.

Japan and the western world up to the mid-nineteenth century

After 1640 Japan had a government that barely pursued foreign relations at all. During the previous eighty years, first Portuguese, then Spanish, Dutch and British missionaries and merchants had arrived and managed quite successfully to convert some Japanese to Christianity and to establish trade. Meanwhile, Japanese traders spread throughout Southeast Asia, and Japan seemed to be on the point of becoming a major trading power in the region. There was no opposition to this from government until the 1590s. By this time, the military leader Toyotomi Hideyoshi had established himself as pre-eminent among the warlords in an age of almost continuous warfare. As he imposed his rule on Japan's southernmost island of Kyushu, several of whose rulers had converted to Christianity, he made clear his opposition to the foreign faith. Adherence to Christianity implied a loyalty to a structure that was controlled from outside Japan. This could all too easily become a means through which foreigners might intervene in Japanese affairs either directly or by giving their support to those critical of Hideyoshi and his successors. Moreover, trade created the opportunity for local lords to build up resources that they could use to purchase arms and build up a fighting force able to resist the central authority.

Hideyoshi died in 1598 and after some jostling for power Tokugawa Ieyasu emerged as a successor after defeating his main rivals at the battle of Sekigahara in 1600. This made him the leader of the hegemonic bloc that controlled most of the 240 feudal domains. He had the emperor designate him and his successors Shogun in recognition of his family's pre-eminent military power. Over the next twenty years a system of governing was devised which isolated those elements most likely to disturb the balance of forces and put them under close control, while the more reliable elements were given a degree of autonomy. In this way, the Tokugawa family was placed unchallengeably at the peak of the political structure.

Previously issued restrictions on the activities of Christian missionaries were strengthened. Trade too was restricted until, by the end of the 1630s, only Dutch and Chinese traders were permitted to remain, and they were confined to a small island in Nagasaki bay. Japanese were forbidden to travel or trade abroad and those still overseas were forbidden to return home. A small trading mission was maintained in Pusan, and over the next 250 years occasional Korean missions were permitted into the country under close supervision. These were the only exceptions to a seclusion policy which cut Japan off from the outside world. Christianity was outlawed.

The Tokugawa Shogun in Edo (modern Tokyo) ruled on the basis of the authority granted to him by the emperor, who lived in Kyoto. However, the imperial family was wholly subordinate to the Shogun's control and for most of the Tokugawa era the reigning emperor was largely confined to the grounds of his Kyoto residence. The house of Tokugawa governed all the productive land in the Kantō plain surrounding Edo, its economic and political base. It also created directly controlled power bases in strategic locations in other regions so that it could keep a close watch on the activities of any lords whose loyalty was suspect. Those who were particularly inept or disloyal could be replaced, but for the most part the Shogun interfered very little with regional government. For their part, the lords controlled their fiefs from castle towns through a local government system composed of their samurai retainers. Most of the population, around 80 per cent, worked on the land, and peasant villages were allowed a degree of autonomy, largely being left alone as long as they paid their taxes and showed no sign of rebellion. Peasants had been deprived of arms in 1588 and forbidden to use surnames, clearly distinguishing them from the samurai who were the only ones permitted to carry swords. During the course of the seventeenth century a series of decrees elaborated status distinctions to separate four main classes: samurai, peasant, artisan and merchant, in descending order of status. Rules defined their dress, restricted their economic activity and forbade intermarriage. Those who fell outside this system were regarded as outcast, not permitted to have normal relations with other members of society and, as far as possible, ignored by it. This system evolved over the 250 years of Tokugawa rule but its basic parameters – strict social divisions, a structure of indirect rule and isolation from the rest of the world – became regarded as immutable elements of Japanese life.

It was only possible for the Tokugawa regime, which had virtually no standing army and no naval power, to sustain a foreign policy based on isolation as long as the rest of the world remained uninterested in Japan. By the end of the eighteenth century, however, western ships began to arrive in the seas around Japan. In the 1790s Russian ships exploring the coast of Hokkaido demanded that the government enter into negotiations. They were instructed to go to Nagasaki. In 1812 British ships arrived in Nagasaki bay and demanded that the Japanese discuss the opening of its ports. The governor of Nagasaki could not prevent the British from landing (and later killed himself in shame), but this was not the start of a sustained attempt by the British, or anyone else, to insist that the Japanese 'open up'. For the time being there were more than enough profits to be made and diplomatic challenges to be resolved elsewhere in Asia.

Meanwhile, domestic crises were becoming increasingly intractable. Despite the low prestige accorded to the activities of the merchant class by the neo-Confucian theories on which Tokugawan rule was based, commerce developed in particular, though not exclusively, between the cities of Edo,

Kyoto and Osaka. It was becoming difficult to maintain the clear distinction between samurai and merchant, and, sumptuary regulations notwithstanding, merchant families tried to improve their social status by marrying into samurai households, often in return for the commutation of loans. Meanwhile, peasant uprisings were becoming more frequent, at times seeming endemic. Central government had no solution to these problems. Certainly, the simple reinforcement of neo-Confucian orthodoxy could no longer be relied on to generate solutions.

Nevertheless, it is possible that the Tokugawa regime could have survived staggering from one crisis to another had there been no external challenge to its rule. Moreover, in some parts of Japan the local regime did manage to reform its administrative and taxation structures to create robust local government. Significantly, these were in areas peripheral to Tokugawa rule, in Satsuma to the south of Kyushu, and Chōshū in the extreme west of Honshu. It was the lords of these areas who would be most critical of the ways the Tokugawa regime dealt with the foreigners and its attempts at reforming central government.

Since the late eighteenth century American ships had been crossing the Pacific to trade in China or in search of whales but hitherto they had sailed from ports in New England on the Atlantic coast. Following the development of the west coast of the United States, the 'manifest destiny' of that country to extend its frontiers across the American continent was reinterpreted to justify the expansion of its influence into the Pacific Ocean and beyond. More concretely, as whalers and traders were more often present in the seas around Japan, so storms forced more American shipwrecked sailors to land there in breach of the isolation policy. Americans also began to realize how useful it would be if their ships could obtain supplies at Japanese ports.

On 8 July 1853 Commodore Matthew Perry, acccompanied by four war-ships, arrived in Edo bay to deliver a letter from US President Fillmore in which he called for 'friendly commercial intercourse' between the two countries. Rejecting the demands that he take his missive to Nagasaki, Perry withdrew to the coast of China only to return in the following February to conclude an agreement which opened two ports to American ships, guaranteed just treatment for shipwrecked sailors and promised future development of commerce. Soon after, albeit in slightly different circumstances, similar treaties were signed with Britain and Russia.

Although the Tokugawa government had maintained a policy of isolation, it was not unaware of developments elsewhere in the world, particularly in Asia. Almost every year the chief of the Dutch traders based in Nagasaki travelled to Edo to present to the Shogun a summary of world news. Thanks to this, the government was well aware, for example, of the devastating impact western powers were having on China. The arrival of Perry's delegation caused panic in Edo. The Shogun consulted his supporters on how he should respond. Some suggested unification of the country, others favoured continuing with the decentralized regime. Having been forced to enter into treaty relations with the USA and, later, Britain and Russia, the Tokugawa government and several of the feudal lords started to establish a defence capacity, building fortresses and acquiring military technology, but this could only be done by either imposing forced loans on the merchants or increasing taxes paid by the peasants, generating more discontent in both these sectors. Meanwhile, there was criticism of the Tokugawa government from within the samurai class and the imperial court for having allowed foreigners to pollute the islands of Japan by their presence. These critics rallied round the slogan of 'honour the emperor, expel the barbarian' – *sonnō jōi*.

Up to this point, the foreigners had dealt mainly with the Shogun, but they realized that as the imperial court supported the anti-foreigner policy it was important to involve the emperor in negotiations. So, from 1865 they insisted that he ratify the treaties too. It was becoming clear to all that expelling the foreigners was not a real policy option, but the slogan 'honour the emperor' continued to imply criticism of the Shogun's regime which had failed to protect the country from external aggression. Two options emerged, one reformist, one revolutionary: either to create a strong, unified country under the control of a revived Shogunal administration, or for the Shogun to return all his authority to the emperor and an assembly of *daimyō* to be convened to debate policy under the control of the emperor. This latter option would give the *daimyō*, particularly those from Satsuma and Chōshū, most influence. Hurriedly, the Tokugawa regime tried to modernize its army with advice from the French and create a navy with the help of the British. In 1866 the Satsuma and Chōshū clans were joined by the Tosa leader Sakamoto Ryōma, and their combined forces were sufficient to defeat the Tokugawa army. That same year Tokugawa Yoshinobu became Shogun, and in 1867 emperor Kōmei, a strong supporter of the anti-foreigner policy, died and was succeeded by a sixteen-year-old, Mutsuhito.

In October 1867 Yoshinobu offered to return power to the emperor. The offer was accepted but he was asked to remain in post until the necessary arrangements could be made. There followed a period of confusion in which there was some fighting between the Satsuma and Chōshū troops and those defending the old regime; however, this was less in defence of Tokugawa rule than in opposition to the growing power of the leaders from the south. Yoshinobu himself vacated Edo castle in February 1868. Quite quickly thereafter the pockets of armed opposition were eliminated and the way was open for the creation of a state structure that would be better able to resist foreign encroachment on Japanese sovereignty.

Most credit for the success of the Meiji government in creating a strong state structure must go to those who guided the reform of Japan in the late nineteenth century, but we should note Japan's good fortune in being granted an interlude of comparative international calm. Not long after gaining access to Japan by treaty, Britain, Russia and many other European nations became involved in the Crimean War (1854–6). Moreover, in 1861 the American Civil War broke out, diverting American attention away from Asia. Thus Japan was able to reform itself at a time when there was relatively little threat of intervention.

The Meiji restoration

The aims of the reformers were later summarized in the phrase 'Prosperous Country, Strong Army' – *Fukoku Kyōhei*. These were the minimum requirements for the successful avoidance of control by one or more of the imperialist nations. However, there was nothing obviously revolutionary in the events of 1867–8; for the time being they seemed no more than a change 'from an old feudal order to a new feudal order' (Toyama, quoted in Tsuzuki 2000: 59). The basic motif of the changes during the next few years was to restore the emperor to a position of political centrality, a position he had supposedly held in the seventh and eighth centuries when government had been modelled on that of China, even though then, as in the nineteenth century, 'imperial power was always less than imperial pretensions' (Beasley 1989: 620). In April 1868 the emperor issued a Charter Oath in which he promised to consult widely in the formation of policy, to abandon 'base customs of former times' and to seek out knowledge from throughout the world. The estates formerly belonging to the Tokugawa were taken over by the new government, becoming its main source of revenue. In March 1869 the four leading han – Satsuma, Chōshū, Tosa and Hizen – offered to surrender their lands to the emperor, and the other lords were expected to follow suit. They gave up their hereditary right to rule but they were reappointed as governors of their fiefs by the emperor, for the time being at least. There was some resistance to this policy and further centralization was introduced. In 1871, after hardly any debate, a decree was issued abolishing the feudal domains and creating in their place seventy-two units of local government, later consolidated to forty-three in the 1888 local government reforms. The existing local militias were disbanded and the castle town headquarters of the lords were confiscated and in some cases destroyed.

The class system was simplified to consist of the nobility (*kazoku*), former samurai (*shizoku*) and commoners (*heimin*). In 1870 all commoners were permitted to take surnames and the principle of freedom of association was established. The following year all restrictions on marriage between classes were removed, the wearing of swords by former samurai became optional and the special restrictions imposed on outcast groups were rescinded. Samurai who had lost their hereditary positions were granted pensions to minimize their opposition to the changes. These were commuted to lump sum payments in 1876 when they were forbidden to wear swords.

Meanwhile, plans to create a conscript army were implemented by a law of January 1873. Men were to report for three years' service at the age of twenty, which was followed by four years in the military reserve. The aim was to create a combined army and naval strength of 31,000 men. There were objections to the scheme from both peasants who did not want to serve and former samurai who felt their status was being undermined. These were ignored, and a modern military force was quickly created, trained on western lines. It was able to deal with domestic opponents of the regime and was capable of service overseas. Its first test came in 1877 when a largely conscript army put down a wholly samurai rebellion in Kyushu.

Right from the start, conscription was conceived only in part as a way to create a standing army. It was anticipated that military training would expose men to nationalist ideas that would continue to inform their everyday lives even after they returned to their villages. Similarly, the introduction of compulsory primary education was at least as much about breaking down class and regional identities and imparting such virtues as obedience and loyalty to the emperor as it was about ensuring minimal levels of literacy and numeracy among the population. By the end of the nineteenth century practically all children in Japan were experiencing four years of schooling.

The third major task was to put government on a sound financial basis, and this meant establishing a national taxation system. In 1869 government income from the former Tokugawa estates only met one half of government expenditure. Income increased somewhat following the abolition of the feudal estates but at the same time the state took on the burden of some of their debt as well as the payments of pensions to former lords and samurai. The first stage of the reform was to standardize the currency and create a banking system based on the US model. Short-term stability of the financial system was assured by a loan from Britain of £2.4 million, but it was reform of the land tax that created the basis for the stability of state finances. Between 1873 and 1881 all land was reassessed for tax purposes, a process that brought some areas of land into the tax system for the first time. Reforms included making the registered landowner responsible for paying the tax, not the village as a unit, fixing taxes on the basis of a percentage of the value of the land (at first, 3 per cent), not the crop in that year, and having the tax paid directly to central, not local, government. The process of reassessment effectively guaranteed possession of their holdings to the large landowners and dispossessed many small-scale farmers, either forcing them off the land entirely or into tenant relations with the big landlords. By 1900 around 40 per cent of those working the land were tenants, sharecroppers who paid for their right to work the land by handing over half of their crop to the landlord. Land tax revenue was the biggest single source of government income throughout the nineteenth century; even in 1900 it was still around 50 per cent of the total.

The structure of government and the new legal system

In September 1868 Edo, the capital of the Tokugawa shoguns and the largest city in Japan, was renamed Tokyo, eastern capital. In November the emperor visited the city for the first time and the following April he returned to make his permanent residence in the castle formerly inhabited by the Shogun. This was the first time a Japanese city had been named by its location, though the practice was common in China. This was not only an indication that Japan's imperial capital had moved from west to east; it also signalled the Japanese assertion that leadership in Asia had shifted from the southern or northern capitals of China (Nanking or Beijing) to the eastern capital of Japan.

China was the source of inspiration for many of the early innovations of the Meiji regime. The new monetary unit, the yen, was at first equivalent to the Mexican dollar, the international currency in East Asia which the Chinese called the *yuan*. The departments of state established in February 1868 had eighth-century (Chinese) names but modern functions – civil affairs, foreign affairs, military affairs, finance, justice and imperial household. The first criminal legal system was based on the Chinese (Ming) code. However, although the Chinese trappings were important, those who were the driving force within the new government were most impressed by the military and economic achievements of the western nations which had, amongst other things, subjected China to a series of humiliating defeats. Throughout the Meiji era, men from the four feudal domains of Satsuma, Chōshū, Tosa and Hizen dominated the political hierarchy. These were individuals who had risen through the reformed administrative structures created in the early decades of the century and who had had direct contact with the western powers. Both Satsuma and Chōshū had not only suffered from attacks by the westerners but had also illegally sent followers to study in Europe.

The Shogunal government had sent missions to the USA and Europe in the 1860s mainly to engage in diplomatic negotiations, but these parties also included individuals such as Fukuzawa Yukichi, who paid close attention to fashion, politics, education, military systems and social structures and wrote illustrated books about them when they returned home. This not only brought an awareness of the developments in the west to the attention of the ruling elite but also to the wider reading public. In 1871 the new government sent the Iwakura mission, a group of senior statesmen, to the USA and European countries. The ostensible purpose was to revise the 'unequal treaties' Japan had been forced to accept in the 1850s and 1860s, but at least as important was to assess conditions in the west in order to work out how best to reform Japan. They spent more than 600 days, following a schedule that included trips to many of the world's major industrial cities where they would visit factories and mines, parliaments and theatres. A record was kept of their travels which was later published. They came to two overall conclusions. First, that the revision of the unequal treaties would require Japan's wholesale restructure, in particular the reform of domestic laws and legal institutions. Secondly, but of equal importance, that the current wealth and strength of Europe originated mostly after 1800 and was pronounced only in the preceding forty years. There was a gap between Japan and the west but it was one that could be bridged.

An important strategy which was adopted to bridge this gap was to employ foreign experts to guide the initial stage of reform while instructing their Japanese subordinates until they could take over. In this way a modern mint was established, a lighthouse system created and a wide range of western industrial techniques were transplanted into Japanese within the relatively short span of fifteen to twenty years.

In a similar fashion were taken measures to revise and modernize Japanese law. Two French scholars were employed and, as a result of their advice, from 1875 all criminal and civil trials were made open to the public and in 1876 torture was abandoned as a routine way of obtaining evidence.

In 1882 a new penal code based on French concepts was introduced, but the civil code proved more problematic. A draft was approved and scheduled to go into effect in 1890 but its implementation was postponed. Following a period of more or less uncritical enthusiasm for western ideas and values in the 1870s, by the late 1880s there was an increased self-confidence among the Japanese elite, who began to worry that a civil code based on 'extreme individualism' would destroy the family-centred traditions basic to Japanese society. Moreover, there was criticism of the universalistic ideas central to French juristic notions of natural law coming from those who drew their arguments from the historical legal tradition in Germany. Somewhat ironically, the Japanese conservatives found support for their neo-Confucian ideas in the writings of German nationalists. The result was the Civil Code of 1898, which purported to protect traditional Japanese family values. At which point we might pause to ask: whose Japanese family values? A survey carried out in the mid-1890s found that 90 per cent of commoners practised 'unorthodox' forms of marriage or household formation (Smith 1996: 168). Thus the new civil code was less a matter of protecting traditional and commonly accepted values and more one of an attempt to impose the 'house system' of the elite on to the whole of Japanese society.

The structure of government evolved from the late 1860s to the late 1880s strongly influenced by the debate on political values which had also influenced the agenda for law reform. On the one hand there were the liberals, influenced by the French and American political ideas, who argued the case for democratic reforms based on notions of rights. Meanwhile, the conservatives sought to protect what they presented as traditional values, supporting their case by reference to German ideas. What is important here is that both sides in this debate were convinced of the need for change, the need to re-create the state in order to be better able to resist western imperialism. The only disagreement was about *how* a strong state capable of standing up to the west could be established and sustained.

The restoration of power to the Meiji emperor created a contradiction at the centre of government in that the revolutionary changes had been led by provincial samurai but their efforts had placed the imperial court, the emperor and court nobles at the apex of political power. Major restructuring of government in August 1869 created an executive body called the Dajōkan, with, at its head, a court noble and two samurai, below whom were four counsellors, one each from Satsuma, Chōshū, Tosa and Hizen. This group advised the emperor and their decisions were carried out through one of the six ministries. As new policies were launched, so new ministries were created. In September 1871 a Ministry of Education was created to train officials and to prepare for the introduction of compulsory primary education. A Home Ministry (Naimushō) was set up in 1873 to supervise the functions formerly carried out by the feudal regime and new ones required by central government such as maintaining a reliable family register system on which to base the conscription process, land surveys on which to base the taxation system and some infrastructural policies such as the creation of a postal system, a road network and a police service. Most of this newly created bureaucracy was manned by samurai, the majority in most ministries coming from the four leading domains.

A western-style peerage was created in 1884, with five titles: prince, marquis, count, viscount and baron. Most of the five hundred names put forward were 'descendants of illustrious ancestors', i.e. former court nobles, but thirty-two were appointed because of their 'distinguished contributions' from the four areas which had engineered the restoration. This created the basis for a House of Peers, but it did nothing to resolve the difficulties at the centre of government. The Dajōkan system worked as long as the complex system of loyalties between those who belonged to the victorious coalition of 1868 could be maintained, but by the 1880s most of the first generation of restoration leaders were dead. As governing became routinized, there was a need for a more coherent government system.

A new structure was announced in December 1885, at the centre of which there was to be a cabinet of ministers – to be called *daijin* – whose activities were to be coordinated by a prime minister – *sōri daijin* – who with the appropriate minister would sign all laws and ordinances issued by the government. The prime minister would also be responsible for major matters of public policy. At an early stage of planning it had been envisaged that the emperor would participate personally in the meetings of the cabinet, but this was later dropped. Thus the emperor was removed from active involvement in politics even though ministers and the prime minister continued in theory to be directly responsible to him.

Over the next few years further reforms were introduced to enforce secrecy, regularize record-keeping and try to eliminate bribery and nepotism. Three grades of civil servant were created, of which the topmost – the *chokunin* (vice-ministers) and prefectural governors – were nominated by the government, nominally the emperor. All other recruits into the bureaucracy had to pass examinations. This could be presented as the implementation of a Chinese, Confucian tradition, but in fact the examinations tested skills that were entirely western in both origin and methodology (Muramatsu 1994: 12). The full implementation of this system completed the move away from inherited status as the prime qualification for government office – and was opposed by the conservatives for this very reason. Nevertheless, for several decades a samurai background continued to be an advantage to those seeking a career in government as patronage continued to be important.

Many of the features of a modern political system had been put into place by the 1880s, but Japan still lacked a constitution. The Meiji Charter Oath had stated that, 'An assembly widely convoked shall be established and all matters of state shall be decided by public discussion', which seemed to amount to a promise to establish some form of representative government. That, at least, is how it was interpreted by the liberals who sought a constitution which would ensure democratic government and guarantees for such rights as freedom of speech, publication and assembly. A Liberal Party was formed and interest in liberal ideas spread rapidly across the country even into rural areas. By the end of 1880 sixty petitions demanding a liberal constitution had been signed by more than 250,000 people. Opposed to them were the mainstream political leaders who sought to develop a system which would keep power in their hands in the guise of exercising it on behalf of the emperor.

Opposition was defused by a combination of concession and repression. The main concession was the announcement in 1881 that the emperor would graciously grant a constitution and convene a national assembly before the end of the decade. Repression came in the form of laws which restricted freedom of press and freedom of assembly. Dissident journalists were arrested – 300 in 1880 – and fined or jailed. An ordinance of April 1880 gave the police powers to supervise the activities of political groups. They attended all rallies and had power to intervene and disband them if people at them made statements 'prejudicial to public tranquillity'. Soldiers, policemen, teachers, students and women were forbidden to attend political meetings or join political parties. Some journalists were expelled from Tokyo and Osaka and were forced to use their skills in regional newspapers they joined or established. The promise to introduce a constitution was crucial in weakening the movement as it robbed the liberals of an aim that all could rally round. After 1881 they split into four groups, none of which survived the 1880s.

This did not, however, mean the eradication of liberal ideas, rather that they went underground. Liberal journalists continued to ply their trade in regional newspapers and keep alive interest in critical ideas. At times when the state relaxed or was forced back, as in the first years of the twentieth century or immediately after the Great War (1914–18), liberal and socialist ideas would reappear and spread rapidly.

At the centre of the new constitution, finally handed down to his people on 11 February 1889, was an emperor, 'sacred and inviolable', who ultimately controlled all the legislative as well as executive powers of state. This was not a constitutional monarch who ruled with the consent of the people by virtue of some kind of social contract; rather, he ruled because he was descended from 'a line of emperors unbroken for ages eternal'. Some concession was made to the rights of citizens, but they were only guaranteed 'within the limits of the law'. There were no rights of the kind that are constitutionally protected in the US political system. A bicameral assembly was created consisting of the House of Peers and an elected House of Representatives. Ministers had the right to speak in both houses but were not responsible to them. The only financial power that the assemblies had at their disposal was to oppose increases; if the government's budget was not passed, that of the previous year would stand.

The conservatives had done all they could to create a constitutional framework that would protect their power with some minimal concessions to the demands from both inside and outside Japan that it include an element of representative government. In the first election held in 1890 just over 1 per cent of the population was eligible to vote, but they did not always vote for the government candidates. The House of Representatives did not have much power, but it refused to be a docile debating chamber and became the focus for democratic activity in the early twentieth century.

Japan and the world in the early twentieth century

In the early 1870s Japan's position had seemed rather precarious. The new leadership was by no means assured of a monopoly of political power, its control over the country as a whole was weak and there was no guarantee that the coalition of samurai and nobility that had orchestrated the restoration would hold together. Externally, the foreigners seemed likely to intervene, perhaps not politically, but economically as their control spread from their footholds in the treaty ports.

Less than thirty years later Japan was a member of the imperialist club, albeit a junior member. Internal revolts had been suppressed and political dissent placed under control. A modern legal system was operating within a constitutional structure that was at least as liberal and democratic as many of those in Europe. Japan had defeated China in the Sino-Japanese war in 1894–5 and made its first imperial acquisition in gaining control of Taiwan. Japan took part in the international expedition in 1900–1 to fight the 'Boxers', sending 10,000 troops, as many as all the other foreign powers combined. This entitled Japan to station troops in Peking and to a share of the massive indemnity that the imperialist powers insisted China pay. Moreover, in 1902 the Anglo-Japanese treaty of friendship not only gave formal recognition to the status of the regime but also gave the necessary guarantees of security to the Japanese generals that would encourage them to make war with Russia in 1904–5. Victory here enabled the Japanese to acquire their second formal colony, Korea, in 1910. Thus equipped, Japan entered the twentieth century with full recognition as a world power.

Conclusion

Much had been achieved in less than fifty years. The constitutional and legal framework had been revised, transforming Japan from a fragmented feudal state into a unitary state with a strong standing army, modern education system and emerging capitalist economy. Foreign expertise had been acquired without allowing the foreigners to gain control of any important aspect of the political or economic structures. This had, however, been a top-down revolution. Liberal ideas, both social and political, spread rapidly throughout the country, in part due to the high level of literacy. Conservatives in government harassed those who joined these groups and prevented criticism of their policies. However, although they had been forced to concede an element of representative government in the constitutional apparatus described in the Meiji constitution of 1889, they were confident that they could keep its influence to a minimum.

2

Political History, 1905–1945

Twentieth-century politics in Japan up to the outbreak of the war in the Pacific is dominated by two interdependent themes. On the one hand there is the liberal, democratic tendency, often informed by socialist ideas, that made demands on the state to enable more people to become involved in the process of government and urged people to take part in politics: a movement coming from below. Meanwhile there was an authoritarian counter-tendency which sought to maintain or increase the power of the state and reduce or eliminate criticism of it. We can think of these political discussions as taking place in a number of environments, though again they were not mutually exclusive. On the one hand there is the development of parliamentary democracy within the parameters set out in the Meiji constitution, along with the gradual expansion of the franchise and the growth in influence of the political parties. There is also the growth of extra-parliamentary groups – trade unions, peasants' organizations, left- and right-wing parties and women's organizations – some of which sought to become involved in the democratic structures, while others totally rejected the parliamentary road.

Parliamentary politics, 1890–1918

The political structure described in the Meiji constitution of 1889 contained an appointed House of Peers and an elected House of Representatives which, it was envisaged, would advise the government. The prime minister was formally appointed by the emperor following the advice of a small group of senior statesmen, known as the *genrō*, all of whom were from either the Satsuma or Chōshū areas which had dominated government in the 1870s and 1880s. This group was not formally recognized in the constitution, but played a crucial role in politics through into the 1930s.

Neither the prime minister nor his cabinet ministers were formally responsible to parliament and there were parts of the government structure such as the Privy Council over which it exercised no control at all. It had no power over the imperial house and some of the Meiji statesmen had urged that the holdings of the imperial estate be hugely increased such that most government functions, including the military, could be funded directly by the emperor (Halliday 1975: 44). This would have put most of the activity of government beyond the reach of parliament, but would have required the transfer of such massive amounts of land to the emperor that it did not prove feasible. However, it was thought that government spending would change very little year on year so that allowing the implementation of the previous year's budget whenever a proposed new budget was blocked by parliament would in practice have much the same effect. Unfortunately for the Meiji statesmen, inflation plus the growing cost of the military in the build-up to and aftermath of the Sino-Japanese War (1894–5) meant that it was essential for the government to win prompt approval for its budgets in order to raise increasing amounts of revenue. The lower house did not turn out to be the docile debating chamber envisaged by the framers of the constitution and the state's need for ever more money gave it political leverage over the bureaucracy.

The uncooperative lower house was dissolved in 1892 and bribery and police intervention (which killed 25 and wounded 388) were used to try to ensure a majority favourable to the government (Tsuzuki 2000: 119). The strategy failed. Liberals who opposed the government held 163 of the 300 seats and they again tried to reduce the size of the budget and impeach the cabinet. The bureaucrats' trump card was the emperor. In 1893 he formally rebuked the party leaders, reminding them that the constitutional role of the house was to aid administration, not to sabotage its activities, and while the cabinet accepted a reduction in the amount of the budget funded by taxation, the total amount remained the same following a contribution by the emperor. At the end of the day, the elected politicians could not outmanoeuvre the oligarchy. Nevertheless, there was a stalemate between the two sides which lasted for six months until the outbreak of the Sino-Japanese War in August 1894. The two sides worked together for the duration of the war, but cooperation broke down as soon as it ended.

Between 1895 and 1900 the bureaucrats adopted a strategy of entering into alliances with groups in the elected house, but the principle was maintained that cabinets should be above party politics – i.e. transcendental. These politician–bureaucrat alliances only lasted as long as the bureaucrats needed them and party leaders became frustrated at this cynical treatment.

In 1898 the voting qualification was revised, almost doubling the size of the electorate. This significantly increased the cost of elections to more than most individual candidates could afford. Thus political parties became important as channels through which funds could be directed to candidates. As of the summer of 1900 there were two political parties: the Rikken Seiyūkai (Friends of Constitutional Politics, usually known as the Seiyūkai) and the Kensei Hontō (The True Constitutional Politics Party, from 1916 the

Kenseikai). These remained the two main parties in Japan until well into the 1930s. The Seiyūkai was created in 1900 under the leadership of Itō Hirobumi, a leading figure in the restoration from Chōshū who had already been prime minister three times and would serve again from October 1900 to June 1901. He was replaced as prime minister by Katsura Tarō in 1901, also a veteran of the restoration process and from the Chōshū clan, but leader of the Kensei Hontō. Itō's place as leader of the Seiyūkai was taken by Saionji Kinmochi (1849–1940), a member of a Kyoto court family. From 1901 to 1913 the post of prime minister would alternate between Katsura and Saionji. As the biggest party, the Seiyūkai could influence policy even when Katsura was in power. Political parties were emerging as important actors, but they were rather different from their counterparts in the UK or USA at this time. Most significantly, they had no coherent ideology or political pro- gramme, no manifesto to distinguish them from their rivals. Although they did at times object to specific cabinet proposals, mostly they approved the demands made of them by the civil or military bureaucracy (Tsuzuki 2000: 135–7).

In the general election of May 1912 the Seiyūkai won 211 seats compared to the 95 of its closest rival, but in December Saionji resigned as prime minister, refusing to accept the army's demands for the creation of two new divisions. It was a regulation at the time that the post of war minister be filled by a serving army officer. When the serving minister Uehara resigned and the army refused to nominate a replacement, Saionji was unable to continue. Katsura took his place and set about forming a party of his own based on anti-Seiyūkai elements. The manoeuvres that put him into office roused the anger of many in the world of politics who felt that the norms of con- stitutional government had been violated, and an opposition movement developed. Public rallies and a press campaign forced Katsura's resignation on 13 February 1913 after less than two months in office. However, the *genrō* were not yet ready for party cabinets or party prime ministers. His replace- ment, Admiral Yamamoto Gonbei, was supported by the Seiyūkai and his cabinet included several party politicians, among them Hara Kei, leader of the Seiyūkai. It adopted some measures of political reform, including the relaxation of the qualifications required of army and navy ministers so they no longer had to be serving officers (Tsuzuki 2000: 187).

In the election of 1915 massive intervention by the government eliminated the Seiyūkai majority. Yamamoto resigned following the House of Peers' decision to cut the navy budget and was succeeded by seventy-six-year-old Okuma Shigenobu, another veteran of the restoration who had first played a role in government in 1868. In October 1916 he was replaced by Count Terauchi, former governor-general of Korea, who formed a transcendental, non-party cabinet. Nevertheless, he had the support of Hara and the Seiyūkai, while the opposition party, the Kenseikai, was led by Katō Takaaki. In late 1917 popular support for Terauchi was fading and his health was failing, but as Hara Kei was the only possible alternative and the *genrō* remained opposed to party cabinets, a decision to replace Terauchi was deferred. Finally, Terauchi took responsibility for the Rice Riots of late summer 1918 (see below) and resigned. Hara was appointed prime minister in an attempt to regain some political legitimacy for the government.

Hara was not only the leader of the main political party, but also a commoner and not linked to any of the samurai or noble families that had played a role in the restoration. After more than twenty years of evolution in a democratic direction, it seemed that the Japanese political structure had taken a decisive step towards the establishment of government controlled by the leaders of political parties who had been elected in contested elections. We will return in a moment to consider how that system would further evolve, but next we turn to examine the development of demands for political change that came from outside the elites.

Dissident ideas pre-1918

Liberal ideas first blossomed in Japan in the 1870s and spread within the popular rights movement. The dynamics of this movement was contained by a combination of concessions and repression which did not so much eliminate it as force it underground. Thereafter, this critical tradition played little part in mainstream political life until the twentieth century.

The late 1890s saw the first signs of a labour union movement and the formation of a Society for the Study of Socialism in 1898 whose members founded a Social Democratic Party (SDP) in 1901. The ideas espoused by these early socialists were derived from Christianity, Darwinism, anarchism and Marxism – all imperfectly understood. Nevertheless, no matter how tiny or uncoordinated, the movement still worried the Meiji oligarchs, who were well acquainted with how powerful the social democratic movement had grown in Germany. In 1900, therefore, a Peace Police Law was passed with the specific aim of obstructing the development of labour and socialist groups. It was this law that provided the legal basis for closing down the SDP less than twelve hours after it had been launched.

Another attempt was made in February 1906 to form the Japan Socialist Party (JSP), with the aim of 'advocating socialism within the limits of the law'. In the spring and summer of that year socialists campaigned against proposed increases in Tokyo tram fares and protested about, though were not directly involved in, the government's use of troops to suppress a riot of 3,600 workers in a copper mine. However, the movement soon became divided between those who were committed to using parliamentary methods to spread their ideas and take control of the state and those such as Kōtoku Shūsui who were advocates of 'direct action', particularly the general strike, as the way to ensure revolution, the abolition of the wages system and the state. At the JSP's second conference in 1907 Kōtoku and the other direct-actionists outnumbered the parliamentarians and the government closed it down.

Military conscription had always been regarded as more than just a way to create a standing army. It was also intended to spread militarist and nationalist ideas back into the villages when the conscripts had completed their service. However, at the start of the twentieth century only 20 per cent of those who took the medical test went to barracks and there was no system which kept ex-soldiers under military discipline. Therefore in 1908 an Imperial Military Reserve Association (IMRA) was created to 'protect the *kokutai* and keep evil, materialistic, foreign ideas from flowing into Japan'. By 1912 the IMRA had a branch in every village and by 1918 it had 2.3 million men in 13,000 branches (Smethurst 1972: 818). This was not much use, though, in dealing with those socialists already under the influence of 'foreign ideas', so in 1904 a Special Police Force (Kōtō Keisatsu) was formed to investigate and control social movements and to suppress radicals who were spreading dangerous foreign ideas. Evidence gathered by this special force was used in 1910 in a secret trial in which Kōtoku Shūsui and twenty-three others were accused of plotting to assassinate the emperor. There was hardly any evidence to support the charges, but all were found guilty and Kōtoku and eleven others were executed in January 1911. After this, nothing 'socialist' could be published, no one dared try to organize a party or group. It was the start of the 'winter years' of socialism.

Alongside the development of the socialist movement, liberal ideas had re-emerged. The Russo-Japanese War had been reported by Japanese newspapers as an overwhelming victory following the destruction of the Russian Baltic fleet in the Battle of Tsushima in May 1905. However, the leaders of Japan knew they could not sustain prolonged warfare and they agreed to a termination of hostilities with the Tsar and negotiated a peace treaty in Portsmouth, New Hampshire, signed on 5 September. In this treaty Japan was granted most of what it wanted except that it had to settle for control of half, not all, of Sakhalin and received no indemnity. Newspapers were very critical of the government and called for rallies of opposition. A demonstration was scheduled to be held in Hibiya Park in central Tokyo, but it was banned. Nevertheless, more than 10,000 demonstrators broke through barriers guarded by 700 police and held a meeting protesting about the Treaty of Portsmouth. Police attacked the demonstrators with sabres, killing seventeen and wounding many more. Outraged, the rioters attacked police stations throughout the city. Rioting in Tokyo ended after three days, but for the next four weeks public meetings were held all over the country in support of resolutions similar to those approved in Hibiya Park (Tsuzuki 2000: 174–5). These demonstrations are often regarded as the starting point of the period known as 'Taishō democracy', a period of political liberalism which contrasts with the authoritarianism of the preceding Meiji period and the following early Shōwa. It was the first time there had been mass protest against a specific government policy. Many of the same people and newspapers who criticized government in 1905 would also become involved in protests in defence of constitutional government in 1912–13 and support demands for universal suffrage in the late 1910s and early 1920s.

Among intellectuals during the 1910s there were attempts to reconcile democracy with the emperor-focused constitutional system. The key word was *minponshugi* – 'politics based on the people' – not to be confused with *minshushugi*, democracy, which in the words of a liberal political theorist could 'easily be confused with the dangerous doctrine of popular sovereignty

Table 2.1   Changes in the size and composition of the electorate, 1889–1947

Total size	Percentage of population	Year of reform	Main voting qualification
450,000	1.1	1889	Male over 25 paying ¥15 or more in taxes to central government
980,000	2.0	1898	Male over 25 paying ¥10 or more in taxes to central government
3,000,000	5.5	1919	Male over 25 paying ¥3 or more in taxes to central government
13,000,000	22.0	1925	Male over 25
40,900,000	52.4	1947	Age over 20

Source: adapted from Fukuoka 2001: 33

implied in a name like the Social Democratic Party' (Yoshino Sakuzō, quoted in Tsuzuki 2000: 193). Yoshino's notion of *minponshugi* was one which would take people's wishes seriously, embraced the idea of universal suffrage but saw sovereignty of the people as impracticable under the Meiji constitution. He saw limited constitutional government as a means by which people might exercise control over government, create solidarity in society and produce a new sense of nationhood. There was no conflict for these intellectuals between demands for greater democracy and nationalism. Indeed, as one of them wrote, 'Nationalism must ultimately end in democracy' (Oyama Ikuo in 1917, quoted in Duus and Scheiner 1988: 680).

The only democratic element included in the 1889 Meiji constitution was the elected lower house, but very few people were actually eligible to vote. Even after the franchise had been extended in 1898 there were still only a million voters in a country of over fifty million (see table 2.1). This relatively small number of electors was thought to enable vote buying, sometimes by the government itself, and other forms of corruption that prevented the democratic structures from effectively controlling government. If the suffrage were broadened to include all the educated middle class, liberals argued, corruption would disappear and 'men of character' would enter politics. In the wave of enthusiasm for democracy that swept through Japan following the end of the Great War in Europe, demands for expanding the suffrage qualification developed into a campaign for universal manhood suffrage and there were even advocates of votes for women. We have seen that Hara Kei was the first premier of a party cabinet, but he was not sympathetic to the campaigns for universal suffrage. All he was prepared to concede was a further reduction in the tax qualification, down to ¥3, which still meant that most city dwellers had no vote.

The Rice Riots of 1918 (see pp. 26–7) had a massive influence on the development of the socialist movement, but they influenced the liberals too. For them, the rioting demonstrated that there was a dangerous gap building up between the governors and the governed. If there was no way that the Japanese people could communicate their concerns through the democratic process, then periodic explosive protests were inevitable. On the other hand, if all were involved in politics through the electoral system, a sense of common interest would emerge to unite the nation. The argument was not immediately accepted, but in 1925 the Universal Manhood Suffrage Act was passed which meant that at the next general election held in 1928 around 12.5 million men could vote, about 20 per cent of the population. A movement for women's suffrage had been founded in 1924. It succeeded in 1930 in getting the support of the then prime minister, Hamaguchi Osachi, and the lower house, but only for the right to vote in local elections. Even this was too much for the peers, who threw it out on the grounds that it would endanger the traditional family system (Tsuzuki 2000: 213).

Parliamentary politics, 1918–32

Hara's elevation to the post of prime minister in 1918 was an important milestone in the development of democratic practice in Japan. A further step towards the normalization of party government was taken when, following the 1920 election, he could command a majority of both houses of parliament. However, this was only limited progress. To start with, parliament was in session for only two months a year, during which time bills were pushed through with very little time for debate. Party leaders treated their followers with scant respect and local party organizations were weak if they existed at all. Hara, his ministers and many of the future party leaders were former bureaucrats who retained links with their ministries and had little commitment to the wider democratic movement. In particular, there was no sympathy for the labour movement.

From 1920 Hara could rely on support from both houses, thus further securing the position of the parties. However, in November 1921 he was stabbed to death in Tokyo station. Takahashi Korekiyo succeeded him as party president and prime minister, but in June 1922 the cabinet split and Takahashi resigned. The next three prime ministers supported by the *genrō* were either non-party or peers, which suggests that the principle of party cabinets had not been established. This became the central issue in the second 'movement for constitutional government'. The three main parliamentary parties made an alliance to fight the May 1924 election focusing on universal suffrage. They won an overwhelming majority.

Following this show of support for the opposition parties, the leader of the biggest party, Katō Takaaki of the Kenseikai, became prime minister. He retained this position, even after the collapse of the party alliance, for slightly more than a year. Finally, it seemed that not only was the balance between parties the mechanism that decided who would be prime minister, but it was the House of Representatives that was the main arena for this inter-party competition. However, we might note that by this stage Saionji Kinmochi was the only *genrō* still alive and he was a supporter of party government, so backing for the principle of party government came also from the extra-constitutional system. When Katō died in January 1926, Wakatsuki Reijirō, who took over as leader of the Kenseikai, became prime minister and until the assassination of Inukai Tsuyoshi in 1932 party cabinets were the rule.

In retrospect, it is clear that it was premature to conclude that the principle of party cabinets had been firmly established but if we compare the political scene at the start of the 1930s with that of the 1890s, the extent and speed of the democratization of Japanese politics seemed impressive. In the course of forty years the elected house of parliament had asserted itself as the pre-eminent structure within the constitution and universal manhood suffrage had been accepted. Cabinets had been able to assert their authority over all the branches of government, including the military, as demonstrated by the reduction in the size of the army in the early 1920s. Institutional developments were also recognized by the leading political theorists. Minobe Tatsukichi, for example, argued that parliament was an organ of the state not empowered by the emperor but representative of the people, and that, of its two houses, 'the one possessed of the main political power must be the one that depends on public election by the people' (quoted in Mitani 1988: 87).

Dissident voices, 1918–40

The first sparks of socialist activity were doused by the arrests and execution of Kōtoku Shūsui in 1911, but the rapid changes in the social and economic circumstances soon created conditions favourable for its re-emergence. First, the rapid economic growth of 1914–18 increased the number of workers employed in factories from 850,000 to 1.8 million. Secondly, the Yūaikai (Friendly Society) was formed in 1912 to provide assistance and relief to industrial workers. It was sponsored by socialist academics, cabinet ministers and even retired business leaders. At first it was oriented towards encouraging labour–management cooperation but as its membership grew, from 1,295 in 1913 to more than 19,000 in 1917, most of them workers in mechanized industries, it became increasingly involved in industrial disputes. In 1919 it renamed itself the Yūaikai-Sōdōmei and in 1921 dropped the Yūaikai from its name, becoming more militant at each stage of this process. Working-class activity increased in 1918 as the once booming factories started to try to reduce wages or lay off workers in the face of the postwar recession. Between 1918 and 1919 more than 300,000 workers were involved in some kind of dispute, not all of them associated with unions or labour federations.

The series of disturbances known as the Rice Riots began in late summer 1918 as peaceful rural protests about the rapidly rising price of rice, but later protest spread to urban areas and involved attacks on rice merchants, coal miners making demands of mine owners and strikes of industrial workers demanding higher wages. The riots lasted for weeks if not months and involved several hundred thousand, perhaps even a million people. In some cities the disturbance was so severe that martial law had to be declared and the army called in. Given the general increase of working-class activity at the time, it is hard to distinguish between protest that was part of the Rice

Riots and protest about wages and working conditions that just happened to include some reference to rice prices.

Any such distinction was academic to working-class activists at the time. The revolution in Russia in 1917–18 had shown that an imperial monarch and authoritarian system could be overthrown and a socialist state founded when the popular discontent of workers and peasants was effectively channelled by a revolutionary party. These riots and industrial disputes demonstrated that there was similar discontent in Japan. For many anarchists and socialists, the creation of a socialist society had hitherto been a desirable, if distant, social change. Events in 1918 suggested to some of them that the socialist revolution was imminent. Precisely because of this, the question of strategy became urgent. The debate between those who urged direct action, the anarchists of various kinds and the social democrats split the union movement. Advocates of direct action lost their most articulate and charismatic spokesman when Osugi Sakae was murdered by police in the aftermath of the Great Kantō earthquake in September 1923. The anarchist movement could claim more supporters than any other left-wing movement throughout the 1920s, but after Osugi's death it ceased to contribute to the debate on revolutionary strategy. Rather, with the formation of the illegal Japan Communist Party (JCP) in 1922, the main debate was between Bolshevik Marxists and social democrats. These debates spread to most parts of the social movement.

The JCP had been formed in secret, but the police soon became aware of its existence and most of its fifty or so members were arrested within a year. However, the police were alarmed to find that many of these people had committed no offence that they could be charged with. The Peace Preservation Law was enacted in 1925 as part of a package that included introduction of universal manhood suffrage and resumption of diplomatic relations with the Soviet Union. This law made illegal groups or movements that advocated the overthrow of the capitalist order or basic changes in the national polity such as the abolition of the emperor system. Punishment for those found guilty of belonging to such a group was up to ten years' hard labour. When it was found difficult to prove membership of an illegal organization, the law was revised in 1928 to make it possible to punish those whose actions had benefited groups which had such aims, irrespective of whether they themselves were members of it. It was now much easier for police to use the law to arrest suspected members as well as sympathizers of the JCP. Mass arrests in March 1928 severely damaged the party and attempts to rebuild it were thwarted by the arrest of key members in April 1929. Subsequent attempts to revive the party failed.

However, once the influence of the JCP had been eliminated, the Peace Preservation Law was used to harass those who remained active in the numerous social movements, both urban and rural. By the early 1930s there were 10,000 arrests each year under this law. Few of those arrested were charged, but many were held for long periods and police brutality was common. Regular detention in prison made it difficult to find work, so the Act effectively deterred all kinds of social activism not approved by the police, with the definition of what activity was permissible narrowing throughout the 1930s.

Some social democratic parties took part in the elections after 1928 hoping that the newly enfranchised workers would support the socialist candidates. However, they had very limited funds compared to the major parties and the police used the Peace Preservation Law to interrupt their public meetings. Only eight out of eighty-eight socialist candidates were elected in 1928.

There was great factional rivalry between the social democratic parties and considerable fear of being infiltrated by communists. However, once the threat from the communists had been eliminated following the arrests of 1928 and 1929, restrictions were imposed on the social democrats too. Two social democratic parties fought the 1932 general election; neither was critical of the emperor system but they were divided over policy towards the new acquisitions of Manchuria and Mongolia. Their combined vote dropped to about half that received by left-wing parties in 1928. The national-socialist factions split off and the remaining social democrats in both these parties united to form the Social Masses Party (Shakai Taishūtō) in July 1932. At the time of its formation, it was opposed to the war in China, demanded state control of staple industries and the provision of comprehensive social services. In the elections of 1936 it received sufficient support to elect eighteen members to the lower house and in 1937 it became the third largest party, with thirty-seven seats. By this time, however, it had declared its support for the war in China and in October 1937 its leader announced that his party was neither 'socialist' nor 'democratic'. That December there was another series of mass arrests of remaining liberals and social democrats critical of government policy. This marked the end of opposition to government policies. In October 1940 all political parties were dissolved to create the Imperial Rule Assistance Association (IRAA) which was supposed to serve as a 'new political structure' in the new era. Once the social democrats dropped their opposition to the aggressive war in China, there was little to distinguish them from the mainstream politicians who also favoured state intervention in the economy and improved welfare services. Nevertheless, these social democrats maintained their identity as a parliamentary group during the war and some of them continued to be politically active after 1945.

Dissidents – anarchist, communist, social democrat – emerged in Japan during the boom in interest in socialism and liberalism. This was stimulated as much by events in the rest of the world as by their awareness of problems facing Japan and the Japanese. The period after 1918 was one of growing affluence and expanding horizons. The newspaper industry was developing rapidly. Nearly half of Japan's eleven million households subscribed to a daily newspaper in 1920. Journalists inherited a tradition of criticizing government policy and supported demands for democratic government. A wide range of weekly and monthly magazines also prospered in the 1920s, feeding the appetite for news from overseas which developed in the relatively liberal atmosphere of 'Taishō democracy'. Radio broadcasts began in 1925. By 1928, 500,000 households had a wireless set and by the late 1930s there were 4 million radios and 20 million listeners. In urban areas practically every household had one (Hanneman 2001: 20; Benson and Matsumura 2001: 168). Radio broadcasting was always monopolized by the state and used to promote ideas and values they deemed desirable. By the 1930s the newspapers too were squarely behind the war effort, not only supporting policies in their pages but collecting gifts and donations to support policy in Manchuria and Mongolia.

Knowledge about what was happening elsewhere in the world provided inspiration for those dissatisfied with conditions in Japan. On the other hand, there was a distinctly Japanese interpretation of liberalism whose origins can be traced back to the 1870s. Socialists, too, did not slavishly import foreign models but, rather, sought to adapt western ideas to the Japanese conditions – and this applied as much to the anarchists as it did to the Bolsheviks and social democrats. However, as the international circumstances changed and as domestic regulation made criticism of government more difficult, those outside the mainstream of politics had to choose between continuing their activity with the strong possibility of arrest and imprisonment, adapting their ideas taking into account the 'trends of the times' or keeping quiet and retiring from active politics either permanently or until the circumstances changed so they could resume political activity. Whichever option was chosen, by the end of the 1930s practically no criticism existed.

Right-wing politics in the 1920s

At the end of the earlier section on parliamentary politics we summarized the political developments of the 1920s in a way that suggested there were good reasons for optimists to feel that a secure basis for liberal democracy had been created in Japan. It is not difficult, however, to describe the 1920s in a very different light. The Peace Preservation Act provided the means by which the state could place restrictions on political discussion, parameters which were gradually narrowed down during the 1930s, and there were other means to restrict the influence of socialist and liberal ideas.

In 1919 the Dai Nippon Kokusuikai (Great Japan National Essence Society) was created with support from the Home Ministry. Prominent among its aims was 'to preserve the essence of the Japanese people'. By the early 1920s it claimed 120,000 members and at its peak more than 500,000, most of them unskilled labourers who were used by landlords and factory owners to intimidate striking workers or tenants (Huffman 1998: 69–70). A Kokuhonsha (National Foundation Society) was founded in 1924, arguing that democracy was alien to and therefore disruptive to emperor-centred Japan. It was the political base for Hiranuma Kiichirō (1867–1952), who during the 1920s was minister of justice, home minister, president of the Privy Council (1936–9) and finally prime minister for nine months in 1939. At one time it claimed 200,000 members and 170 branches (Hunter 1984: 97), but it was dissolved in 1936 when Hiranuma was embarrassed by its links to the right-wing revolutionaries involved in the attempted coup of 26 February. Even allowing for exaggeration of their size, these two organizations still had more active grassroots support than the political parties. Moreover, members of these groups and those like them were used by local elites to intimidate supporters of left-wing or liberal political movements.

Education had always been used as a way of fostering national unity, and from 1903 the Ministry of Education controlled the content of all primary school textbooks, using them to inculcate strong nationalist sentiment. There was some acknowledgement of the pacifist democratic trends in the textbooks as revised in the period 1918–23, but even at this time the history books presented Japan's mythical origins as fact. Thereafter, the textbooks became increasingly nationalistic and supportive of Japan's military objectives in Asia. Budget cuts in the early 1920s had reduced the size of the army and it was decided to redeploy some of the now unemployed army officers in schools. From 1925 every school above primary level had an officer attached to it. This not only provided employment for redundant soldiers, but encouraged the spread of militarist ideas into the school system. Only 20 per cent of the nation's youth attended school after the age of 16 and from 1926 all males aged 16–20 were ordered to report to local 'training centres' for a total of 800 hours of military instruction spread over four years; mostly it was drill, but there was also time for 'ethical instruction'.

The Imperial Military Reserve Association (IMRA) had been created as part of the package in the late Meiji period to prevent the spread of dangerous foreign ideas. By 1918 it had 13,000 branches and 2.3 million men enrolled with as many as 80 per cent of those eligible joining in rural areas. Factory branches were formed from 1914, and from 1915 a youth group was created, the forerunner of the military training centres mentioned above. In 1932 a women's association was created under the control of the army ministry to spread the military ethos among wives and mothers. As a result, by 1935 there were between eleven and twelve million people who belonged to one of these organizations, many of them high in the rural social hierarchies (Smethurst 1974: 37–40). Ideas supportive of the army could be spread very rapidly through this organization, and it was used by the ministry as a political pressure group, for example using mass rallies to demand that the government leave the League of Nations or to oppose the spread of liberal ideas such as those of the constitutional scholar Minobe Tatsukichi.

In other words, quite contrary to the optimistic account suggested earlier, it is not hard to describe the 1920s as a time when nationalistic, anti-democratic structures were put in place which began to close down political debate, a role they would take on with greater energy in the 1930s. It is not necessary to choose between these two accounts. Both currents were present and there was no inevitability about which would prove dominant. Even as late as 1937 there was a general election in which a social democratic party could attract more than a million votes and in the same year Japan became involved in warfare in China with hardly any criticism at home.

Japan in the world, 1900–33

Japan obtained control over Taiwan following the Sino-Japanese War (1894–5) somewhat less than the army wanted, given that they had also successfully invaded northern China. Japan was forced to give back the

Liaotung peninsula following the 'Triple Intervention' of Germany, France and Russia. Russia's defeat in the Russo-Japanese War (1904–5) established Japan's paramount position in Korea, as well as possession of half of Karafuto/Sakhalin and two key ports on the Liaotung peninsula, Port Arthur (Lushun) and Dairen (Dalian). This again was somewhat less than many in Japan had expected, but it paved the way for Japan to annex Korea in 1910. A treaty with Britain effective from January 1902 acknowledged the common interest of these two states in opposing Russian expansion and its revised version in 1905 recognized Japan's hegemony in Korea. Thus far, Japan's imperialist ambitions were accommodated within the international system even if the country did not get all it wanted.

At this point there was debate in Japan about the direction its foreign policy should take. Some of those associated with *minponshugi* ideas argued that Japan should abandon its imperialist ambitions, give independence to Korea and Taiwan and build a compact island welfare state based on industry and trade (Hata 1988: 273; Tsuzuki 2000: 192). This was a minor theme within political discussion, although one that would be endorsed by dissident critics of government policy in the 1920s and 1930s. Meanwhile, within the mainstream the only division was over whether the next phase of Japan's expansion should be to the north, into Manchuria, in which case the main threat came from Russia, or to the south, into south China and Southeast Asia, in which case the main obstacle was posed by Britain and the USA. Whereas the army looked north, the navy faced south. Should Japan prepare for the next phase of its foreign policy by expanding the army, or the navy, or both? Would it be possible for Japan to move in either direction without upsetting the structure of international relations which was dominated by the USA and the Europeans?

Japan might have remained neutral in the Great War, but three days after Britain declared war on Germany, Japan was asked to destroy the German fleet based in Tsingtao and take control of the Mariana islands in the Pacific. By the time war ended, Japanese military forces were operating freely on the Asian continent from Lake Baikal to the west of Sinkiang and to Micronesia in the south, an area almost as big as that occupied by Japanese forces in 1942. So extensive were these possessions that it was almost inevitable that at the Versailles conference the Americans and the British would try to roll back Japan's advances. Indeed, there was a feeling among Japan's military leadership that the postwar settlement deprived Japan of almost everything it had won in the war. All that was gained was recognition of Japan's special interest in Manchuria and Mongolia, which had in any case been claimed by Japan before 1914.

A new international order, one which mainly served the interests of the USA and Britain, was created by the combined impact of the Versailles and Washington treaties of 1919 and 1921–2. Germany was punished by this settlement, having to pay reparations. Italy and Japan, though on the winning side, felt inadequately rewarded. Meanwhile Russia, by now the Soviet Union, lay outside the new system of international politics, committed in theory, at least, to its overthrow. Japanese troops remained in Siberia until

1922, the last remnant of an international expedition aimed at preventing the spread of Bolshevik rule into the Russian far east. Now Japan was back to the borders within which she had operated in 1914 on land, while the effect of the Washington Naval Treaty was to keep the Japanese fleet inferior to that of the USA and the UK in the Pacific. Moreover, acceptance of the framework of international politics represented by the League of Nations meant that in the future Japan had to rely on economic diplomacy to further its interests and to agree to non-intervention in China's domestic affairs.

By 1928 the Kuomintang (KMT – the Chinese Nationalist Party) had unified nearly all China proper apart from Manchuria. Japanese policy in China was inconsistent and lagged behind that of the USA and the UK, which were both prepared to make concessions to the KMT regime. However, the government in Tokyo was unable to exert much control over the army in Manchuria. In 1928 senior army officers arranged for the assassination of the warlord Chang Tso-lin in an attempt to provoke an uprising that would justify further military action. This time it failed, but a similar incident in September 1931 engineered by a small group of officers led to troops advancing into Manchuria in a move that had not been approved by the central army authorities, still less the cabinet. By March 1932 the occupation of Manchuria was complete and a new and nominally independent state of Manchukuo had been created under close Japanese supervision.

Great Britain, the United States or the Soviet Union might have intervened, but as none of their interests was directly threatened none of them did. The KMT, too, sought to avoid military confrontation and chose instead to appeal to the League of Nations to recover Manchuria. Lord Lytton chaired a commission of four to investigate the situation, and its report rejected the Japanese version of the course of events. When the League of Nations voted in February 1933 by 42 to 1 to accept the Lytton report, Japan withdrew.

Domestic politics and international crises

The reputation of the party cabinets was not high in the early 1930s. Domestically they seemed unable to deal with the economic crisis, while in their foreign policy they had been forced to accept further restrictions on the size of the navy at the 1930 London Naval Conference. The growing anti-party, pro-military mood prevented the cabinet from taking punitive actions against the army officers who had acted unilaterally in Manchuria. Both at national and local levels the activities of groups like the Kokuhonsha and branches of the IMRA could influence the policy climate at a time when the influence of the socialist and social democratic groups was fading under police pressure. Attacks by right-wing patriots on politicians accused of betraying Japan became more common. Prime Minister Hamaguchi was shot and wounded in late 1930, resigned from his post and died from his wounds in 1931. Abortive *coups d'état* were planned by right-wing army officers for March and October 1931. The Minister of Finance and a leading industrialist were

the USA following the attack on Pearl Harbor, and with the British Empire following the simultaneous attacks on Malaya on 7/8 December 1941.

Events on the battlefields need not concern us, but we might note that the onset of total war did not result in the elimination of parliamentary politics. To be sure, criticism of government was muted and most members of parliament could be relied on to support the government, but not all. In 1941 the government tried to form a House of Representatives section of the IRAA, but only 70 per cent of the house signed up for it. A general election was held in April 1942 and the government tried to make sure that only its candidates were elected. It secretly gave each of them ¥5,000 to use on election expenses, and used the state-controlled radio and press to urge people to vote for them. Independent candidates were permitted to run – 613 in all – and they won over a third of the total votes: 85 of 466 seats (Shillony 1991: 23–6).

From the start of the war in the Pacific, control over parliamentary sessions increased. Speeches had to be cleared in advance with the cabinet and the government insisted on the rapid approval of bills. Nevertheless, within these limits it was possible to express discontent with government policy, elected politicians continued to serve in the cabinet (though they did not form a majority) and consultative committees oversaw the work of each ministry. That said, there was no meaningful opposition to war, the extra-parliamentary political force was completely crushed. It remains significant, though, that, even in 1944–5, when Japan's future looked bleak, there was no attempt to abolish or suspend parliament. To that extent at least, parliamentary politics was firmly established as part of the machinery of state.

Conclusion

The key question about the pre-war era is whether there was anything about the nature of the Japanese state at the end of the nineteenth century which led to defeat in the middle of the twentieth. We have tried to consider this question from three perspectives: from that of those who controlled state structures, those who opposed them and the international situation.

It is clear that those who designed the 1889 Meiji constitution were not democrats. They did not want the elected house to contribute much to government. The state intervened to try to ensure a cooperative house in the elections of 1892 and 1915, and one might argue that the Peace Preservation Acts of 1900 and 1925 institutionalized the ability of the state to interfere in the electoral process. This did not completely prevent organized opposition, but it did enable the state to exert some control over its critics. And, there were other informal means at its disposal. The IMRA spread nationalist ideas and acted as a lobby for the army. The Kokusuikai, Kokuhonsha and similar groups led by men close to central government not only propagated ultra-nationalist ideas but also were involved in attacks on leftists at meetings and as they walked home afterwards. Such actions at the local level supplemented police supervision of social movement organizations. Meanwhile, the assassinations of leading liberals in government and business, particularly between 1930 and 1936, added to the climate of fear which deterred critical thought.

In the 1910s and 1920s some liberals were arguing that democracy was not possible within the structure of the Meiji constitution. Certainly, there were some parts of the state structure that were formally beyond the reach of elected politicians, for example the Privy Council and the right of the military to report directly to the emperor. On the other hand, the Meiji constitution had displayed an impressive degree of flexibility which had enabled it to absorb and expand democratic practice. Progress in a democratic direction was particularly impressive from the perspective of 1930. My own view is that the Meiji constitution impelled political practice in an authoritarian direction, but did not compel advance in that direction. One can quite easily imagine a scenario in which the Privy Council became irrelevant to the normal practice of politics and for party cabinets to have become firmly rooted as the only form of government. That this did not occur was largely due to the international situation, which suited the authoritarian militarist world-view.

The desire to resist control by the imperialist powers had led to Japan creating a powerful military establishment which soon adopted an expansionist agenda. Moreover, from 1919 Japan could identify with Italian and German complaints that their interests were ignored by the major powers, mainly the UK and USA. As long as Japanese expansion was limited to the wastes of Manchuria and Mongolia, the leaders of the international community would not do more than express their disapproval in the sessions of the League of Nations. However, when there was a direct threat to British and American economic and strategic interests there was bound to be a response. War in Europe created the possibility that Japan could secure control over such strategic raw materials as oil only by further advance into Asia. It hoped to win the support of local elites by emphasizing its anti-western credentials. In this it was only partially successful. A much bigger mistake was that the Japanese underestimated the US determination to avenge the humiliation inflicted at Pearl Harbor.

3

Postwar Re-creation of the Japanese State: Occupation and Aftermath

---

There are two main sets of interpretation of the events in Japan in 1945–51, the years of the occupation of Japan by the Allied Powers. One emphasizes the extent of the changes imposed by the occupiers, reforms that went well beyond anything that the Japanese would have devised for themselves but which established the basis for political, social and economic progress in the 1950s and beyond that led to recovery and economic power. The other argues that there was little of lasting importance that the occupiers introduced to Japan that did not build on foundations laid down by the Japanese themselves before the war. How much continuity/discontinuity was there between pre-war and postwar Japan?

It might be thought that some light might be shed on this problem by examining the nature and intentions of the occupiers. Certainly the occupation was well planned, but the occupiers were a mixed bunch. There were deeply conservative, career army officers such as the US General Willoughby, who exchanged cigars for sherry every Christmas with General Franco and who, as early as December 1945, was urging the strengthening of Japan in preparation for the coming war with the Soviet Union. Meanwhile, at various levels of the occupation hierarchy were men and women who had joined the army to fight fascism and who advocated 1930s American-style 'New Deal' liberal values. Setting the agenda, and often the pace, was the US General MacArthur, who was Supreme Commander of the Allied Powers (SCAP) from 1945 to 1951 and at least in the early months he seems to have been inclined to accept a liberal reform agenda.

The main aims of the occupation were set out in the 1945 Potsdam Declaration by the US, Soviet and British leaders and can be summarized as 'democratization' and 'demilitarization', in order to 'insure that Japan will not again become a menace to the United States or to the peace and security of the world' (Initial Postsurrender Policy, quoted in Dower 1999: 76). No one was sure how long this would take; some suggested at least twenty-five years. There was also disagreement about how extensive and punitive the demilitarization programme should be. At first, it was proposed to dismantle much of Japan's heavy industry and transport it to the neighbouring states that had been ravaged by war as a form of reparations. This programme began, but was soon stopped as more emphasis was placed on rebuilding the Japanese economy in preparation for confrontation with communism.

First of all, we should note some general characteristics of the occupation. There had been extensive planning which had started quite soon after the outbreak of war and involved several leading social scientists. The USA insisted on having control of the occupation. Not all the occupying forces were American: some parts of Japan were 'host' to Commonwealth troops, but control was centralized. There was no zoning, as happened in Germany. The other Allies were represented on such bodies as the Allied Council for Japan or the Far East Commission, but these had very limited influence. Moreover, it was MacArthur who played the key role. He was responsible directly to the US President, not to the other Allies or to any department in Washington, and he could (and did) claim credit for many of the reforms.

However, again unlike Germany, at the point of defeat the state structure in Japan remained intact. Once established in Tokyo, SCAP made it clear that it intended to work through existing state structures, not supplant them. The policy process then was that the general outlines were set by Washington but SCAP was given considerable discretion to decide how and when the reforms were to be implemented. The detail of reform was worked out within the ministry, aided or supervised by the appropriate section of SCAP which existed alongside the ministry. The advantage of this approach was that those who were responsible for carrying out the policies were Japanese with good local knowledge who did not provoke resistance among those who were being forced to change. The disadvantage was that it meant there were countless opportunities for bureaucrats high and low to resist the formulation or implementation of policy they opposed.

Resistance of the people of Japan to the occupation was much less than expected. Nevertheless, the first phase of the occupation was 'saturation-type'. Troops were sent to even the smallest villages and remotest islands to deal with any last-ditch resistance (of which there was very little) and to bring home the reality of defeat. This was followed by a retreat to the prefectural capitals in early November 1945. At the level of the ruling elites, those considered responsible for the war were charged with war crimes and put on trial. Those closely identified with the prosecution of the war were purged from positions of power, many until after the end of the occupation. Some of them re-entered the political world not only unaffected by the purge but actually stronger (Dower 1999: 213). Very few bureaucrats were affected by the purges: they made up only 0.9 per cent of the total number of purgees. Most continued in their posts, some even benefited, leaving their ministries to take up careers in politics and filling the gaps created by the purge of wartime politicians.

Later in this chapter we will look at the political structure created to serve the new Japan, but before that let us consider two fundamental reform policies implemented in the early years: in land ownership and education.

Land reform

The major problem for the government following surrender was how to feed the population. People were starving, the official rations did not supply enough for even basic nutrition. There were food demonstrations in central Tokyo led by socialists and communists which on one occasion culminated in raids on the imperial kitchens. An immediate priority shared by the Japanese and Americans was to return to agricultural self-sufficiency as soon as possible. One way to encourage this was land reform which would put the ownership of the land into the hands of those who farmed it, giving them direct incentives to improve productivity.

Land reform also fitted in with the Allies' political aims. It was believed that much of the popular support for ultra-nationalism had come from the landlord class, which had exercised extensive power over their tenants. If the material basis of their power could be eliminated, the likelihood of a revival of extreme nationalism could be reduced. On the Japanese side there had been support for land reform within the ministry of agriculture since the 1930s. In part it derived from a fear of rural radicalism. The agricultural depression in Japan lasted from 1920 through into 1936 and led to a number of disputes between tenants and landlords generating support for radical ideas in rural regions. The situation, already bad in 1945, was bound to get worse over the following months with the return of demobilized soldiers and those who had moved to farm land in Korea or north China. There was a fear that rural radicalism might revive to form the basis of a revolutionary movement, as had happened in China. Fears of revolution aside, there were also those in the bureaucracy who were genuinely sympathetic to the problems of the tenants and realized the need to reduce rents and prevent evictions. In December 1945 a land reform bill was presented by the Ministry of Agriculture and Forestry for consideration by MacArthur. The cautious proposals of the Japanese were rejected by the Americans as too moderate and they put forward a much more radical bill in October 1946 which aimed to 'break the economic bondage which has enslaved the Japanese farmers through centuries of feudal oppression' (quoted in Livingston et al. 1976: 188).

To summarize the reforms: all land of absentee landlords (those not living in the village) was bought by the state at a fixed price and sold, usually to the tenant; local landlords who did not work the land were permitted to retain one *chō* (about 2.45 acres) but had to sell the rest; those who did farm their land were permitted to retain up to three *chō* they farmed and one *chō* they rented out. In the future all rent was to be paid in cash (not a proportion of the crop as hitherto), restrictions were placed on the reacquisition of land and formal contracts were devised where land was rented (to replace informal agreements which could be interpreted to suit the needs of the landowner). Tenants who wished to buy their land paid at a fixed price in instalments over a period of thirty years. The process of redistribution took place in 1947–8, controlled by local land commissions composed of tenants, owner farmers and landlords, with the former in the majority. These committees implemented the rules, taking into account the productivity of the land and other local factors.

In most respects the reforms were a great success: 70 per cent of farm households benefited. Generally, the result of the reforms was to transfer the title of a piece of land from its owner to its erstwhile tenant. Land prices were in any case set quite low, but the burden on the purchasers of land was much reduced by the rapid inflation of the late 1940s which made the repayments insignificant. It created a large landowning class which had a stake in the occupation programme. Reform seems to have encouraged productivity: rice production went up from an average of 9 million tonnes in 1945–50 to 12.4 million tonnes by 1955. This kept food prices low, assisting the stabilization of wages and releasing foreign currency for the purchase of technology and machinery rather than food.

It is less clear whether land reform restructured rural social and political relations. Many farmers – 43 per cent in 1949 – held too little land to support a family and needed to lease some land, thus recreating a dependency relationship. Forest land, two-thirds of the land area, was left untouched by the reforms and was a basis for the retention of social and political influence (Halliday 1975: 192–3). Ex-landlords formed a political lobby demanding compensation for the very low prices paid by the state and in 1965 were rewarded by the Liberal Democratic Party (LDP) with government bonds in recognition of their cooperation with the land reform process (and support of the LDP).

Education

The Americans saw the landlord class as being one of the pillars supporting pre-war militarism and blamed the education system for spreading those ideas throughout the population. The education system was therefore another major target for the reformers. Reform began with a purge of the teachers to eliminate the militarists: between August 1945 and April 1947 about 120,000 left the profession, one quarter of the total, most of them resigning. The next priority was to revise what was taught. At first this amounted to just the elimination of objectionable passages from textbooks, but later new sets of books were commissioned which highlighted democratic values. The control of education was also democratized by creating locally elected boards which were independent of the Ministry of Education (MoE). Responsibility for curriculum and textbooks was devolved to the individual schools and teachers, with the role of the ministry being limited to issuing guidelines, making suggestions and producing teaching guides.

The complex, multi-track, elitist education structure was radically reformed and compulsory education extended from six to nine years. Henceforth, all children would spend six years in primary school followed by three
in junior high school. Comprehensive senior high schools were created and
higher education was reformed on a four-year model. Thus, a 6–3–3–4 system
was set up, very similar to the US structure. Systematic discrimination against
girls was eliminated: equality of opportunity and co-education were to be the
rule, at least in principle. Even within the classroom there was to be a change
of ethos to emphasize child-centred teaching methods.

These reforms, which were gradually introduced and largely welcomed by
teachers, did not amount to a 'settlement' of the problem. Conservatives were
very critical of the changes, which they regarded as having been forced upon
Japan. Bureaucrats in the MoE were concerned at their loss of control over
local authorities, the curriculum and textbooks. Education has been a major
battlefield on which the forces of conservatism have contested the 'progressive' control of education from the 1950s through into the twenty-first
century. Resistance from the Japan Teachers' Union (JTU), supported in
parliament by the Japanese Socialist Party (JSP) and its allies, slowed down
the reassertion of central control, but pressure from the right continues to
be remorseless. In 1956 the system of local school boards was abolished. In
future they would be set up at prefectural or municipal level, appointed by
the prefectural governor or mayor, and be subject to the demands of the
MoE. Two years later the MoE made its curriculum mandatory, textbooks
had to conform to this curriculum and they were inspected for compliance
by ministry-appointed 'reviewers'. From 1963 selection of textbooks was
taken out of the hands of individual teachers and given to the school boards
of the responsible local authority. Meanwhile, the ministry tried, ultimately
successfully, to regain control over the teaching profession through an
efficiency-rating system.

Because of its presumed links with industrial growth, law and order and
national morality, education policy is a heavily politicized area in most states.
In Japan, the policy debates have been conducted with more than usual vehe-
mence because overlaid onto these purely domestic concerns were the deeper
and broader concerns of Japan and the world. On the one hand, the struggle
between the JTU, prominently supported by the JSP and JCP, and the conservative reformers in the MoE and the LDP was a domestic reflection of
the Cold War struggle between communism and capitalism, internationalists
against nationalists. At other times the conservative campaigns were characterized as being in support of Japanese traditional ethics which had been
swept aside by the poorly informed American educationalists in their efforts
to infuse the school system with alien notions of 'democracy' and 'individualism'. Relations between the MoE and the JTU only started to improve
– that is, they started to talk to each other – in the early 1990s as the Cold
War divide lost as much of its relevance at home as abroad. But the issue of
nationalist ideas in the educational system remains centre stage as debate
continues to rage over the content of history textbooks.

The constitution

The cornerstone of the occupation reforms, the central issue in the debate on the nature of the postwar Japanese state, is the constitution. One commentator has even gone so far as to argue that 'Japan cannot be a normal state as long as the Socialists, the constitution and the security treaty remain' (Kataoka 1991: 219). The crux of the conservative case is that the constitution is based on ideas alien to Japanese tradition and that it was forced on a reluctant Japanese government in 1946 accompanied by a vague threat that if they resisted, the emperor might be indicted as a war criminal. For some time the fiction was maintained that the constitution was produced by a collaborative effort between the Americans and the Japanese. Subsequent research has demonstrated that this was a rather misleading interpretation of the sequence of events.

In late 1945 the Japanese government was invited to submit proposals for constitutional reform, and in early February 1946 a draft was presented to SCAP but was rejected as being too conservative. Meanwhile, a Far East Commission was being established, composed of representatives of eleven nations which would have to agree to any changes in Japan's constitutional structure. It was known that the Soviet Union and some other countries wanted the emperor tried in person as a war criminal and that neither his constitutional role nor that of his successors could be guaranteed. If the debate on the constitution had been drawn out, not only would the preservation of the imperial institution be at risk – the main concern of the Japanese conservatives and regarded as crucial to the success of the occupation – but, more generally, the ability of the Americans to control the final version of the constitution would have been seriously diluted. It was, then, in the interests of both SCAP and the Japanese government to move quickly.

A small group of twenty-four was set up in the government section of SCAP on 4 February 1946, and within six days they completed a draft which was presented to the Japanese cabinet on 13 February and accepted by them 'in basic principle' on 22 February. The only major concession was the substitution of the bicameral for a unicameral assembly – an elected House of Councillors would replace the House of Peers. An election was held on 10 April 1946, the last under the old constitution, and it was this newly elected assembly that debated the constitutional proposals in the summer of 1946. The new constitution was approved by the lower house by 421 to 8 votes (six of those who voted against the proposals were communists) on 24 August, passed by the House of Peers on 6 October and approved by the Privy Council on 29 October. It came into effect on 3 May 1947.

There are three notions fundamental to the 1947 constitution and which set it apart from its predecessor: popular sovereignty, pacifism and human rights. Under the Meiji constitution, sovereignty lay with the emperor, but the main thrust of the new constitution was to marginalize the role of the emperor both as a person and an institution and to focus attention on the people of Japan. In the words of the preamble to the 1947 constitution, the authority of government is 'derived from the people, the powers of which are exercised by the representatives of the people and the benefits of which are enjoyed by the people'. Henceforth, the emperor is no more than 'the symbol of the State and of the unity of the people, deriving his position from the will of the people with whom resides sovereign power' (Article 1).

The most controversial section of the constitution is Article 9, the peace clause in which Japan apparently renounces the right to wage war and to maintain any armed forces. There are two rival explanations for the origins of the peace clause. In testimony to the US Senate given in May 1951, MacArthur claimed that the suggestion that the new constitution contain a renunciation of war came from Shidehara Kijūrō, prime minister from October 1945 to April 1946 (Stockwin 1999: 167). Others point out that in 1935 the Philippines, where MacArthur had served immediately prior to the outbreak of the war in the Pacific, adopted a constitution in which at Article II, section 2, 'The Philippines renounces war as an instrument of national policy' (Kataoka 1991: 37).

The extent to which you conclude that the 'peace clause' was imposed on Japan depends on which of these two versions you believe. In any case, as Stockwin demonstrates, significant changes were made to the wording as it passed through the lower house. For example, whereas the original draft is quite unequivocal:

> War as a sovereign right of the nation is abolished. The threat or use of force is forever renounced as a means for settling disputes with another nation.
> No army, navy or airforce or other war potential will ever be authorised and no right of belligerency will ever be conferred on the state. (Tsuneoka 1993: 97)

the final version declares: 'the Japanese people forever renounce war as a sovereign right of the nation and the threat or use of force as a means of settling international disputes' (Tsuneoka 1993: 18), which could be interpreted as permitting defence against invasion or participation in international operations.

Already by the summer of 1946 the USA might have been happy to see the force of Article 9 reduced and in 1953 Vice-President Richard Nixon asserted that it had been a mistake (Stockwin 1999: 168). Ironically, in view of the later arguments that it was imposed on Japan by the USA unfairly to constrain the development of an independent foreign policy, PM Yoshida referred to it in the 1950s to resist American pressure on the Japanese to increase defence spending. Equally, it is a strange quirk of postwar political history that left-wing critics of US foreign policy have been the strongest defenders of the peace clause and indeed the constitution as a whole.

The third element of the constitution is its commitment to human rights, which is present in three places. In the preamble, it refers to the Rooseveltian notion that 'all peoples of the world have the right to live in peace, free from fear and want . . . [and] . . . that laws of political morality are universal'. Towards the end, Article 97 states:

> The fundamental human rights by this constitution guaranteed to the people of Japan are fruits of the age-old struggle of man to be free . . . and are conferred

upon this and future generations in trust, to be held for all time inviolate. (Tsuneoka 1993: 88)

However it is Chapter 3, 'The Rights and Duties of the People', which lists the rights and freedoms in political, economic and social activity, claim rights on government – to choose and dismiss public officials – and rights related to criminal justice. It specifically guarantees the right to academic freedom, to minimum standards of wholesome and cultural living, to an education corresponding to ability and to organize, bargain and act collectively. A considerable body of judicial case law has accumulated on these rights first set out in the constitution, although, as we will see, there has been both domestic and international criticism of Japan's record on human rights.

The Japanese constitution is now one of the twenty oldest constitutions in the world of a total of more than 180 and one of the few that remains completely unrevised. Some argue that the Americans made it deliberately hard to change – amendment needs the support of at least two-thirds of each house plus a simple majority in a referendum. However, the Japanese government passed up an opportunity to review it in 1949 and many Americans expected that Japan would revise its constitution once it regained independence. Certainly, there have been many demands from conservatives that it be completely revised. A Commission on the Constitution sat between 1957 and 1964, but its recommendations were not acted upon. Interest in the constitution re-emerged during Nakasone's term in office, 1982–7, but it was only the apparently terminal decline of the JSP in the late 1990s that opened up the possibility for constitutional revision.

Public opinion shows itself to be in favour of some kind of constitutional reform and in early 2000 both houses set up 'research committees' to discuss the constitution. (English summaries of the discussions of the lower house committee can be found on its Diet website: http://www.shugiin.go.jp/itdb_main.nsf/html/index_e_kenpou.htm.) This is the first step towards serious consideration of constitutional amendment which could occur by 2010.

Bureaucracy

The purges which forced many politicians to leave public life had barely any impact on the bureaucracy and there was only limited reform of its structure. A comprehensive civil service law was enacted, a central personnel agency – the National Personnel Authority – was created and attempts were made to introduce modern (i.e. American) concepts and procedures of public management. However, the Japanese bureaucracy proved resilient to change and many of the old patterns persisted.

There was some change in the division of powers between ministries. In the early 1930s the Naimushō (Home Ministry) had exercised wide-ranging powers: police, health, welfare, local government. The Ministry of Health and Welfare (MHW) was created in 1938 to supervise the expanding welfare services; in 1947 those sections of the MHW that were responsible for labour administration became a ministry in their own right; the Ministry of Labour (MoL). Naimushō was regarded by the Americans as having played a crucial role in encouraging the spread of nationalism through its control over state Shintō, the suppression of democracy through the censorship system and both the ordinary and 'special' police. It was therefore a target for the US reformers and was finally dismantled in December 1947, with its remaining functions being distributed to the Ministry of Construction, the National Police Agency (located in the prime minister's office), the National Land Agency and Local Autonomy Agency (in 1960 promoted to full ministry status). Censorship functions were taken on by SCAP.

The wartime Ministry of Munitions became the Ministry of Commerce and Industry, but in 1949 it merged with the Board of Trade to create the Ministry of International Trade and Industry (MITI). The Ministry of Justice was reconstructed following the establishment of the Supreme Court, which directly controlled the court system. Before the war the legal profession had been under close ministerial control, but in the spirit of the 1947 constitution a new national association was created in 1949 – the Japan Federation of Bar Associations – with a high degree of independence from the state. A new Practising Attorney Act was passed which defined the primary duty of lawyers as 'to protect fundamental human rights and to ensure social justice'. The legal profession has been a key player in the promotion of human rights in postwar Japan.

The drive for the democratization of government was not limited to the national level. Not only was authority over education taken from the MoE and given to locally elected school boards, but control over the police was transferred to locally controlled public safety commissions. There was a thorough democratization of the chief executives in local government: governors and mayors were henceforth not appointed but selected via direct elections, and the locally elected assemblies were the final decision-making bodies for local policy.

During the 1950s some of this decentralization was reversed. In 1954 juris-diction over the police service was placed under the control of appointed public service commissions and the prefectural police chiefs became national, not local, officials. In 1955 strict central controls were imposed on local government finance and in the following year the school board system was revised (Muramatsu 1997: 24–5).

Capital and labour

The initial phase of economic policy was intended to ensure that Japan would not re-emerge as a significant regional power. A plan was formulated in December 1945 by an 'Ambassador for Reparations', E. W. Pauley, by which Japan would not only send reparations payments to those countries that had suffered wartime destruction, but also required that some industrial plants should be dismantled and shipped out to East Asia. This was intended to build up their economies to the same level as Japan's and to prevent Japan from using reparations payments to consolidate its economic supremacy over its neighbours. The 'Pauley plan' would have radically reconstructed Japan's industrial structure concentrating on food production and light industry, permanently reducing it to the same levels as the other countries in East Asia. Needless to say, this did not coincide with the aims of the Japanese government, which was already planning the regeneration of the economy through the stimulation of heavy industry. Nor did it coincide with American interests, at least not by the summer of 1946 when the USA was moving towards strengthening its anti-Soviet alliance and was beginning to realize how expensive the occupation policy was. In May 1947 MacArthur ordered all reparations to stop and resolution of the issue was postponed until the San Francisco Peace Treaty of 1951. In the end, only 30 per cent of the facilities designated for transportation were moved, half of them to China.

A similar pattern emerged in the occupation policy to the *zaibatsu*, the major industrial conglomerations whose control over the economy had increased during the war. *Zaibatsu* dissolution policy flowed directly from the early US policies of demilitarization. It was thought that they were both monopolistic and militaristic and that breaking them up would strengthen the 'peaceful disposition of the Japanese people' (Halliday 1975: 177) as well as making it difficult for them to direct economic activity to military ends. Yasuda, one of the big four companies, along with Mitsubishi, Mitsui and Sumitomo, devised a plan for 'voluntary' dissolution in October 1945 which satisfied MacArthur for the time being, but a more radical plan was devised in the form of the Deconcentration Law and Anti-Monopoly Law of April and December 1947. MacArthur was enthusiastic about this programme and 300 companies were listed for dissolution. However, there was considerable US investment in Japan which would have been adversely affected by the deconcentration programme and US companies allied with the *zaibatsu* to lobby vigorously against it. Meanwhile, between late 1947 and early 1948 there was a decisive shift in US policy away from demilitarization and towards building up Japan as an ally in the anti-communist struggle. From an original list of 1,200 firms, 19 were listed for deconcentration, of which only 9 were dealt with before the programme was closed.

Assessments of the dissolution programme vary. Kosai suggests that it decreased concentration of the economy, encouraging competition which permitted the growth of new companies in the high growth period after 1955 which had no connection with the *zaibatsu*. He notes in particular the reduction in monopolistic control in such areas as iron and steel, shipbuilding, beer-brewing and paper-making as well as the dissolution of the Mitsui and Mitsubishi trading companies and the breaking up of their holdings (Kosai 1988: 497). Others point out that already by 1951 three firms producing pig iron accounted for 96 per cent of total output, only three firms were producing aluminium and three producing beer. Mitsubishi Trading Company was recreated in 1954 and Mitsui Trading Company in 1959, by which time most of the conglomerates had reformed. In the long term the only significant effect of the deconcentration efforts was to modernize the management structures of the *zaibatsu*, eliminating or greatly reducing the influence of the members of the families which had built them in the nineteenth and early twentieth centuries. Contemporary critics such as T. A. Bisson argued that the dissolution programme failed to create or maintain a competitive economy and any changes in Japanese business life were incidental (Schonberger 1989: 107).

Critics suggest that during 1945–7 the cabinets consistently opposed occupation policies whether they were releasing political prisoners or ending controls on freedoms of speech, press, assembly and religion, the purge orders, or *zaibatsu* dissolution. Indeed, only with a change of emphasis after 1947 from reform to recovery was there a degree of collaboration between the conservative bureaucrats and the US shadow government. Nowhere is this pattern clearer than in the policies towards the union movement.

The pre-war union movement had reached a peak in 1936 when there were 420,000 organized workers, 6.9 per cent of the industrial workforce. In 1939 industrial unions were reorganized into the Industrial Patriotic Society, Sanpo, which might have been the organ representing labour within the IRAA if that body had developed the corporate structure that was at one time envisaged. Sanpo was dissolved in September 1945 at the same time that SCAP was proclaiming its recognition of elementary rights, which included the right to form unions. A union law was passed in December 1945 and the number of labour union members grew rapidly from 900,000 in January 1946 to more than seven million, half of the total workforce, by 1949.

The situation of the Japanese worker in later 1945 was desperate. The average monthly wage of a 40-year-old worker was ¥213 at a time when ¥509 was needed to support a family of four (Schonberger 1989: 115). Economic hardship was the principal reason for joining the unions but the very high levels of inflation constantly undermined whatever gains were made in specific struggles. So grave were the economic circumstances that unions felt they could not afford to engage in strike activity for fear that their demands might force the company into bankruptcy. Some unions adopted the radical tactic of 'production control' whereby workers dismissed the management and ran the companies themselves. The *Yomiuri* newspaper was run successfully by its workers for a time in 1946, as was a Mitsui coalmine in Hokkaido and the Keisei Electric Railway company (Dower 1999: 257–8). In most cases output increased under workers' control, but the tactic threatened one of the most basic notions of capitalist society – private property – and it could not be sanctioned by government. From spring 1946 SCAP began to cooperate with the Japanese government on the introduction of measures that would bring the union movement under control.

Not only were some workers adopting deeply subversive tactics, but the movement as a whole seemed to be slipping under the control of the communists. In August 1946 attempts to create a single union federation failed. One of the union federations, Sōdōmei, was relatively weak, with only 900,000 members and had links to the right wing of the JSP. Another, Sanbetsu Kaigi, claimed 1.5 million members and was more militant, being closely associated with the JCP. Moreover, some of the largest individual unions, for example the National Railway Workers' Union and the Teachers' Union, were believed to be aligned to the JCP. This meant that although the membership of the JCP itself was quite small – probably no more than 100,000 – as many as four million workers were aligned with it in 1947.

Not only did this alarm conservatives in the Japanese government but it was regarded as an affront by the liberal members of the occupying force, who were almost as anti-communist. In September 1946 a Labour Relations Adjustment Law was introduced with three main anti-union provisions: a ban on strikes and unions among policemen, firemen and prison guards; a ban on strikes (but not unions) among general government employees, which included teachers and railway workers; and enforceable 'arbitration procedures' in the case of strikes by workers in 'public utilities', with the government having the power to designate any enterprise a public utility. Inflation remained very high – at monthly levels of 70–80 per cent – which devalued whatever increases unions were able to negotiate from management. The Sanbetsu Kaigi found it easy to organize a protest movement against the government's economic policy, which seemed incapable of dealing with inflation and only sought to contain the left-wing workers. Their campaign was due to culminate in a general strike on 1 February 1947. Informal efforts to have the strike called off failed and so on 31 January 1947 MacArthur intervened to ban the strike.

This was the start of a more consolidated campaign to combat the influence of the Sanbetsu Kaigi federation and to restrict the activities of government employees. Democratic Leagues – Mindō – were created as anti-communist cells within the Railway Workers' Union in 1947 and were strong enough to challenge the communist faction in 1948. Mindō groups from other Sanbetsu Kaigi affiliated unions tried to take control of the national organization in June 1948, failed and were expelled (Halliday 1975: 217–18).

By the end of 1948 total production was still at only 65 per cent of 1930–4 levels when the population had been fifteen million fewer. Supporting the Japanese economy continued to be a drain on US resources and the slow recovery meant that Japan was a potentially weak link in the chain of reliable bases for US forces that stretched from Alaska to the Philippines. J. M. Dodge, a banker, was called in to recommend policies that would control inflation and gear industry towards exports. He suggested three main policies: achieve a 'balanced budget' by cutting expenditure and increasing income (mainly by tax increases); create a 'tight money' policy by restricting credit; and set a single yen–dollar exchange rate (eventually $1 = ¥360) to integrate the Japanese economy into the global capitalist system. Inflation was cut to only 24 per cent in 1949 compared to 80 per cent the previous year. However, the need to balance the budget forced government to reduce expenditure. In the railway industry 20 per cent of the workforce was made redundant (126,000). As many as 700,000 lost their jobs in the period of retrenchment of 1949–50 despite well-supported and occasionally violent strikes (Halliday 1975: 218). Most industries and corporations experienced serious management problems at this time. Strikes were called to oppose wage cuts or redundancies. Management responded with lockouts or attempts to create a second union which would be more compliant with management wishes. These second unions would exclude the militant workers and usually only be as big as the minimum number the company needed to employ at the time of maximum retrenchment, a core workforce. Thus, out of this period came two elements of the labour management structure, which was later to be called the Japanese Employment System: weak labour organized within a company union, plus a workforce that was made up of permanent employees, who were represented by the union and who were guaranteed employment and good working conditions, and temporary employees, who had none of the benefits of security of tenure, good wages or union support. Overall, the union movement was seriously weakened in the three years after 1949, losing one million members, with the unionization rate dropping from 53 to 43 per cent.

Meanwhile, the government and SCAP sought to reduce the wider influence of left-wing ideas. Early in 1949 SCAP began to call for the exclusion of communist professors from universities. A 'Red Purge' began in the public sector at the end of 1949, including the dismissal of teachers and professors, and it spread to the private sector too. On 3 May 1950 MacArthur announced that the drive to root out 'destructive communist elements' would be stepped up and by the end of 1950 about 22,000 public and private employees had been fired (Schonberger 1989: 154). This domestic drama was played out in the context of the Communist Party victory in China and the outbreak of the Korean War in which Japan supported US and UN responses to 'communist' aggression.

Repression of radical union leadership was accompanied by support for the Mindō cells within unions. Sanbetsu Kaigi lost support, rapidly dropping from 1.5 million at its peak to 47,000 members in 1951, and down to 13,000 by 1953 (Halliday 1975: 220). A new federation was formed in 1950, Sōhyō, which was more supportive of Japanese management practices, such as company unions and seniority wage systems. However, it did not turn out to be a dependable anti-socialist, pro-American labour centre. Not only did it oppose the terms of the San Francisco and Security treaties of 1951, it also allied with the JSP and JCP in opposing the reimposition of central control over the police force and education system and took a leading role in the 1959–60 struggles against the revision of the Security Treaty.

Party politics

Government operated at two levels during the occupation. On one level prime ministers were elected and cabinets formed, which appeared to be responsible for the formation of some and the implementation of all policies. Meanwhile, in the shadow there were the various divisions of SCAP supervising the demilitarization and democratization of Japan. Even at the time, it was difficult to assess the division of responsibility between the two and how far the Japanese side was able to resist or reinterpret the American policies. There were also times, for example during the implementation of the 'Dodge plan', when it suited the Japanese government to give the impression that a policy was an American imposition in order to deflect criticism. Assessment of responsibility was all the more difficult because of the strict censorship imposed by SCAP about which no comment was permitted. For example, the discussion of the draft constitution was not as free as it seemed, as no overt criticism of it was allowed. Information and discussion of the atomic bombings of Hiroshima and Nagasaki were tightly controlled. However, even if they operated within parameters enforced by the Americans, party politics did return to some kind of normality by the late 1940s and set patterns for political activity that would last through the 1950s and beyond.

Prince Higashikuni Narihiko was appointed prime minister on the day of surrender, 15 August 1945, to oversee the transition to the occupation. It was thought that generals overseas would be less likely to disobey orders to disarm if they came from a close relative of the emperor. Higashikuni signed the surrender document and coped without mishap with the early requests of the American forces. He was also quite amenable to the demands from big business to continue payment on war production contracts and indemnity claims for war damage. Johnson (1982: 178) suggests that the ¥26.6 billion paid out in the three months after surrender amounted to a third of the total paid out for this purpose between September 1937 and August 1945. Moreover, these payments continued until June 1946. Meanwhile, favoured businesses and individuals were allowed access to the foodstuffs and raw materials stored in military warehouses. Given the high rate of inflation and the rapidly changing exchange rate, it is hard to put a figure on the value of the hoarded goods that passed into the hands of the business community, but all are agreed that it substantially exceeded the $2.2 billion of American aid paid during the entire period of the occupation. Keeping food off the market in the early phase of the occupation fuelled inflation and contributed to the dire state of the urban Japanese, who had very little to eat (Schonberger 1989: 37; Cohen 1987: 338–48).

On 9 October Higashikuni was replaced by Shidehara Kijūrō, a member of the House of Peers who was a liberal with a record of having opposed the war. During his seven months in power he cooperated with the implementation of reform, ending restrictions on political, civil and religious freedom, introducing union legislation, votes for women and the early debates concerning the new constitution.

Former Seiyūkai members led by Hatoyama Ichirō set up a Japan Liberal Party in November with 43 members. Former Minseitō members and one faction of the Seiyūkai established the Japan Progressive Party, composed of 274 serving members of the lower house. A third conservative party, the Japan Cooperative Party, was formed in December with 23 members. SCAP issued purge orders against nearly all of those who had served as lower house members during the war. As a result, in late 1945 and early 1946 the Progressives saw 260 of their 274 members purged, the Liberal Party lost 30 out of 43 and the Cooperative Party 21 of 23 (Tsuzuki 2000: 345). The first postwar election used the 'large multi-member constituency system', in which each constituency returned 4–14 members with voters having 1–3 votes depending on constituency size. So many politicians had been purged that 80 per cent of those returned in this election were new. No party won a majority, but it was expected that Hatoyama, leader of the Liberal Party with 140 seats, would lead a coalition with the Progressives (94 seats). On the same night that an agreement between the parties was settled, SCAP announced that Hatoyama was purged from political life. After another flurry of negotiations, Yoshida Shigeru, Hatoyama's deputy, was agreed as a replacement. During his first term as prime minister, which lasted until May 1947, land reform was implemented, education reform introduced and parliamentary debates on the constitution took place. This period also included the defeat of the labour movement over the general strike, at which time MacArthur announced that a general election would be held at the end of May 1947.

There was much criticism of the Yoshida regime. The JSP had reformed in November 1945 and before the 1947 election was a powerful and united political force. Meanwhile, the conservatives were divided between the Liberal Party and the Progressives, who were now calling themselves the Democratic Party. Two weeks before the election Yoshida decided (with SCAP support) to revise the election law replacing the 'large' constituency system with the 'medium-sized' constituency system (2–5 representatives each) with a single vote. This gave significant advantage to the party in power whose wealth could be used more effectively. The decision is reported to have cost the JSP fifty seats (Schonberger 1989: 103). The JSP came out of the election as the biggest party, with 143 seats, but well short of a majority and facing a Liberal Party with 131 seats and the Democrats with 126. A coalition cabinet was formed by the socialist, democratic and cooperative parties led by Katayama Tetsu of the JSP, Japan's first socialist prime minister. However, he had to make major concessions to his coalition partners, including keeping his left-wing colleagues out of the cabinet, a dilution of their coal nationalization programme and a promise not to reveal state secrets. This latter referred to the extent of SCAP intervention in the policy-making process and the results of investigations into the disappearance of 'hoarded goods'.

The Katayama cabinet lasted only eight months, being brought down in part by internal dissension. It was followed by a cabinet led by Ashida Hitoshi, leader of the Democratic Party, but which included some JSP members. The presence of socialists in the cabinet did not prevent them from approving SCAP orders to ban government employees from calling strikes or engaging in any form of collective action. In October 1948 the Ashida government fell following accusations that senior ministers (including Ashida himself and his deputy) had accepted bribes in return for arranging low interest loans. All were eventually cleared.

This paved the way for Yoshida Shigeru to return to the post of prime minister, which he would retain for the next six years, making him the key figure in the transition from occupation to independence. In the election of January 1949 Yoshida's Democratic Liberals won a clear majority, while the JSP was humiliated, winning only 13.5 per cent of the votes and 48 seats. Recriminations within the JSP culminated in a split into left and right between 1951 and 1955. The JCP won 35 seats with 9.7 per cent of the vote. Communist

influence did not last beyond the Red Purge and the outbreak of the Korean
War. They compounded their difficulties when at their October 1951 conference they rejected the parliamentary road to socialism and adopted a stance
of opposition to American imperialism and capitalism that included guerrilla
warfare tactics. This prompted arrests by the police of leading members.
Those not arrested went underground or fled to China.

Yoshida was sympathetic to the political and economic aims of the occupation, whose priorities were now to make Japanese industry internationally
competitive and to undermine the influence of the labour unions and left-
wing parties, but this was not a stable or happy time for Japan. There was
sharp internal rivalry within Yoshida's own party, which, despite its majority
in the lower house, did not control the House of Councillors. Strikes continued and in the first quarter of 1950 business confidence fell so low that the
Tokyo Stock Exchange dropped from 150 to 101. Yoshida's position was only
saved by the outbreak of the Korean War, which provided additional justification for the anti-communist policy and brought an immediate $40 million
in special procurement orders for Japanese companies from the US military.
This grew to a total of $4 billion by June 1954, providing a kick start for
Japanese industrial growth (Calder 1988: 81).

There were other, less welcome consequences of war. As American troops
left their bases in Japan to fight in Korea, it was felt there was a need to create
a force that could be used to suppress any internal dissent that might be led
by the JCP or other leftists. In July 1950, less than a month after the outbreak
of the Korean War, Yoshida agreed to an American request that a 75,000-
strong National Police Reserve be created. Former officers of the imperial
army were appointed to lead it (Bailey 1996: 61). This would be equipped
with artillery and tanks the following year, and renamed the Self Defence
Forces (SDF).

Factional rivalry within the conservative coalition intensified with the
lifting of the political restrictions on Hatoyama and others purged in 1945–6.
He, along with 138 other 'depurgees', was elected to the lower house in
October 1952. For the next two years Yoshida would cling to power, facing
mounting criticism from Hatoyama and defending his party colleagues from
another round of charges of bribery in 1954. In the years just before and just
after Japan's reversion to independence there was little evidence of political
stability and most economic growth seemed to depend on supplying US
forces in Asia.

Japan and the world at the end of the occupation

The end of the occupation came at the price of accepting dependence on the
USA and was agreed in three parts. First came the Peace Treaty, signed on
8 September 1951 (to be effective from April 1952) at a stage-managed
ceremony in San Francisco attended by the forty-nine European and Latin
American allies of the USA. The Soviet Union was opposed to the treaty
and the mainland Chinese government was not recognized by the Americans,

so it was a 'partial' peace treaty and Japan's diplomatic relations with the USSR and the People's Republic of China were left unresolved. Later that same day a bilateral Security Treaty was signed by Yoshida and US Secretary of State Dean Acheson, whose details were only gradually revealed to the Japanese people. Somewhat later, in January–February 1952, an administrative agreement was made in secret between the Japanese and American governments.

Although it came in three instalments, the end of the occupation amounted to a single package. In the Peace Treaty Japan agreed to renounce all claims to former imperial territories, but was freed of any obligation to pay further reparations to them or anyone else. Japan was not required to maintain any of the occupation reforms, but was obliged to accept the continued US occupation of the islands of Okinawa. Japan did not renounce claims for the return of Sakhalin and the Kurile Islands by the Soviet Union. In accepting the Security Treaty, Yoshida was agreeing to the presence of an undefined number of US military personnel on Japanese soil, at the time about 210,000 US troops in 300 bases (Calder 1988: 416). The USA had the authority to suppress disturbances within Japan and had no obligation to consult with the Japanese government if troops based in Japan were sent into action in a third country. By the administrative agreement, the US military in Japan was given the right to take control of those areas they required for military purposes. They could arrest Japanese citizens causing disturbance even outside US bases, while American courts had jurisdiction over all Americans in Japan, even when off duty and away from the base. Many saw this as a modern unequal treaty, including a new form of extra-territoriality.

Yoshida was convinced that the new Chinese communist regime did not pose a threat to Japan. Moreover, he and much of the business community saw China as a natural market for Japanese goods and indeed some companies had already succeeded in resuming exports to the mainland. He was compelled, however, to accept US policy on China, abide by the trade boycott and sign a treaty with the KMT based in Taipei in April 1952. Thus Japan was bound both in its defence and foreign policy not to contradict, if not always to serve, the main aims of US policy in the Pacific. Such subordination was resented and criticized by many, both on the left and right of the political spectrum.

The impact of the occupation

Japan's conservative elite in mid-1945 feared that revolution would be the inevitable consequence of defeat. When by autumn 1945 it was clear that this was not going to happen, the priority shifted to minimizing the impact of the US reform programme. Japanese liberals, socialists and communists released from prison or freed of restriction welcomed the occupying forces and cooperated positively with the reform process.

Meanwhile, on the American side there was a division. The majority regarded the wartime nationalism as an aberration which had forced Japan

off the path of modernization and peaceful cooperation with the western
capitalist countries. This group was very positive about the immediate impact
and long-term consequences of the occupation-induced reforms. Herbert
Passin even goes as far as to assert: 'The American Occupation of Japan
certainly ranks as one of, if not *the* proudest achievements of post-war
American foreign policy; it was among other things central to the development of Japan's "modern miracle"' (in Cohen 1987: xi). Other commentators
stressed that the roots of authoritarianism went much deeper and can be
traced back to the state structure devised in the Meiji period. Basic and
thoroughgoing reform, including the removal of the emperor from the
political system, would have been needed to eliminate the old power structures and permit genuine democratization of the system. Not only were these
views a minority in the late 1940s, they were identified as 'communist' in the
witch-hunt atmosphere of the early 1950s, and cost both jobs and outlets
for publication. Only in the 1970s did scholars emerge who would attempt to
reassess the often extravagant claims of the 'conservative' school.

My view is that there was a socialist, liberal, anti-establishment 'tradition'
in Japan, which can be traced back to at least the 1870s and which was open
to critical ideas which it attempted to implement at times when the authority of the state ebbed. We saw earlier examples of this happening in the first
and third decades of the twentieth century, and then again in the fifth. The
main difference was that in the second half of the 1940s it was Americans in
Japan who were encouraging the implementation of liberal ideas which many
conservatives wanted to resist and would indeed 'roll back' in the 1950s. To
generalize, it was only where a social group was in a position to defend the
integrity of the reforms that it was able to resist the 'roll back' process: the
teachers in their classrooms or the tenant farmers in their fields.

Contrary to the claims of conservatives both in Japan and in the USA, the
occupation was never as radical as it seemed. The US forces did not intervene as forcefully as they might have done to prevent the hoarding of goods
or compensation of cancelled contracts in the first weeks and months, which
provided the material basis for the urban elites to retain their economic
power, political authority and social status. And while land reform did deprive
landowners of their prime source of income, most landowning families
retained their social and political positions within their communities and in
any case received compensation in the 1960s. The 'peace clause', which the
US government was soon to regret, did not prevent a strong and probably
intentional continuity between the leadership of the imperial army and the
officer class of the SDF. Even as late as 1970, 80 per cent of the top personnel of the SDF came from the pre-1945 military.

There was continuity too in the political elites. Not only did the Liberal
and Democratic parties regroup around the remnants of the pre-war Seiyūkai
and Minseitō, but the massive influx of 'depurgees' in 1952 meant that the
personalities in postwar Japanese politics were linked to pre-war patterns.
The early commitment to union rights was not sustained in the face of
attempts by union leaders to use those rights to force concessions in negotiations about employment practices. Similarly, the attempts to weaken the

control of the major conglomerates were abandoned as soon as they might affect economic growth.

Very little had been resolved by the end of the occupation. The political parties were either divided or weakened by factional rivalry. The economy was growing, but only, it seemed, because of the good fortune of military procurement. It still seemed fundamentally weak. A reformed political structure and constitution existed, but many, including the Americans, expected that Japan would revise its constitution soon after independence. The occupation had set Japan off on a new trajectory, but many of the personnel and attitudes remained unchanged.

Part II
Parties

4

Conservatives and their Allies

The Liberal Democratic Party's (LDP) dominance of government is the single most important fact in Japan's postwar political history. At the time of writing, it is still the party in power, even if its control of politics was no longer as secure as it had been at the start of the 1990s. Until 1993 it was common to regard LDP rule as inevitable, unchallengeable and likely to continue for 'half an eternity'. Meanwhile, this scenario condemned opposition parties to a permanent presence on the sidelines of politics, able to make loud noises but never able to influence the course of play. As things were to turn out, all the opposition parties, with the exception of the JCP, were to take some part in government in the mid-1990s and LDP weakness in the House of Councillors means that it is likely to depend on some kind of coalition arrangement until at least 2004. However, the events of the period after 1992 will be considered in chapter 9. The purpose of this chapter is to outline the process which allowed the conservatives to occupy the driving seat in Japanese political life for most of the time from 1945 until the early 1990s – the rise and rise of the '1955 system'.

In the earlier chapter on the occupation we saw how the conservative parties created in the occupation period claimed links with the pre-war parties, the Seiyūkai and Minseitō, but that the purge severely reduced their ranks: of candidates wanting to stand in 1946 only 10 of the 274 Minseitō, 10 of the 43 Seiyūkai and 2 of the 23 Cooperative Party candidates escaped the purge and only 38 of the 456 elected in 1946 had been in the previous parliament (Pempel 1998: 88, 99). Following the end of the occupation, all restrictions were lifted and the question was whether or not fundamental changes had been made to the architecture of political life so that old patterns would reassert themselves.

In what follows we will be chiefly concerned to explain the development of the LDP, but to make the topic more manageable we will start with a

section on the 'pre-history' of the system, then look at the LDP from the time
of its foundation to 1972, the year when Satō Eisaku ceased to be prime
minister, trace the sequence of events from Tanaka to Takeshita in 1972–89
and conclude with what turned out to be the coda to LDP domination, from
Uno to Miyazawa.

The LDP: pre-history and formation

Yoshida Shigeru became prime minister in April 1946 only because
Hatoyama Ichirō, leader of the Democratic Party, was purged by the occupation authorities. The Socialist Party, led by Katayama Tetsu, emerged as
the largest party in the elections of May 1947 and with the support of the
Democrats formed a coalition government. This arrangement proved unstable and all attempts to sustain a left–centre party coalition ceased in 1948
when Ashida Hitoshi, leader of the Democrats and prime minister, Nishio
Suehiro, leader of the JSP, and 62 other ministers and officials were arrested
on charges of bribery and corruption. Yoshida took over once more and in
the election of January 1949 his party, now called the Democratic Liberals,
won a clear majority – 264 of 466 seats – and the conservatives appeared to
be back in charge, a trend confirmed when 33 Democrats joined Yoshida's
party. Between October 1950 and August 1951 nearly 100,000 of those purged
for their wartime activities were allowed to return to public life, including
Hatoyama Ichirō and Kishi Nobusuke (see below) who immediately resumed
political activity.

However, Yoshida refused to step aside to permit Hatoyama to take over
as prime minister, forcing him to set up a faction in January 1952. Meanwhile,
Miki Takeo, who had led his Cooperative Party into an alliance with the
Democratic Liberals, set up a Reform Party (Kaishintō) in February 1952 and
Kishi established a Reconstruction League in April 1952. The Liberal Party
remained formally united with Yoshida at its head, but only retained a narrow
majority in the October 1952 elections in which the left and right wings of
the Socialist Party regained much of the ground lost in 1949. They stepped
up their criticism of government policy, especially the re-creation of the
armed forces, while Hatoyama led criticism from the right. This two-pronged
attack culminated in a vote of no confidence being proposed by the socialists, which was also supported by the dissident conservatives so that the government was forced to call another election in April 1953. Yoshida's Liberals
came out of this with 199 seats as the largest party but had to enter into a
coalition with the Reform Party to stay in power. Meanwhile, Hatoyama's
liberals won 35 seats and they continued to snipe at government policy. In
April 1954 the socialists narrowly failed to pass another no confidence motion
in the wake of a ship-building scandal that was so serious that Yoshida had
personally to intervene to prevent the arrest of the Liberal Party's general
secretary, Satō Eisaku. By this point, opposition to Yoshida had spread even
to his coalition partners, and leaders of the Reform Party proposed in
October 1954 that a new conservative party be formed after Yoshida had

been removed from office. On his return from a two-month overseas trip in December 1954, Yoshida was forced to resign, his post being taken by Hatoyama. Some see this as being a more important watershed than the formation of the LDP some ten months later. Certainly Yoshida's removal from office reduced the personalized conflict from the heart of conservative politics. Moreover, December 1954 was the time when conservatives and business leaders agreed on the need to unify the forces of conservatism.

The LDP and the business community

In January 1955 an Economic Reconstruction Council (Keizai Saiken Kondankai) was formed with the support of the four business organizations – the Keidanren, Nikkeiren, Keizai Dōyūkai and Nisshō – to act as a channel for contributions to the conservative party. These four organizations provided crucial support for the LDP and made important contributions to the policy-making process from this time. Largest and most important is the Keidanren (Federation of Economic Associations) which is composed of more than 800 of Japan's largest corporations and 110 industry-wide groups. At any one time it has up to thirty-two permanent committees developing policy proposals in close contact with counterparts in the LDP and the ministries. Nikkeiren (Japan Federation of Employers' Associations) is composed of more than 30,000 employers organized in forty-seven regional and fifty-one industrial associations. Its most conspicuous role is to engage with organized labour, particularly at the time of the *Shuntō* (Spring offensive – see below) negotiations. The Keizai Dōyūkai (Japan Council for Economic Development) is made up of around 1,400 individuals, most of them senior executives in major corporations. It has coordinated welfare-oriented policies that have crossed ideological and party lines. Finally, Nisshō (the Japan Chamber of Commerce and Industry, JCCI), founded in 1878, coordinates the activities of the 478 regional chambers of commerce. Particularly since the 1970s, it has championed the cause of small and medium-sized industries in negotiations with the LDP (Calder 1988: 197–201).

In 1961 the LDP was streamlining its structure in a futile attempt to eliminate factions, and at the same time the central fundraising unit was reorganized to create the Kokumin Kyōkai (People's Association) (Halliday 1975: 267–8). In 1975, in the wake of the Lockheed scandal (see pp. 70–1), changes were made in the law on political donations and the organization changed once more and became the Kokumin Seiji Kyōkai (People's Political Association). The main function of this body has been to channel funds from business into the LDP. Over 90 per cent of the LDP's official income came through it (Dower 1993: 16).

To return to the 1950s: despite the agreement between politicians and business leaders on the need for a consolidated conservative party, personal rivalry delayed its creation. In the end it was formed less as a positive force to support a raft of conservative ideas and more as an anti-socialist coalition. In the election of February 1955 the two wings of the socialist party won sufficient seats (sixty-seven for the right, eighty-nine for the left) to block constitutional revision. At the same time the labour federation, Sōhyō, was mobilizing its followers, 800,000 of them in one demonstration, in what subsequently became known as the *Shuntō* ('Spring offensive') in which the unions demanded industry-wide wage increases. Moreover, during the summer of 1955 left- and right-wing socialists overcame their differences and reunited on 13 October. The left as a whole seemed to be gathering a momentum which might take it back into government.

Following the creation of a single funding mechanism and a single opposition party, the conservatives could not afford to be divided. Despite lingering rivalries among the Liberal Party leadership, and with the encouragement of the USA (whose CIA provided funds), the Liberal and Democratic parties merged their forces of 112 and 185 respectively to create the Liberal Democratic Party on 15 November 1955 (Pempel 1998: 101). At the next election, May 1958, the LDP won 287 seats to the JSP's 166. A two-party system was formed. Or so it seemed.

The years of stable growth

Hatoyama Ichirō had waited almost ten years to lead his party and country, only to serve for two years until 1956. He was replaced by Ishibashi Tanzan, who was only in office a few months before resigning for health reasons in July 1957. Ishibashi and Hatoyama were part of a cluster of politicians within the LDP who favoured positive rearmament, a constitution revised to eliminate Article 9 and a build-up of troops. They were unhappy with a foreign policy that depended on unquestioning acceptance of US strategy and sought the implementation of Keynesian economic measures to stimulate the economy along with a package of subsidies and protection for key industries. A second group, linked to the former Democratic Party, was critical of the Security Treaty, favoured a tilt in foreign policy towards Asia, but was almost social democratic in its advocacy of closer links with unions and increased economic planning to correct the 'abuses of capitalism'. This group contained Miki Takeo and Ashida Hitoshi, among others. The mainstream, however, were the successors to Yoshida: Ikeda Hayato, Satō Eisaku and Fukuda Takeo. In foreign policy they were content with the close alignment with the USA as long as it did not require an expansion of Japan's own military, and in economic policy they sought tight control of government spending, while emphasizing growth (Pempel 1998: 106).

Kishi Nobusuke was detained as a war criminal for three years because of his links with the Ministry of Munitions, but released in 1948 with no charges brought. This did not prevent him from succeeding Ishibashi in February 1957. Some recentralization of the police force had taken place in 1954, partially reversing the US reforms, but under Kishi a bill was put before parliament that would have substantially increased the police powers of interrogation, search and arrest and control over demonstrations. To the socialists, this seemed like an attempt to recreate aspects of the pre-war authoritarian state, infringing the basic human rights set out in the constitution. Boycotts and barricades in parliament were accompanied by strikes and demonstrations on the streets, which finally persuaded the government to shelve the proposal. An efficiency rating system for teachers was introduced to increase the control of the MoE within schools and weaken the militant teachers' union. This too aroused mass protest, but was eventually passed.

In many industries there had been serious confrontation with labour in the late 1940s or early 1950s as managements had sought to rationalize manpower and rid themselves of troublesome union activists. From the early 1950s oil refineries started to reopen and, faced with this competition, owners of coalmines began plans to run down the industry: to cut back on investment and to seek to dismiss workers. An earlier attempt in 1953 to cut the workforce by the Mitsui Mining Company had been successfully resisted following a 113-day strike. In 1959 the company announced another 'rationalization' plan that would make more than 4,500 miners redundant. The Miners' Union (Tanrō), with the support of Sōhyō, opposed this and the Miike branch went on all-out strike from January 1960. As had often happened in strikes in Japan, it was not long before a new union was formed which declared itself averse to the 'class struggle' tactics of the main union and said that it wanted to start work. Not surprisingly there were violent scuffles between the members of the two unions, in one of which a gangster supporting the new union and management stabbed and killed a Tanrō member. On 7 July, Sōhyō organized a rally of 40,000 outside the mine. The outcome in the short term was the defeat of the radical union, recognition by management of the moderate second union and negotiation of a solution. In the longer term the coal industry was heading for rapid contraction: the share of coal in primary energy supply dropped from 31.3 per cent to 6.1 per cent between 1961 and 1971 (Tsuzuki 2000: 391–2).

These domestic crises were compounded by a crisis about defence and foreign policy. The Security Treaty (*Ampo*) was signed by the US and Japanese governments in San Francisco in 1951. In it, Japan accepted the continued presence of US bases on Japanese soil, agreed not to allow any other country to base their troops in Japan without US permission and even gave the US the right to intervene in the case of domestic disturbance; all in return for US military protection. This suited Yoshida, who wanted to restrain military expenditure so that resources could be concentrated on economic growth, but it was characterized as subordination to US imperialism by the left and regarded by many within the LDP as equivalent to the 'unequal' treaties imposed on Japan during the nineteenth century. Formal negotiations to revise the treaty began in November 1958 and in February/March 1959 a People's Council for the Prevention of the Revision of the Security Treaty was formed by members of the Socialist and Communist parties. Over the next twelve months Kishi led negotiations which resulted in Japan substantially increasing its independence of action without reducing the US commitment to the defence of Japan or committing Japan to an increase in military expenditure. The agreement was signed by Kishi in the White House on 19 January 1960 and he then returned to Japan to seek parliamentary ratification.

The anti-security treaty movement (known as anti-*Ampo*) would accept nothing less than the complete abrogation of the treaty and organized demonstrations in major cities and in parliament. Parliamentary business was in any case being disrupted by debates on the Miike crisis. Delaying tactics prevented the treaty from being passed by the lower house before the end of the normal session, 26 April, but it had to be approved by 19 May if all the remaining stages were to be complete before the arrival of US President Eisenhower on 19 June. Burly members of the JSP and their secretaries, who prevented the Speaker from leaving his office to call a vote, were expelled from the building on Kishi's orders. Later that night, in a chamber attended only by LDP members, a vote was taken to ratify the treaty. That did not end the crisis. Demonstrations continued into June, the most violent taking place on 15 June, which left hundreds of students and police injured, 196 students arrested and 1 dead. The planned visit by Eisenhower was cancelled, as his safety could not be guaranteed. Kishi put SDF troops and tanks on alert to be brought in to put down the violence (Tsuzuki 2000: 386).

However, Kishi did not have the support of all of his party. Some were critical of the deal he had done with the Americans, others simply disliked the way he had pushed the treaty through the ratification process. Several key members of the party had absented themselves from the midnight session of 19/20 May – Ishibashi Tanzan and Miki Takeo among others. Political violence and instability affected the stock market and the value of Japanese bonds abroad. The major business federations called in public for political stability and in private for a replacement for Kishi (Calder 1988: 95).

Two days after the most violent of the demonstrations, Kishi was replaced by Ikeda Hayato. Despite having a reputation for a brusque lack of sympathy for the poor or the bankrupt, Ikeda's first moves as prime minister were conciliatory. He introduced measures that facilitated the settlement of the Miike dispute and was less confrontational with the opposition parties. More generally, he adopted 'low-posture politics', placing economic growth at the centre of his and the LDP's agenda. He famously committed the government to an 'income doubling plan' which not only promised to double all incomes over the next ten years but also to improve social security, increase spending on education and science and assist the development of the industrial infrastructure. Ikeda's income doubling plan was less a prediction and more a political agenda. When it became clear that the Japanese economy was in fact growing faster even than the planned rate, the LDP could take the credit.

Despite all its problems in the first half of the year, the LDP won 296 (of 467) seats in elections of November 1960, which was 13 more than in 1958. This success at the polls was repeated throughout the 1960s even though there was a slow decline in its overall electoral support: it got 54.7 per cent of the total vote in 1963 and 47.6 per cent in 1969. In 1964 Ikeda was elected to an unprecedented third term as president of the party, but illness forced him to resign, and his place was taken by Satō Eisaku. Both of these prime ministers who served in this 'golden age' of LDP rule deliberately sought to avoid divisive domestic conflict. The commission on the constitution ceased activity in 1964 after ten years of controversy. Ikeda and Satō were both content to play a low-key role in international affairs beneath the protection of the US 'nuclear umbrella' with a defence budget that fell below 1 per cent of GNP, where it remained for the next twenty years.

Meanwhile, the economy grew rapidly. Total GNP surpassed the pre-war total in 1955; thereafter, it grew an average of 8 per cent each year from 1955 to 1959 and 12 per cent from 1960 to 1964. A severe recession struck in 1964–5 which was overcome by the issue of national bonds as a stimulus for recovery (Tsuzuki 2000: 397). An annual growth rate of around 9 per cent was resumed for the rest of the 1960s only to be interrupted by the 'shock' of Nixon's new economic policy of 1971 and after. This rate of growth meant that Japan's total GNP exceeded that of the UK and Italy in 1964 and by the end of the decade it had accelerated past that of West Germany to make it the third largest economy in the world, only behind that of the USA and the USSR. In 1964 Japan became the first non-western nation to join the OECD. Moreover, the benefits of growth were felt by many Japanese. Few people owned any electric consumer goods in the 1950s but by 1964 27 per cent had a vacuum cleaner, 61 per cent had a washing machine, 38 per cent a refrigerator and nearly 90 per cent owned a television. Owner-ship of these basic consumer items would reach almost 100 per cent by the end of the decade.

This was a time of rapid urbanization of the country and industrialization of industry, but the new prosperity was not confined to urban areas. Policies originally intended to encourage food production in the late 1940s were elab-orated in the early 1960s to provide generous subsidies to rice farmers. This not only prevented social division between the rural and urban areas but also kept the rural vote loyal to the LDP. During the late 1940s and early 1950s the farming community had been organized by the Ministry of Agriculture, Forestry and Fisheries (MAFF) into cooperatives collectively known as Nōkyō (Agricultural Cooperatives Association). More than 4,000 coopera-tives were created as the basic units of a vast organization that includes the entire farming population and has more than 500,000 employees. Nōkyō bodies handle supply and marketing for its members as well as providing insurance and banking services. Government subsidies go through the Nōkyō bank. MAFF specialist advice is provided through Nōkyō channels. Until at least the 1970s the LDP had weak grassroots party organizations: for many LDP parliamentarians, the Nōkyō branch in their support organization *kōenkai* acted as their grassroots support group. It is said that at least 60 per cent of the LDP were tied to Nōkyō. Constituency boundaries remained unchanged from the late 1940s until the mid-1990s, which ensured that the rural communities were over-represented in parliament. So despite the dwindling importance of the agricultural sector within the economy, the political significance of the agriculture lobby (i.e. Nōkyō) remained high, at least until the electoral reforms of 1994 (see Mulgan 2000).

Satō remained prime minister until July 1972, during which time the LDP experienced a period of unprecedented internal tranquillity. The party could claim credit for the rapid economic growth of the 1960s and in 1969 it increased its number of seats in the lower house to 288, despite a looming political scandal. Satō's faction was the largest in the party and was unchallenged. In its foreign policy, Japan had negotiated a treaty with South Korea in 1965, paving the way for closer economic links. In November 1969, US President Nixon agreed to the return of Okinawa to Japanese sovereignty, which finally took place in May 1972. Thus, two of the outstanding postwar issues were settled.

Opposition to government policy could still rouse extra-parliamentary protest. There had been massive demonstrations against the normalization of relations with South Korea in 1965. A period of violence on university campuses in 1968–9 began as protests against increased charges for higher education, but merged with wider issues such as protest about Japan's involvement in the Vietnam War. The Security Treaty was up for revision again and a second anti-*Ampo* campaign began in 1969 which was supported by more people than that of 1959–60. The issue was defused when it was agreed automatically to extend it until either country give notice of annulment one year in advance.

Satō might have continued as prime minister for several more years had his position not been undermined by US policy change. In 1971 Japan experienced two 'Nixon shocks'. The first came in July, when, with little warning and no prior consultation, President Nixon announced he would visit China. This reversed the anti-China policy that Japan had supported at considerable political and economic cost over the previous twenty years. The second shock came in August, when America put an end to the dollar's convertibility into gold, thus upsetting the international exchange rate system within which the yen was pegged at ¥360 = $1. Within the floating exchange rate system the yen strengthened against the dollar, making export goods less competitive in world markets. Two years later a third shock – the oil crisis – further damaged the faltering economy, and the rate of growth fell back to 3–4 per cent throughout the 1970s.

In spring 1972 Satō announced his intention to retire. There was fierce competition among the faction leaders over who should succeed him. Fukuda Takeo (b. 1905), a graduate of Tokyo University, had been in the Ministry of Finance (MoF) until entering politics in the late 1940s. By virtue of both seniority and expressed preference of Satō, he was expected to take over. However, Tanaka Kakuei (b. 1918) made up for his relative youth, lack of university education and absence of bureaucratic background by his vast personal wealth and the fact that he was poised to take over Satō's faction. In the end it was cash that was the trump card. Tanaka had more of it and he used it more brazenly to win over those who were hesitant to support Fukuda. In July 1972, Tanaka became prime minister. There was considerable resistance to Tanaka within the party and factional rivalry continued at a high level throughout the 1970s, at times seeming likely to split the party. This, then, is an appropriate place for a digression on factions in Japanese politics, particularly the LDP.

Factions (habatsu)

Sociologists point out that most Japanese social institutions have patron–client relations as their basic building blocks. This creates patterns of personalized relationships within organizations whose importance will usually transcend any particular attachment to method (in the arts) or ideology (in politics). In turn, this can lead to sets of 'local' loyalties that may be stronger than loyalty to the organization as a whole, such that when the organization encounters a crisis, whether internally generated or because of a change in external circumstances, a senior dissenting individual may defect from the organization taking most if not all of his or her followers to create a rival group. Japan's social and cultural history is replete with examples of internal factional rivalry culminating in division, as disagreement over doctrinal interpretation or appropriate method or strategy proves not to be resolvable by compromise.

Not all political parties in Japan have had to cope with problems generated by factions (*habatsu*). Kōmeitō (CGP – the Clean Government Party) and the JCP have imposed tight internal discipline to prevent the emergence of factions. On the other hand, factions have been almost as troublesome for leaders of the JSP as they have been for the LDP, except that factional infighting there has been linked to the kind of ideological disputes common to democratic socialist parties all over the world. One of the unusual features of the factionalism within the LDP is that it has very little to do with ideological or policy issues. In the LDP's case, the origins of the factional structure are closely linked to the way the party was formed from a number of conservative groups with little more in common than an anti-socialist bias and a desire to be funded by big business. We have already pointed out that there were in the mid-1950s three main groups which had their origins in the Liberal, Democratic and Progressive parties, although these labels did not signify much, either then or later. A genealogy of factions can be drawn up which shows that few faction leaders manage to hold on to their positions for more than ten years. On their death or retirement from politics, either the faction is dissolved or it is taken over by one of the leader's close followers, not infrequently following a squabble over who is the rightful heir to the post.

Factions within the LDP have been sustained by the multi-member constituency system which was the basis for all elections until the 1994 reform in the method for electing the lower house (see figure 4.1). This made it easy for the LDP to be launched in 1955, as few if any elected conservatives lost their seats as a result of unification, unlike, for example what would have happened if there had been single member constituencies. Thereafter, where there was more than one LDP candidate in a constituency (i.e. nearly all of them), another candidate from the same party was as much, if not more, of a threat to someone's chances of re-election than were the opposition parties. Funds from the party made up only part of what a candidate needed to ensure election. Some money could be raised locally through a *kōenkai*, but the cash

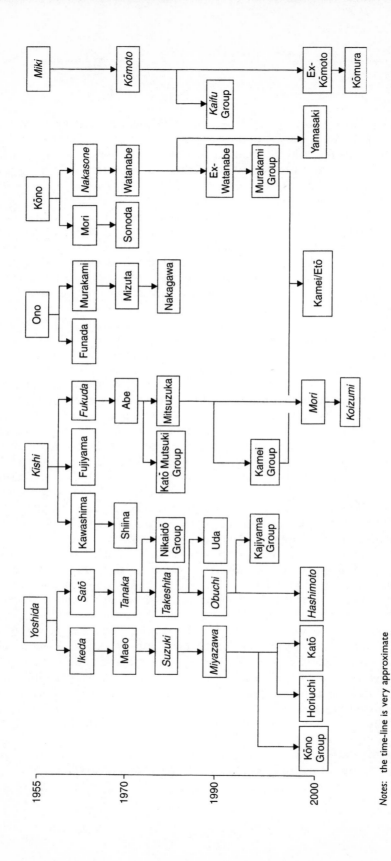

Notes: the time-line is very approximate
        names in italics indicate those who have been prime minister
Source: adapted from Fukuoka 2001: 150

Figure 4.1   Development of the main factions in the LDP, 1955–2001

supplied by a faction could make the difference between success and failure – and we are not talking about small sums of money here: in the 1974 upper house election, Fukuda supplied each of his faction's candidates with ¥5 million; Tanaka provided his faction with ¥30 million each (approximately $17,000 and $100,000 respectively; Weir 1999: 60). In 1992 it was estimated that even in a non-election year a parliamentarian needed $1.4 million when the salary and party subsidy amounted to $400,000 (Pempel 1998: 184). A major function of factions has been to act as a channel for funds to bridge this gap.

The other resource with which a faction leader can supply his followers is access to positions in government. Prior to each cabinet reshuffle, the faction leaders present the prime minister with a list of the people they wish to see in government. Those factions that supported the prime minister in his bid to become president of the party will get more seats, but it is important for all factions to be represented in cabinet to keep the party united. A faction leader will want full cabinet posts for himself or the senior members of his faction (those elected five or six times), particularly those who have not had a turn as a minister, and posts such as political vice-ministers for those elected just two or three times. Government posts, particularly seats in the cabinet, can be regarded as resources which the prime minister and faction leaders can use to reward party and faction members and thus maintain unity. The amount of resources available can be doubled by shuffling the cabinet every year rather than every two years. Thus, irrespective of how well a prime minister or cabinet is performing in terms of policy-making, six to nine months after the formation of a cabinet, he will come under pressure from within his party to carry out a cabinet reshuffle. When Tanaka Kakuei was prime minister, he shuffled his cabinet four times in twenty-nine months.

A post in government, even its lowly echelons, can significantly improve a person's chances of re-election by enhancing his standing in the eyes of his supporters. It can also put him in touch with parts of the bureaucracy that may be able to ensure that projects are more likely to benefit his supporters rather than those of rivals in the same or neighbouring constituencies.

But what does the faction member give in return for this cash and preferment? Ultimately, it comes down to just one thing: unquestioning support in the elections to the post of LDP leader. The president of the LDP is elected for periods of two years. There has been some tinkering about with the system over the years, but it is still the members of parliament who are the main electors. The leader of a large faction will play a major role in the selection of the party leader and will expect to take on that role at some time in his career. However, the personal nature of the patron–client relationship and the limits to the amount of money any one man can raise has meant that it has proved hard to sustain factions with more than 100 members. At its peak, the Tanaka faction had 119 members, but the optimum size seems to be between 40 and 70. Given that at any one time there are between 350 and 400 LDP members in both houses, it will require a coalition of faction leaders to ensure the success of one of them. In the votes that are taken, a leader must be able to depend on his followers voting for the agreed person. The rewards for loyalty, then, are cash and posts; the penalty for disloyalty is expulsion from the faction. This not only cuts the individual off from resources, but will put him to the back of the queue should he join another faction, since it is seniority in the faction that counts, not age or seniority in the party or house. This discourages movement between factions, although the pattern of the factions is a constantly changing picture.

The LDP from Satō to Suzuki

The faction led by Satō had 102 members by the early 1970s. In 1972 he had been in power for nearly eight years and one of his senior supporters, Tanaka Kakuei, was building up a group that was becoming dependent on his cash handouts. Even before Satō announced his decision to retire, 81 of the 102 members in his faction pledged their allegiance to Tanaka. Fifteen years later, after Tanaka was incapacitated by a stroke, Takeshita Noboru, his principal lieutenant, would use a similar tactic to build up a personal following which later became the basis of a new, Takeshita faction. Although culture places a strong value on loyalty – Tanaka's actions were described as 'patricide' – and rewards it, when the prospects of cash or personal advancement are greater from joining a break-away group than staying, loyalties are easily set aside.

Satō had become prime minister when the economy was growing rapidly, and within a year after taking power three of his factional rivals died. Tanaka was not so lucky. The economy was stalling in the face of the revaluation of the yen and the quadrupling of oil prices. The years of rapid growth were over. Within the LDP, Tanaka was surrounded by rivals, not only Fukuda Takeo, but also Ohira Masayoshi and Nakasone Yasuhiro. Furthermore, although the LDP had a majority in the lower house, the LDP vote was steadily falling such that it was predicted that by 1974 the party would lose its overall majority. Already in 1971, the combined socialist/communist vote in Tokyo was over 60 per cent, while the LDP vote was below 30 per cent (Calder 1988: 107). It seemed that only the over-representation of rural areas was keeping the LDP in power. There was criticism of the LDP from the business community, and there was talk of an imminent split in the party that would lead to a major realignment. Miki Takeo, leader of one of the more centrist factions, began to explore the prospects for a cross-party coalition that might take power if a split were to happen. In the autumn of 1974 there were revelations about some of Tanaka's murky financial dealings that proved so serious that he resigned in December. In the midst of this crisis the LDP sought a candidate for prime minister who could rescue it from its sleazy image and Miki was the obvious choice, even though it was clear from the start that he would only play a transitional role.

Miki did indeed only serve one two-year term, but it was one in which there were important developments. First, evidence was presented to a US Senate committee that executives of the Lockheed company had given several million dollars in bribes to Japanese politicians. Miki might have been able to protect his party colleagues as Yoshida had protected Satō in 1954, but he allowed the investigators free rein. In July 1976 Tanaka was arrested and made to answer charges about his role in the affair. He was finally found guilty in 1983, sentenced to four years in prison and fined ¥400m. He at once appealed, but had a stroke in 1985, dying in 1993. His sentence was confirmed in 1995 (Tsuzuki 2000: 432).

An immediate consequence of the Lockheed investigations was the defection of six younger LDP members to form the New Liberal Club (NLC) in protest against corruption within the party. In the election of December 1976 the NLC won 4.2 per cent of the vote, much of it from the LDP, whose support dropped from 46.9 per cent in 1972 to 41.8 per cent. This gave it seventeen seats and it seemed set to be a significant, if minor, actor at the centre of Japanese politics. Over the next ten years it was associated with discussions about the creation of a centre party which would give voters a credible alternative to the LDP on the right and the JSP on the left. These discussions never led to anything, and interest in the NLC dropped away such that in the 1986 election they got only 1.8 per cent of the vote. Soon after the election, the party was dissolved and the six MPs rejoined the LDP.

Returning to the 1976 election, the LDP won a bare majority, leaving it unable to control all the house committees. Miki was forced to take responsibility for the election result and Fukuda took his place. The LDP seemed to be in a process of irreversible decline and there were confident predictions that in the 1980s the LDP would lose power entirely to be replaced by a coalition of opposition parties. Meanwhile, the LDP's problems were not over. While Miki was prime minister a new two-stage method of selecting the party leader was devised for situations when there were three or more candidates. In the primary stage all members of the party would vote and the two candidates with most votes would go through to the next stage, where the final choice would be made by the LDP members in parliament. Four candidates contested the election in 1978: the incumbent Fukuda, Ohira, Nakasone and Komoto Toshio. Fukuda, confident of victory, proposed that to take the selection process to the second stage risked unnecessary conflict within the party and therefore whoever won in the first stage should be accepted as the party leader. Meanwhile, Ohira as secretary general of the party, with Tanaka's backing, had created an extensive support base. He beat Fukuda by a large margin in the first phase of voting. Fukuda agreed to step down.

This did not reduce factional in-fighting, particularly after the party did marginally worse in the 1979 election than in 1976 as a result of a comment during the campaign by Ohira about his intention to introduce a new sales tax. The party was so divided after the election that it could not decide whether to propose Ohira or Fukuda as prime minister, so it nominated both of them. Ohira, with Tanaka's backing, mustered most votes and was confirmed as prime minister. In May the following year, the JSP proposed a vote of no confidence in the government, the Fukuda faction refused to vote with the government and it was soundly defeated. The LDP appeared on the brink of self-destruction.

The lower house election precipitated by this no confidence vote was held on the same day as the upper house election, making it Japan's first ever 'double election'. During the campaign Ohira died of a heart attack and, partly due to a sympathy vote, the LDP was returned with an overall majority sufficient for it to control all the committees. Suzuki Zenko, who had inherited control of the Ohira faction, also succeeded him as prime minister.

Meanwhile, Tanaka Kakuei had not been idle. Although he had resigned his membership of the LDP shortly after his arrest and spent most of his time preparing for the court case and subsequent appeal, he was determined to become prime minister once more, or, if that was not possible, to continue to exert control within the LDP. He had disbanded his faction in 1977, but maintained a number of informal support groups which he brought together in October 1981 to form a 92-member faction – the Mokuyōkai – which was the biggest in the LDP (Weir 1999: 59). Over the next two years it would continue to grow to reach a total of 119. Not only was it the largest, it also had the broadest geographical spread – only five prefectures had no Tanaka faction member. This gave Tanaka a decisive say in all party affairs, including the selection of the leader.

Kōenkai

By the mid-1980s the LDP had been in power for thirty years. At the national level, the reason for its success was that its policies were bringing prosperity to most Japanese. The success of individual members of the party was due to their ability to maintain a *kōenkai* – a personal support group. All parties rely on *kōenkai*, even the JCP (Lam 1996: 369–73). What they have in common is that they are organized by the candidate not the party, and are more important than the local party office. They became more elaborate structures in the LDP because the multi-member constituency system meant that nearly every LDP candidate had to face competition from someone else from the same party. *Kōenkai* are based on family, school and university friends and business associates, but often grew well beyond personal links to include Nōkyō, neighbourhood associations and local business federations. Keeping them loyal by sending out cards at New Year and midsummer, as well as presents and visits at appropriate times (births, marriages and deaths), is expensive and is one reason why LDP candidates sought support from the factions. *Kōenkai* are expensive to run but even more expensive to create from scratch and difficult for an outsider to take over when the incumbent dies or retires. This explains why 38.2 per cent of LDP members (89) and 19.6 per cent of DPJ members (25) elected to the lower house in 2000 had inherited their *kōenkai* from a relative, usually a parent. In the 2000 election 72 per cent of the 'hereditary' candidates were elected (Kaneko 2001: 24–5).

Tanaka Kakuei was one of the first to see the potential of the *kōenkai* system and he invested his money to develop a large one. It was inherited by his daughter, Tanaka Makiko. *Kōenkai* are blamed for several features of Japanese political life: the weaknesses of the parties, the power of the factions and the parochial orientation of Japanese politicians. One of the hopes of the reformers in the 1990s was that electoral reform would reduce their significance (Stockwin 1999: 145–8).

Nakasone to Takeshita

Nakasone took over from Suzuki following another two-stage electoral campaign. Tanaka's influence was clear: seven of the twenty cabinet members came from his faction, but his support was a mixed blessing. On 23 October 1983 he was found guilty of corruption charges, reminding the electorate of LDP sleaze in the run-up to an election held in December 1983. The LDP managed to acquire a bare majority and it entered into a coalition with the NLC.

Nakasone's five years as prime minister, from 1982 to 1987, were marked both in domestic and foreign policy by an energetic leadership that was unusual in postwar Japan. He had been involved in the process of administrative reform under Suzuki, and as prime minister he pushed forward a programme of reforms premised on financial retrenchment and reducing the role of the state. The theme of 'small government' was not new in Japan, but it was an idea that was being taken up by Thatcher in the UK and Reagan in the USA, and Nakasone was not slow to present his policies as part of the international trend. He focused his attention on the 3 Ks – *Kokutetsu*, *Kome* and *Kokumin hoken* (the Japan National Railway system (JNR), rice and the health insurance system) – as the three main drains on national expenditure.

The JNR had accumulated a massive deficit partly because of the central control exerted by the MoT. It was split into nine units, which were permitted to engage in activities other than simply running a railway – developing stations as shopping malls, for example. Large areas of land were sold off for development, paying off some of the JNR debt. The sell-off also weakened Kokurō, the railway workers' union, which had been a staunch supporter of the JSP, a critic of government policy and a fierce opponent of attempts to rationalize the workforce. NTT, the domestic telephone carrier, was also transformed from public corporation into a joint-stock company, although it maintained most of its monopoly until the 1990s.

By the mid-1980s the annual cost of the rice-related budget was over ¥1.3 trillion ($9.29 billion), more than ¥10,000 for every Japanese man, woman and child (Schwartz 1998: 215–17). Most years, more rice was being produced than consumed, and overall consumption was steadily dropping. There was international criticism of the closed Japanese rice market and, though strongly opposed by Nōkyō, a consensus was developing that agriculture policy had to change.

Reform of the health system was complex and we will have more to say about that in a later chapter. For the moment, it is sufficient to note that after 1973 the state took on an increasing burden of the welfare of its citizens, but that from 1983 the emphasis was once again on the need for people to contribute to their own families' health care. In 1973, for example, the over-70s became eligible for free medical care, but in 1983 payment was reintroduced, albeit at a low level.

Nakasone was always regarded as being more nationalist than his contemporaries within the LDP leadership. Consistent with this, he was committed to making Japan more assertive in international affairs and less dependent on the USA. This resulted in significant changes in both foreign and defence policy. Briefly put, following talks with US President Reagan in January 1983, Nakasone pledged to stand shoulder to shoulder with the USA against the USSR, and he promised increased cooperation between Japan's defence forces and the US military. He abandoned the 1 per cent GNP ceiling on military expenditure announced by Miki in 1976, although there was not much change. But despite this and his attempts to project himself as being on first-name terms with 'Ron', relations with the USA were tense, as Congress criticized Japan's trade policy and a trade war seemed to loom. Meanwhile, at home the opposition parties criticized his 'war-mongering' rhetoric.

In the eyes of the voters, though, Nakasone was popular, and the economy was booming again. He took advantage of this to call a general election in July 1986, another 'double election'. This was a great success. The LDP won 58.6 per cent of the lower house vote – 300 seats out of 512 – while the JSP vote slumped to 16.6 per cent – only 85 seats. The Nakasone and Tanaka factions did well. Although Tanaka had had a stroke in February 1985, it was said not to be serious and he stood again in the 1986 election. By the end of that summer, though, it was clear that he was not going to recover.

Nakasone was at the peak of his popularity. Although the LDP was still riven by rivalry, it was stronger than at any time since the 1960s. It was so grateful to Nakasone that he was granted an additional year as party president. Perhaps because he personally had nothing to lose – he would not get a further extension to his time in power – in his final year he supported two risky policies. First, he reduced the price paid to rice producers – an economically and administratively correct decision, but one that risked alienating the important rural vote. Secondly, in February 1987, he proposed the introduction of a sales tax despite having promised not to do so in the election campaign. This provoked strong resistance in parliament – a series of 'cow walk' voting sessions – and also opposition among small business. This combined resistance persuaded him to drop the idea in May.

By now, the race was on to decide who would succeed him. There were three contenders: Miyazawa Kiichi, leader of a faction with 89 members; Abe Shintarō, who had 85; and Takeshita Noboru, who had the support of all but the most loyal of the Tanaka faction, 113 in all. Size matters in the LDP, and Takeshita became the next prime minister in November 1987, perhaps on the understanding that when he stood down Abe and Miyazawa would get their turn. The economy continued to grow rapidly, too rapidly as it turned out. The LDP had a comfortable majority, and Takeshita was renowned as a wily political operator who had no king-maker to deal with and two rivals apparently willing to wait their turn for the top post. There seemed no reason why he would not serve at least two two-year terms. He continued his predecessor's policies of 'balancing the budget' by changing the tax system through the introduction of a sales tax. Despite massive opposition in and out of parliament, it was set at 3 per cent and implemented from 1 April 1989.

At this point a major scandal engulfed the LDP: the 'Recruit Scandal'. In summer 1998 Recruit-Cosmos, a recruitment company, distributed unlisted stocks to many politicians which they could sell at a profit when they were listed. Nakasone or his secretary received 19,000, which would give a profit of ¥43 million when sold (Tsuzuki 2000: 442). Subsequent investigation showed that most senior members of the LDP and several opposition party members too had benefited from Recruit shares. At first, Takeshita denied any link, but proof soon emerged that either he or his secretary had received some of these shares and so, with a popularity rating that had dropped lower than the rate of his sales tax, he resigned in April 1989.

Uno and Kaifu: the beginning of the end

In fact Takeshita had offered to go earlier, but no one could be found who would take on the post. Most of the senior liberal democrats, including Abe and Miyazawa, were shown to have taken Recruit shares. The reduction in the rice support subsidy and the lifting of restrictions on beef and citrus fruit imports had alienated most of the farming community. The introduction of the sales tax aroused opposition from small businesses and housewives. It was practically certain that the LDP would do very badly in the 1989 upper house election, so nobody wanted to take on the post of prime minister. Finally, Uno Sōsuke, foreign minister in the Takeshita cabinet, was persuaded to take over. At a time when things looked bad for the LDP, he only succeeded in making things worse. In the run up to the election he was implicated in an affair with a former geisha. Although the story did not at first have much impact, when it was taken up by the foreign press he was criticized for his shameful actions. The story had particular resonance because the new and popular leader of the JSP was a woman, Doi Takako. The LDP did even worse than expected, winning only 27 per cent of the vote in the national constituency, holding only 3 out of 24 seats in rural constituencies and overall going down from 142 to 109 (out of 252) seats. They had lost control of the upper house for at least six years.

Uno had no choice but to resign after just two months in the job. But who could succeed him when most of the party was regarded as tainted? Just as in 1974 when the LDP had turned to Miki as a clean transitional figure, this time it turned to Kaifu Toshiki, of the same small faction (33 members). The previous high point in his career had been as Minister of Education and he was regarded as of so little importance that the Recruit Cosmos company had not bothered with him. It was never likely that he would be able to exert much power over the big beasts of the Japanese political jungle: Abe (with a faction of 86), Miyazawa (with 84) and Takeshita (with 104).

A lower house election had to be held before summer 1990 and, although Kaifu does not seem to have been the one who made the decision, the election took place on 18 February 1990. Some had feared that, following opposition party gains in the Tokyo metropolitan elections in June and the upper house elections of July 1989, this might be the breakthrough that would remove the LDP from power. But this was not to be. The LDP held 275 seats, a comfortable majority, although the JSP did well, up from 83 to 136 seats. The LDP had been shaken by the events of 1989, but there was no reason to anticipate the imminent demise of the 1955 system. Indeed, the gain in strength of the JSP seemed to suggest that the system had reserves of resilience.

There were, however, changes within the broader context. First, the end of the Cold War between the USA and USSR, the subsequent collapse of communism in Eastern Europe and the restructure of Russia all marked a massive change in international circumstances, although it was unclear what impact this would have in East Asia. Secondly, the Shōwa emperor died in 1989 and was succeeded by one who spoke standard Japanese, not the archaic court language, and who declared his support for the constitution. Thirdly, and most importantly, the economic boom of the 1980s came to an abrupt halt in 1991: growth was only 1.2 per cent in 1992 and would remain at that level or lower for the rest of the decade. There had been economic slowdown, even recession, in the past, but this had always previously been attributable to a foreign crisis – the oil crisis of 1973, for example. This was the first time it was internally generated. Would the political system be able to cope with this new kind of crisis?

Conclusion

Although several pre-war politicians reappeared in key posts after the American occupation, the 1950s did not see a reappearance of pre-war patterns of politics. On the other hand, it was not clear what new pattern was emerging until the early 1960s. In this chapter we have described how the dominance of the LDP produced a complex faction system (*habatsu*), a personalized support system (*kōenkai*) and a system of support from the business community. In chapter 8 we will explore the way 'policy tribes' (*zoku*) emerged from within the LDP, acting as intermediaries between pressure groups, *kōenkai* and *habatsu*. These new structures kept the system dynamic despite the length of LDP domination. *Habatsu* occasionally nearly split the party, but kept the leadership alert to the needs of the party. Demands from *zoku* and *kōenkai* were self-serving, but prevented bureaucratic domination of the policy process. Challenges that might have come from the opposition parties came from within the LDP. So let us next look at what the opposition parties did in the '1955 system'.

5

Socialists and their Allies

The Japanese Socialist Party (JSP) won more seats than any other party in the first election under the new constitution of 1947 and would have won fifty more if it had not been for last-minute changes in the electoral system insisted on by Yoshida (Pempel 1998: 99–100). So, although the JSP had 143 seats, it did not have an overall majority, since the Liberal, Democratic and Cooperative parties had 132, 121 and 31 seats, respectively. Nevertheless, the leader of the JSP, Katayama Tetsu, became prime minister at the head of a coalition cabinet composed of Socialist, Democrat and Cooperative party ministers. As we have already seen, this coalition was short-lived and in October 1948 Yoshida became prime minister once more. April 1947 until October 1948 was the only period before 1993 that a left-of-centre party had posts in the cabinet. For forty-five years, left-wing parties were excluded, apparently permanently, from direct influence over central government. In this chapter we will explain the developments within the parliamentary opposition during this period, and in the next chapter outline the unexpected series of events that gave them a brief taste of power.

In power and opposition, 1945–55

The JSP was not the only socialist party with parliamentary representation. The Japan Communist Party (JCP) had first been formed in secret on 15 July 1921, but was crushed by the state in the late 1920s and '30s. It re-established itself soon after the occupation, with senior positions being taken over by old campaigners who were either newly released from prison or who had returned from exile in China. In its early phase the US occupation forces had seen the JCP, particularly those who took the moderate line advocated by its general secretary, Nosaka Sanzō, as pursuing ends consistent with their plans for the democratization of Japan (Oinas-Kukkonen 1996: 207–14). Meanwhile, the JCP analysis was that the US occupiers were completing the bourgeois revolution that the Meiji restoration had left 'incomplete'. Nosaka was a gradualist who believed that Japan would go no further than democracy in his lifetime. At its Fifth Congress held in February 1946, the party adopted a programme of peaceful revolution 'based on support for parliamentarianism and reliance on mass organisation' (quoted in Day 1999: 7). It won 8 seats in the elections of 1947, 4 each in the upper and lower houses, but increased its support in the next lower house election in 1949 to 35 seats, with just over 10 per cent of the popular vote.

By this time the context had changed. Anti-communism within US foreign policy had become more strident and the decision to purge communists and communist sympathizers led to the sacking of more than 1,000 teachers in schools and universities, plus about 22,000 others in positions of influence in the media and unions (Schonberger 1989: 154). At the same time there was criticism of the JCP strategy of a parliamentary route to socialism within the international communist movement. As a result, the National Congress held in October 1951 pledged itself to the goal of national liberation, which could embrace violent means. This line supported guerrilla tactics, including bomb attacks on police stations. Not surprisingly, this provoked the Japanese police to take action. The outbreak of the Korean War in June the previous year created the prospect of a communist threat from just across the Korean straits and sabotage at home. Some leaders of the JCP went underground again or, like Nosaka, took refuge in China. Popular support for the JCP dropped to less than 2 per cent and the communists disappeared as a force in domestic politics until the mid-1960s.

The JSP, meanwhile, took some time to overcome the recriminations following its fall from power in 1948. Not only was there an internal debate about the compromises made during its brief time in power, there was growing disagreement about the terms of the San Francisco Peace Treaty and the Security Treaty that ended the US occupation. Those in the centre and right-wing factions supported the treaty, but those on the left were adamantly opposed. They demanded a 'total peace': a peace treaty with all of Japan's former enemies, including the USSR and China, not just the USA and its allies who were the signatories to the San Francisco Treaty. They sought the withdrawal of foreign troops – i.e. the removal of all the US and Commonwealth troops who remained in Japan. They advocated permanent neutrality, which implied opposition to the Security Treaty with the USA, and stressed the constitutional prohibition on armed forces contrary to US policy, which was encouraging Japan to re-arm. This amounted to opposition to US foreign policy in Japan and East Asia. Passions ran so high that the party formally split in 1951. When it reunited in October 1955, the ideological debate between Marxist socialists and social democrats had not been resolved.

Nevertheless, after the next general election held in May 1958 there were just two main parties: the LDP with 298 seats and the JSP with 167 seats (the JCP held just 1 seat). It seemed as though after ten years of instability a two-party system was emerging in which the JSP would develop into a socialist party which, like its European counterparts, would one day take power.

Socialist parties and the union movements

Just like their European equivalents, the left-wing parties sought and received substantial financial and organizational support from the union movement. Sanbetsu Kaigi, the most radical union federation affiliated with the JCP, dwindled to just a few thousand in the early 1950s and was dissolved in 1958. Meanwhile, the largest union federation Sōhyō was promoted by the Americans as an alternative to the communist front organizations, but it was weak because of internal disagreements about the activities appropriate to a union movement. On the left were those who regarded themselves as part of the class struggle which manifested itself not only in the workplace but also in wider society. The aim of this class struggle was social revolution, which justified union participation in demonstrations and other activities opposing the reorganization of the police force, increased centralized control over education and the renewal of the Security Treaty. Moderate unionists, however, argued that their only legitimate concern was to improve the working conditions and living standards of their members within the existing economic system. They argued that unions should not waste their energy on political activities. A split took place in the union movement in 1954, resulting in the creation of a centre left union federation which ten years later regrouped and called itself Dōmei (aka Zen Nihon Rōdō Sōdōmei – All Japan General Federation of Labour). Finally, there was Chūritsurōren (Neutral Labour Unions Liaison Conference), formed in 1956 as a labour federation which deliberately did not ally itself with any political party.

The union movement grew rapidly in the late 1940s such that by 1950 50 per cent of the workforce was unionized (Pempel 1998: 46). This growth was not sustained as the industrial workforce expanded in the 1950s and beyond, but it did suggest that a union movement might have become powerful in Japan. The Japanese unions' weak point was that they were recreated after the war within the company structures. They were enterprise unions, not trade unions (as was common in the UK) or industrial unions (as was often the case in the USA or Germany). These enterprise unions had difficulties organizing within an industry and so in 1955 a group of Sōhyō leaders tried to organize a joint offensive in the spring just before the renegotiation of most labour contracts. This became known as the *Shuntō* – Spring Offensive.

From the late 1950s a pattern was emerging. Plans for *Shuntō* would begin the previous December at the time the government was finalizing its plans for the next year's budget. Some time early in the New Year a target wage increase would be agreed, either a flat increase – say ¥5,000 per month which tended to favour the poorer paid – or a percentage. Once agreement was reached between the union leaders, as organized by Sōhyō, Chūritsurōren and (later) Dōmei, one industry would be targeted, usually an industry that was thought to be able easily to afford the proposed raise (Halliday 1975: 221).

If management, usually supported by the business organization Nikkeiren, was reluctant to grant the pay rise, the union might launch a one-day strike to demonstrate its resolve, or indulge in some other show of non-cooperation. If and when the union in the target industry achieved the desired pay increase, it set the standard for other negotiations between management and unions involved in the *Shuntō* and indeed for all union negotiators whose success or failure was judged on the basis of the *Shuntō* norm. As the strategy developed in the 1980s, the wage demands were sometimes accompanied by requests related to working conditions or overtime payments. During the 1990s in *Shuntō* and, indeed, other negotiations, the stress was on resisting wage cuts, and where demands for increases were made they were very small.

From a two-party system to 'one plus several'

In early spring 1959 a 'People's Council for Preventing Revision of the Security Treaty' was formed with the backing of the left-wing JSP, the JCP and various left-wing unions and student groups. It coordinated demonstrations against the renewal of the Security Treaty with the USA from November 1959 until June 1960 in the anti-*Ampo* struggle. The socialists' case was that the treaty represented the subordination of Japanese interests to the needs of US imperialism and thus created a situation where Japan might become involved in a war (with the USSR, for example) in which Japan had no direct interest. Ultimately, the series of protests proved ineffective and the Security Treaty was ratified. However, the crisis pushed the LDP to the verge of collapse amid criticism of Kishi's management skills. The LDP was accused of a lack of concern for the clearly expressed anxieties of the Japanese people. Opposition parties were accused of lacking respect for parliamentary procedures and the principles of democratic government. More broadly, questions were asked about the suitability of democratic practice to Japanese culture.

At the start of the crisis in January 1960 a group of forty socialist members of parliament broke from the JSP to form a Democratic Socialist Party (DSP). Promising to have a share of political power within five years, it put up 104 candidates in the election the following December – one in almost every constituency – but only seventeen were elected (Fukuoka 1993: 140). In that election the DSP attracted just 8 per cent of the total vote and its electoral support never exceeded that over the subsequent thirty years. Its 'natural supporter' within the labour movement was the centre-left Dōmei.

Meanwhile, another party was emerging to occupy the centre ground of Japanese politics, the Kōmeitō, the Clean Government Party. Kōmeitō was, and in most ways still is, the political wing of a religious organization, Sōka Gakkai, which at its peak claimed twelve million believers. Sōka Gakkai is the biggest of a large number of 'new religions' which have been founded outside the Buddhist and Shintō traditions. They grew rapidly in the 1950s and 1960s and some developed into powerful organizations. Some, like the Rishōkōseikai with more than five million members, and Reiyukai with nearly two million, have routinely supported the LDP, but Sōka Gakkai developed its own political ambitions. Sōka Gakkai thought combines western ideas about education with aspects of Nichiren Shōshū Buddhism. Its members first stood in local government elections in 1955. In 1956 it won three seats in the House of Councillors and in 1964 Kōmeitō was launched. In 1967 Kōmeitō stood candidates in lower house elections for the first time and won twenty-five seats. At the next general election in 1969 it almost doubled in size and won 10.9 per cent of the vote. At this point political commentators within Japan and abroad began to worry that it was an intolerant religious group that aimed to take power in order to impose its ideas on Japan through the creation of a Buddhist state. Certainly, there were some examples of excessively 'enthusiastic' attempts to convert non-believers and some evidence of an authoritarian internal structure that was devised, among other things, to prevent the formation of factions. There were also some documented examples of it preventing the publication of critical books and articles. To allay some of these fears, in 1970 Kōmeitō formally separated from Sōka Gakkai and announced its commitment to the principle of 'separation of politics from religion'. This did not completely satisfy its critics and the activities of Sōka Gakkai/Kōmeitō still generate strong feelings.

However, the vote for Kōmeitō has never exceeded the 10.9 per cent it reached in 1969, although it won as many as 57–8 seats in the 1960s. Its strength is that it has a well-disciplined support base, which can be relied upon to turn out to vote no matter what the weather or how boring the election campaign: 80 per cent of Sōka Gakkai members can be relied on to vote for Kōmeitō. Moreover, it became adept at calculating in which of the multi-member constituencies it had the best chances of winning a seat; very few votes were wasted. However, the Kōmeitō never managed to attract much support beyond its membership. In terms of its position in the political spectrum, it began by standing centre-left, lining up with the JSP/DSP in its defence of the pacifism of the constitution and in favour of social welfare provision. Meanwhile, many of its members are owners of, or employed in small and medium-sized enterprises, and it has favoured policies that have benefited this sector. In terms of political strategy, Kōmeitō has been ambivalent. It took part in negotiations with the JSP and other centre parties in the 1970s and 1980s when it was thought this was the only way to end the LDP monopoly of political power. At the end of the 1980s the Takeshita cabinet was negotiating with the DSP and Kōmeitō to create a conservative coalition, but then it joined with left-of-centre parties in criticisms of LDP corruption, even though there were occasions when Kōmeitō members of parliament also were implicated in similar scams.

In 1955 the JCP abandoned its ultra-leftist line and returned to the idea of peaceful revolution. During the early 1960s it became identified with the Chinese side in the Sino-Soviet dispute, which damaged its image in the eyes of the Japanese electorate. At the Tenth Congress in 1966, it broke with the Chinese and announced its policy of a 'Japanese path to Communism', which involved opposition to the rule of American imperialism and Japanese monopoly capitalism in order to carry out peaceful democratic revolution within the framework of capitalism and parliamentary democracy. This was a period

Table 5.1   JCP members and *Akahata* readership

Party Congress	Membership	Readership of Akahata (Red Flag)
1961 (8th)	over 80,000	340,000
1966 (10th)	nearly 300,000	over 1 million
1973 (12th)	over 300,000	2.82 million
1977 (14th)	nearly 400,000	3.26 million
1982 (16th)	nearly 480,000	over 3 million
1987 (18th)	490,000	over 3 million
1994 (20th)	360,000	over 2.5 million
2000 (22nd)	386,517	1.99 million

Note: the JCP announces its membership and *Akahata* readership at its congresses
Source: *Daily Yomiuri*, 17 July 1997, and Resolution of the 22nd Congress of the JCP, 24 November 2000

of rapid economic growth, but also a decade when the 'negative externalities' of urbanization and industrialization became apparent. Many of those suffering from cramped housing and environmental pollution, and those who sympathized with them, saw the JCP as offering a real political alternative. The JCP vote increased from 2.9 per cent in 1960 (3 seats) to 10.9 per cent in 1972 (40 seats). Thereafter the number of seats it won varied between 19 and 41, although its popular support stayed around 10 per cent.

Like the Kōmeitō, it has a disciplined following which can be relied on to turn out at elections. At its core is the party membership which, as table 5.1 shows, grew to more than 300,000 during the 1960s and peaked at 490,000 in the late 1980s. Beyond this is the Zenkoku Kakushinkon (National Reform Group) which has around 4.5 million members who support the JCP without being full party members. When in 1989 the main union federations united to form Rengō, the JCP-oriented unions formed Zenrōren (National Labour Union Federation). There are also women's groups, a student federation and several consumer cooperatives linked to the JCP, and even a small business federation that has 370,000 members in 615 branches (Takizawa 2001: 81–3). Finally, the party is able to exert influence through a number of publications including a daily newspaper, *Akahata*, which claims up to three million readers.

Uniquely, the JCP image at home was strongly influenced by events abroad. The Soviet invasion of Afghanistan in 1979 damaged the domestic image that portrayed communism as a force for peace and welfare. Similarly, the nuclear accident in Chernobyl in 1986 and the attacks on the pro-democracy movement in Tiananmen Square in 1989 harmed the JCP's attempts to portray itself as supportive of an anti-nuclear policy and human rights protection.

To summarize: although in the early years of the development of the '1955 system' Japan seemed to be moving in the direction of a stable two-party democracy, over the next ten years, three more parties emerged to eat into their electoral support base such that by the early 1970s the conservative LDP

could command only just over 45 per cent of the total vote and a bare majority in the lower house, and the JSP had just over 20 per cent of the vote. The
situation was made even worse, of course, following the defection of the NLC
in 1976, which took another 4.2 per cent of the vote with it. Some suggested
that the LDP was condemned to a steady decline and that it was only a matter
of time before it was replaced by a coalition of the opposition parties. The
problem was that it proved difficult to negotiate a common platform which
could unite the opposition parties (Johnson 2000).

Opposition parties and policies

The opposition parties exerted very little influence within the policy-making
process. Most bills are formulated outside the legislature. Proposals come
from within the ministries and agencies and, following approval by the
appropriate LDP committees and subcommittees, they are presented for
the endorsement of cabinet before they are put into their final form by the
Cabinet Bureau of Legislation. Only at this stage is the bill introduced into
parliament and the opposition given a chance to comment. Very little amendment of government legislation takes place, and what does is rarely substantive. Not even the JCP routinely opposes government bills, as is usual in the
UK parliament. In fact, Pempel shows that over the period 1966–79 opposition parties became increasingly likely to approve government bills: approval
rates increased from 80 to 90 per cent for the DSP, 80 to 85 per cent for the
CGP, 63 to 75 per cent for the JSP and even 10 to more than 60 per cent for
the JCP (Pempel 1998: 174–5).

Where they were opposed to a policy, the parties had to decide whether
simply to express their disagreement by voting against the measure in the
committee or in the house as a whole or to go further and try to prevent its
adoption by disruptive tactics. Whichever strategy was adopted, it was possible for pro-government politicians to criticize the opposition as unwilling
to compromise and unable to contribute positively to policy formation. In
fact, there is considerable evidence of the informal contribution of opposition party suggestions in the development of education, welfare and even
foreign policy, but this is rarely recognized by LDP leaders who prefer to
denigrate and understate the role played by opposition parties.

Opposition in retreat

It turned out that the mid-1970s was the nadir of LDP popularity; by the 1986
election it had fought its way back to 49.4 per cent of the vote, with 300 seats,
and even more after the NLC rejoined. Support for the opposition parties
dropped correspondingly, in the case of the JSP from 19.5 to 17.2 per cent,
112 to 85 seats. Why had the opposition parties been unable to finish the LDP
off in the mid-1970s when it had seemed so mortally wounded by a series of
scandals? Some blame the ineffectiveness of the opposition. It was said that
after so long out of power the opposition parties only knew how to oppose.

In particular, the JSP was accused of being fettered by outmoded Marxist theory. Nakano (1997) has shown, however, that even in the 1970s the JSP was prepared to respond pragmatically to events and revise its policies to make them compatible with its potential partner parties when there was a chance that it might lead an anti-LDP coalition. Others suggest that as the largest opposition party there was no incentive for it to adopt a risky strategy of devising new policies which might alienate its existing supporters either on the left or right. As a result, the JSP continued through the 1980s without any fundamental review of its policies. So although the party was riven by ideological rivalry, as is not uncommon in left-wing parties, this did not generate new policy proposals. A significant source of JSP support came from the rural areas, a somewhat similar profile to that of the LDP. However, whereas the LDP was able to find new supporters in the urban and sub-urban sector, the JSP found itself outflanked by the DSP and Kōmeitō to the right and the JCP to the left.

The main source of JSP support came from the unions. In the early 1970s the union movement was divided between three federations:

Chūritsurōren, with 1.4 million members and 11 per cent of the unionized workforce, took no political stance but its members probably voted for the JSP and DSP in equal proportions.

Dōmei had 2.21 million members in 1977 and 18 per cent of organized workers, 90 per cent of whom were in the private sector and gave both cash and campaign support to the DSP.

Sōhyō was the biggest union federation, with 4.5 million members and 36 per cent of the unionized workforce, but two-thirds of its members worked in the public sector and thus were forbidden to strike. Sōhyō was the most radical union federation and it gave its support to the JSP, but it was weak in that its members were unable to participate freely in the full range of industrial activity.

Overall union density – union membership as percentage of employees – dropped from 35.1 per cent in 1970 to 28.9 per cent in 1988. Moreover, unions were recruiting only a small proportion of those who were entering the work-force in the 1970s and 1980s.

In the early 1980s the federations started negotiations to create a united front in an attempt to increase the attractiveness of union membership. The first stage was discussions between Chūritsurōren and Dōmei which resulted in the creation of Rengō in 1987. A separate organization called Dōmei Yuai Kaigi was also set up to collect funds for the DSP. The next step was to nego-tiate with Sōhyō to create an 8 million-strong federation in November 1989 and, once again, a residual body, the Shakaitō Tsuyomerukai, was set up to channel funds to the JSP. This was accompanied by a plan to ensure that the unification of the labour movement would provide the basis for a united opposition.

There was a great deal of optimism that the process of creating Rengō would reinvigorate the labour movement and enable the unification of the centre-left parties in opposition to the LDP. Thirteen Rengō candidates stood in the 1989 upper house election, many of them in constituencies that only returned one member. The other opposition parties agreed not to put up a candidate, giving voters a straight choice between Rengō and the LDP. This created a small group of eleven Rengō members of the upper house between 1989 and 1995. However, the tactic was not successfully repeated and none of the eleven was re-elected in 1995.

The 1986 'double' election had been a major success for the LDP and its leader Nakasone. LDP representation went up from 250 to 300, the JSP down from 112 to 85 and the DSP from 38 to 26, while the Kōmeitō and JCP more or less maintained their levels of support. This was a particular disappointment for the JSP, which earlier that year had abandoned the platform originally adopted in 1964 based on Marxist principles and issued a policy for the 'New Socialist Party'. Chairman Ishibashi Masashi, who had led the modernization process, took responsibility for the electoral results and resigned, his place being taken by Doi Takako, who became the first woman to lead a major political party.

Despite the fact that the economy was growing faster than at any time since the 1960s, there were some sectors of society that were feeling left out. Farmers were suffering from the liberalization of the beef and citrus fruit markets and felt their livelihoods to be threatened by changes in the rice price support policy. Younger urban residents were finding housing excessively expensive, as speculation sent land prices ever higher. The LDP government was criticized for its introduction of the 3 per cent consumption tax in 1989, despite election promises not to do so. Moreover, in 1988–9 there were almost daily revelations about the extent of the Recruit scandal, which eventually showed that it even included prime minister Takeshita, despite his initial denials. No members of the JCP were involved with Recruit, and only one member of the JSP (and he resigned immediately and suggested all other similarly compromised members of parliament should do likewise), but several in the DSP and Kōmeitō were shown to have taken Recruit shares.

Doi, though relatively unknown and inexperienced, established a good relationship with the media through which she appealed to sections of the electorate that had ceased to support the JSP; in particular, she appealed to female voters. She encouraged unions to be more active in recruiting and pro-moting women; she encouraged women to stand in by-elections, in the Tokyo municipal elections of June 1989 and the House of Councillors elections of July 1989. Her opposition to the consumption tax endeared her to house-wives, as it was they who were paying the extra 3 per cent added to their grocery bills. She announced a strategy of 'hop, step and jump'. The hop was the Tokyo municipal elections, the step was the House of Councillors elec-tion and the jump was the House of Representatives election which had to take place some time before July 1990. In Tokyo the JSP succeeded in increas-ing its number of seats and in the House of Councillors election the LDP lost overall control for the first time since 1955. Not only did Rengō do well, but within the national constituency the JSP won 35.1 per cent of the vote com-pared to 27.3 per cent who voted for the LDP. On the basis of these results, it was not impossible that the LDP might be forced out of power at the next election.

In 1989 Hirohito, Shōwa (Enlightened Peace) emperor, who had been on the throne since 1926, died. In 1990 the inaugural ceremonies took place to mark the start of the reign of his son Akihito, whose era would be called Heisei (Achieving Peace). Would this new era see the formation of a non-LDP government? An election was called for 18 February 1990, but the hopes (or fears) that the LDP might lose power proved unfounded. The LDP did not do well. Its overall support was down 3 per cent compared to 1986, but it retained 275 seats, a comfortable majority. The JSP did better than at any time since the 1960s, winning 24.4 per cent of the vote and 136 seats. Meanwhile, all the other parties lost seats – the DSP went from 38 to 26, Kōmeitō from 56 to 45 and the JCP from 26 to 16. The LDP remained in power, but the JSP was confirmed as the pre-eminent opposition party, poised, conceivably, to engineer the replacement of the LDP later in the decade. Just over a year later, however, both commentators and opinion polls were agreed that the JSP had lost direction.

Two things discredited the JSP. First, the party was unable to put forward any positive proposals in the debate over how Japan should respond to the Gulf War. It resolutely opposed government policy but withdrew from discussions with the LDP, DSP and Kōmeitō about possible policy options. Not only did this isolate the JSP; it also pushed the Kōmeitō and DSP into the conservative camp, as their support was needed if any bill were to pass through the upper house. Secondly, the JSP's inability to take a positive lead was demonstrated in the run up to the Tokyo governor elections in 1991. The LDP and Kōmeitō had supported Suzuki Shunichi in the previous three elections, but Kōmeitō was unhappy with his performance. Possibly as the price of Kōmeitō support for LDP Gulf War policy, the LDP Secretary General Ozawa Ichiro refused to back Suzuki in the next election, who decided to stand as an independent. With the conservative vote split, a strong JSP candidate could have taken the post but it could not decide on a candidate. Someone was found late in the day, but he won only 7 per cent of the vote, less even than the JCP candidate. When Doi Takako resigned as leader in June an opinion poll showed only 17 per cent support for the JSP, the lowest ever recorded (Stockwin 1999: 76–7).

Thus, the momentum that seemed to be pushing the JSP towards a more central role in government had almost completely disappeared by 1991. This was confirmed in the 1992 upper house elections, when the JSP won only 22 seats compared to the 69 of the LDP. Ozawa had maintained links with the DSP and Kōmeitō, dividing the opposition and enabling the LDP to continue to rule. DSP support for the government's Gulf War policy prevented any progress in negotiations between it and the JSP. The results of the 1992 election pointed to a further decline in DSP support, as its position became hard to distinguish from that of the LDP. The Kōmeitō retained its support from Sōka Gakkai members, but it got few, if any, votes beyond this solid core. Both during the Recruit scandal and after, it became almost as common to discover that Kōmeitō politicians were receiving bribes or other benefits as

LDP members, tarnishing their image as supporters of 'clean government'. Only the JCP was untouched by these allegations. It had maintained its integrity during the Recruit scandal and steered an uncompromising but consistent line during the funeral of the Shōwa emperor and the installation of his son. However, between 1989 and 1992 the communist party states and parties of Western Europe had virtually disappeared and neither of the nearby communist regimes, the People's Republic of China and the Democratic People's Republic of Korea, were inspiring models. What role could there be for a communist party in a post-Cold War, post-Marxist world?

Conclusion

In 1955 there seemed to be a two-party system in the process of formation. Admittedly, one of them had twice the parliamentary seats and twice the electoral support of the other one, not to mention the backing of big, medium and small business. Nevertheless, the socialists had the support of the union movement, resulting in a conservative/socialist confrontation resembling that in many contemporary capitalist states. But instead of a bipolar structure, by the 1970s Japan had acquired a 'one plus several' party system in which the opposition parties seemed doomed to eternal opposition. Between 1989 and 1991, it seemed possible that the opposition, with the JSP in the vanguard supported by Rengō, Kōmeitō and even the DSP, might be able to bring an end to the LDP monopoly on political power, but Ozawa's skilful strategy plus the JSP bungling in the Tokyo governor elections suggested that the old system had survived the challenge.

Confrontation between political parties in Japan was guided by international and domestic parameters that usually overlapped. On the international level there was global confrontation between capitalism and communism, and at home confrontation between those opposed to the occupation reforms and those in favour of them (Kabashima 1999: 11). Up until 1989 these parameters made sense to both politicians and the ordinary voter. By 1992 it was clear that old certainties in international politics had disappeared and this raised serious questions about the conduct of domestic policy too. There was a need to think in terms that went beyond the 'occupation settlement'. As the old parameters of politics broke down, it soon became apparent that alliances unthinkable within the pre-1989 system would become possible and even necessary.

6

Party Politics 1992–2000: Towards a New System

In the summer of 1991, Stockwin wrote that 'reform [of the electoral system] would provide strong incentive for the formation of a new party of opposition, combining elements of the old opposition parties, together perhaps with centrist elements from the LDP as well' (1991: 6). At the time it seemed unlikely that this prediction could come true. And, indeed, as things stand in the early 2000s, although the political scenery is somewhat different from that ten years earlier, the party system can still be described as 'one plus several'. So did anything change? As we will see, there were some quite dramatic events. The LDP became an opposition party between August 1993 and June 1994, a leader of the JSP was prime minister from June 1994 to January 1996, leading a JSP/LDP coalition cabinet; both these events seemed unlikely in the extreme, even in 1992. But by the end of the decade the LDP had only been out of power for eleven months and the main difference now is that only a trace of the JSP remains within the political system, while its successor to the title of main opposition party, the Democratic Party of Japan (DPJ) is no more, perhaps less, united than its predecessor. Fundamental changes have taken place in the international context of politics. Has there been any corresponding change within the domestic practice in Japan?

The unravelling of the LDP

The process began in a very unportentous way. Kaifu Toshiki, an indecisive prime minister with a weak power base within the LDP, had been selected mainly because of his 'clean' image at a time when most of the party was revealed to have taken shares from the Recruit company. During 1991 he tried to assert his leadership by proposing radical reform in the electoral system. Although there were some in the party who favoured such reform, the mainstream was opposed and it was decided that Kaifu would have to go. In November 1991, Miyazawa Kiichi took over. He was leader of a mainstream faction, had had a classical elite career in Tokyo University and the Ministry of Finance, followed by distinguished political service in the LDP which had led to positions in the ministries of International Trade and Industry (MITI), Finance (MoF) and Foreign Affairs (MFA). His period in office began well. The LDP through Ozawa persuaded the DSP and Kōmeitō of the importance of passing the Peacekeeping Operations bill which would enable Japan to play a more positive role in UN activities. The LDP needed this support to get the bill approved in the upper house. Moreover, in spite of a series of scandals implicating LDP politicians, it regained popular appeal, winning 69 seats to the JSP's 22 in the 1992 upper house election. This did not mean that the LDP regained control of the upper house, but it was a reversion to the pattern of House of Councillor results of the 1980s and earlier, and suggested that the 1989 results had been an aberration with no deep significance (see figure 6.1).

One new development was the election of four representatives of the Japan New Party (JNP). This had been founded earlier in the summer by Hosokawa Morihiro, formerly an LDP member of the upper house and governor of Kumamoto. Relatively young (b. 1938), and certainly young-looking, he is the grandson of Prince Konoe Fumimaro who had been prime minister just before the outbreak of the Pacific War. The aristocratic background attracted media attention, but there was little that was distinctive about the party's policies apart from their stress on decentralization. Small parties had won seats in the upper house before and there was nothing to suggest that it would be of any significance.

However, in retrospect it is clear that the old order was starting to unravel in the autumn of 1992. In September Kanemaru Shin, the effective leader of the Takeshita faction, was found guilty of having received ¥500,000 from Sagawa Express in violation of the Political Fund Regulation Law. He was fined ¥200,000, provoking protest at the paltry penalty. He immediately resigned from the Takeshita faction and stood down from his parliamentary seat in October. Strains then appeared among the leadership of that faction, as a result of which Hata Tsutomu and Ozawa Ichirō set up a group they called Reform Forum 21, which was committed, among other things, to changes in election methods and the political donation system. About half the Takeshita faction had joined this group by December, with the rest remaining loyal to Takeshita's successors, Hashimoto Ryūtarō and Obuchi Keizō.

Shortly after Kanemaru's resignation, the prime minister, Miyazawa, made a speech in which he said:

> It is most regrettable that public confidence in politics has been badly shaken. ... I strongly feel that public distrust in politics has never been so deep as today. ... Our reform programme would make political funds transparent, political activities less costly and elections fought on policy proposals. (quoted in Mitchell 1996: 127)

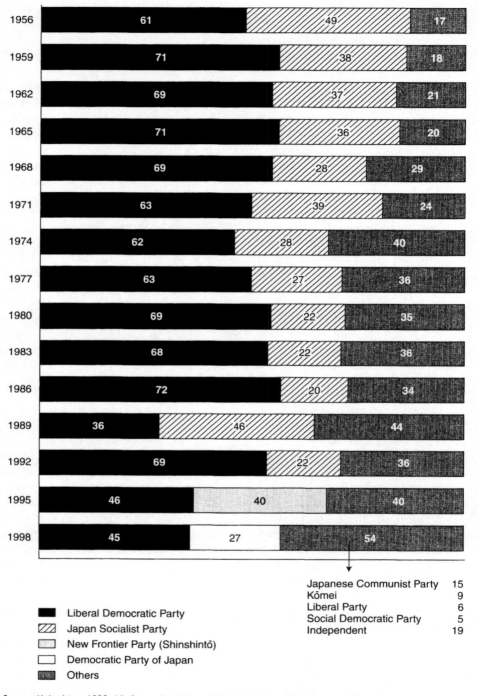

Source: Kabashima 1998: 10. Reproduced by permission of the author and publisher

Figure 6.1   Seats captured in upper house elections, 1956–98

There is some doubt though about how committed Miyazawa was to the implementation of this reform programme. In January 1991 the LDP had apparently accepted the need for change, and by August three bills were ready that would have made the lower house electoral system resemble that in Germany – a combination of single member districts (SMD) and regional blocs using a proportional representation (PR) system. There was some discussion about how appropriate this was for Japan, which does not naturally divide into regions, there being no equivalent to the German *Länder*. There was also disagreement about how many seats should be apportioned between the SMD and PR systems.

Miyazawa's plan for reform in 1993 would have made political funding more transparent and redrawn constituency boundaries to eliminate imbalances, but it was based entirely on single member districts using a first-past-the-post system. Such a system would have meant that the LDP would win 80 per cent of the seats, wiping out most of the smaller parties. The opposition parties therefore refused to consider it. The JSP and Kōmeitō suggested a variant of the German system. Negotiations between the parties broke down, as Miyazawa must have known they would, and in June 1993 the government announced that it was shelving all reform proposals.

LDP: out of power

Meanwhile, on 6 March 1993, public prosecutors announced their intention to arrest Kanemaru on charges of tax evasion and two days later police, accompanied by TV cameras, searched his house and discovered ¥3 billion worth of securities, tens of millions of yen in bank notes and 100 kilograms of gold bullion (Pempel 1998: 140). It was not clear whether he was hoarding this wealth for personal use or to be the financial basis for a new political party. His trial began on 22 July 1993 but had not reached a verdict when he died in March 1996. Even after the series of financial scandals of the previous ten years, there was public outrage at the scale of these revelations. The LDP leadership seemed to assume complacently that it would blow over, as had previous crises, along with the debate about electoral reform. It was wrong.

All the non-communist opposition parties backed a motion of no confidence in the Miyazawa administration on 18 June. In the vote thirty-nine LDP members, including thirty-four from the Hata–Ozawa group Reform Forum 21, voted with the opposition and a further sixteen deliberately absented themselves. Parliament was dissolved and a general election was called for 18 July. On 21 June a small party was formed of centre-left politicians led by Takemura Masayoshi (formerly LDP, Abe faction) calling itself Shintō Sakigake (New Harbinger Party). Two days later the Hata–Ozawa group launched a new party under the name of Shinseitō (Renewal Party), with the support of forty-four LDP members from both houses. There followed a confusing election campaign in which three new parties ran for the first time in the lower house: the JNP, Shintō Sakigake and Shinseitō. The result left the

Table 6.1 Parliamentary parties, August 1993

	Representatives	Councillors
LDP	227	99
JSP/SDP*	76	73
Shinseitō	60	8
Kōmeitō	52	24
Sakigake-JNP	52	0
DSP	19	11
JCP	15	11
JNP-DRP		15
Niin Club		5
Independents	10	6
TOTAL	511	252

* The JSP changed its name to the Social Democratic Party in January 1996
Source: Compiled from various sources

LDP well short of a majority for the first time since it was formed in 1955. In fact, the LDP candidates had not done badly – the party had one more seat after the election compared to before. Moreover, nearly all of the fifty-five Shinseitō and thirteen Sakigake members had been LDP members three months earlier and could have given a conservative coalition a clear working majority. Indeed, the LDP gerontocracy seems to have assumed that it would be easy to coax them back in to an LDP-led coalition. In the days just after the election the chances of the party putting together a two- or three-party coalition looked better than those of the opposition cobbling together an agreement among six or seven parties.

Nevertheless, the deals were done and on 9 August 1993 an eight-party coalition government was formed (see table 6.1). Hosokawa was prime minister. His JNP, standing in a lower house election for the first time, had won 35 seats and he gave the government a fresh face. Ozawa's group won the most seats in cabinet (6) although Ozawa himself took on no ministerial post. The JSP (with 5 cabinet posts) led by Yamahana Sadao found its support down to 70 (from 136 in 1990), but though weak it was still the largest opposition party and an essential component in the coalition. The fourth key figure was Yamagishi Akira, leader of Rengō, who persuaded the JSP and DSP to serve in the same cabinet.

Having kicked the LDP rascals out after thirty-eight years, a great deal was expected of the new government. An ambitious programme was announced which included reform of the lower house electoral system, anti-corruption legislation, substantial deregulation of industry, commerce and banking and the devolution of some central government functions to local authorities. It was reform of the electoral system, however, that had brought the coalition together and even then there was substantial disagreement between the coalition parties about the detail. The JSP wanted more PR seats and tough anti-corruption regulations, while others preferred more SMD seats and a more relaxed funding regime. Compromises moved the SMD/PR balance from 250:250 to 274:226 to 300:200 between the initial presentation of proposals in August 1993 and the final passage of the bill at a joint session of both houses on 29 January 1994.

Prime minister Hosokawa expected to be able to keep this coalition together to implement some of the other reform proposals, but the LDP, now of course an opposition party, discovered a relatively minor financial indiscretion in Hosokawa's past and he was forced to resign. Hata Tsutomu, leader of the Shinseitō, took over as leader of the coalition, but his task was made difficult when it leaked out that Ozawa was trying to unite all the coalition parties except the JSP into a single party, Kaishin (Reform). At this, the JSP, now led by Murayama Tomiichi, once regarded as on the left wing of the party, withdrew its support and Sakigake too pulled out of the coalition. This left Hata with just 160 supporters in the lower house, very much a minority government, although the JSP and Sakigake agreed not to undermine the government until the budget had passed. This complete, intensive negotiations began to try to entice them back into the coalition. Meanwhile, they were also talking to the LDP, and on 29 June 1994 it was announced that an agreement had been reached in which Murayama would become the next prime minister and Takemura Minister of Finance, and the JSP would have three more cabinet posts and Sakigake one. The rest would go to the LDP, which was thus back in power after an absence of just eleven months.

What had been achieved? The passage of the electoral reform bill was no small victory. Hosokawa himself put great emphasis on enforcing the relaxation of the total ban on rice imports. Certainly, neither of those would have been possible under an LDP administration. Just as important was that it placed an agenda of reform, much of it outlined in Ozawa's 'Blueprint for a New Japan' first published in 1993, at the centre of the political arena (Ozawa 1994). Subsequent cabinets could no longer ignore such issues as deregulation, decentralization or the restructuring of government. Although politicians continued to be widely distrusted, there had been a significant shift of emphasis away from bureaucrat-dominated decision-making and towards elected politicians taking the initiative.

Four elections and a funeral? The end of the JSP

Murayama became the first socialist prime minister since 1948, less than a year after his party suffered its worst electoral result since 1949. If he had reflected on postwar history, the lesson would seem to be that socialist party leaders do not benefit from leading coalition cabinets. Why then did he do it? Why was the LDP so eager to enter into a coalition with its erstwhile enemy? The second question is easier to answer. As the party in power, the LDP had been closely associated with the administration and LDP members cemented their links with their *kōenkai* and constituents mainly by virtue of their ability to deliver material benefits. Unable to do this, they feared they might risk election defeat. This fear may well have become so strong that LDP parliamentarians would defect to the Hata or Hosokawa parties simply in order to renew the links that could guarantee the flow of resources. If the LDP had stayed out of power for much longer it might have collapsed. Neither ideology nor party loyalty have been important characteristics of the LDP.

On the other hand, ideology had always been crucially important within the JSP. Indeed, its critics argued that its political impotence before the 1990s was largely due to the fact that it was constricted by an outdated ideological strait jacket. So what had changed? Though excluded from Kaishin by Ozawa, the JSP might still have been able to negotiate a key role for itself in a Hata-led coalition. Murayama would not have been prime minister, but the party would have had more influence over policy-making. It may be that sense can be made of it by reference to, if not ideology, then policy orientation. There were perhaps fewer differences in 1994 between the LDP and the JSP than there were between the JSP and the neo-liberal agenda that was being advocated by Ozawa and which was informing the agenda of the Kaishin. Traditionally, the LDP had been reluctant to include labour in the policy-making system, but from the late 1980s it began to accept that Rengō might be able to play a legitimate role within government. If it could work with Rengō, why not the JSP? International politics by 1994 had ceased to be dominated by Cold War confrontation and it was also becoming clear that the old domestic politics which focused on protecting/revoking key reforms of the occupation was no longer the only game in town.

Not long after forming his cabinet, Murayama surprised many grassroots supporters of his party by jettisoning many of its signature policies. Henceforth, the existence of the Self Defence Forces would not be regarded as problematic, either illegal or unconstitutional. The party would no longer oppose the US–Japan Security Treaty and it would end its campaign against the compulsory use of the *Hinomaru* (Rising Sun) flag and *Kimigayo* anthem in schools. These policy reforms were approved at the September party conference, but serious strains threatened to split the party.

Meanwhile, the parties that had belonged to the coalition led by Hata began talks about the formation of a single opposition party, which resulted in the creation of Shinshintō (New Frontier Party, NFP) in December 1994. This was composed of the DSP, Kōmeitō, the JNP, Shinseitō and a handful of defectors from the LDP led by former prime minister Kaifu. In total, it could claim 178 members in the House of Representatives and 36 in the House of Councillors. Was this the party that Stockwin had predicted in 1991?

The first test of these new arrangements was the 1995 upper house election in which those who had faced the electorate in 1989 sought re-election. Turn-out was poor, only 44.5 per cent. The two parties of the ruling coalition did badly: the LDP won 46 seats, better than in 1989 (36) – though nowhere close to the 'normal' range of the 1960s and after, which had hovered around 70 – and the JSP won only 16 seats. Meanwhile, the NFP won 40 seats, giving it a total of 56, the largest opposition party in the upper house. Also performing well was the JCP, which won 8 seats overall, apparently attracting votes from former JSP supporters. The message coming out of this election was unclear, partly because of the low turn-out. The two parties with the best disciplined supporters, the JCP and Kōmeitō, now part of the NFP, did well. Neither the JSP nor the LDP had much to be pleased about – the results were less than a ringing endorsement of their policies.

Murayama had a difficult eighteen months as prime minister. On 17 January 1995 a major earthquake hit Kōbe, causing 5,502 deaths, the collapse of overhead highways and the disruption of rail links between east and west Japan. On 20 March several cans of the nerve gas Sarin were planted on underground trains that would pass beneath Kasumigaseki station at 8.30 a.m., presumably aimed to kill top bureaucrats on their way to work. Ten commuters died and more than 5,000 became ill. This was what might have been the first stage in a bizarre *coup d'état* by a 'new, new religion', Aum Shinrikyō (Supreme Truth Religion), which already had a 'shadow government' with ministers of defence, welfare, etc., and whose beliefs included a prophecy that the religion would emerge triumphant following some kind of cataclysmic collapse of civilization that the Sarin attacks aimed to provoke. The aftermath of both these events would last many years. Kōbe and district were rebuilt, while politicians debated how to construct a crisis management system that could cope with problems such as earthquakes. Meanwhile, the legal system had to deal with those accused of the terrorist attack and work out how to cope with groups professing bizarre and possibly dangerous ideas while protecting constitutional rights to freedom of belief and expression.

In both cases the Prime Minister's Office (PMO) was shown to have been unable to handle the crisis, while various ministries proved to have been inflexible, slow to share information and to have acted in ways inappropriate to the emergency. An often-quoted example is the way dogs trained to search for survivors in collapsed buildings were prevented from entering Japan by officials who insisted on compliance with quarantine regulations. Ozawa's proposals for the reconstruction of government and strengthening of the PMO were endorsed.

Two other serious political problems of 1995 were caused by the rapid rise in the value of the yen and the fiftieth anniversary of the end of the war. The rapid economic growth of the late 1980s was followed by a period of stagnation, as the 'bubble' burst to reveal a series of unwise investment decisions made by banks and other financial institutions. So serious were some of the problems caused by the massive 'bad debts' that some feared for the existence of the banking system itself. And, if the Japanese banking system collapsed, it would take most of East Asia with it. These doubts did not prevent the rise in the value of the yen in mid-1995 up to 'parity' with the dollar ($1: ¥100) and briefly to $1: ¥80. Many Japanese companies had argued for some time that anything below an exchange rate of $1: ¥120 made exporting very difficult. At these very high rates the trend for companies to relocate manufacturing in Southeast Asia was accelerated, causing still further problems for the domestic economy.

Many in the JSP, and indeed on the left in general, wanted the fiftieth anniversary of the end of the war to be commemorated by an apology for

Japan's acts of aggression. Those on the right, including Hashimoto Ryūtarō of the LDP and some in the NFP, were strongly opposed to this, arguing that Japan had nothing to apologize for, particularly not to western countries. A resolution was eventually agreed on 9 June, but it was weaker than many on the left would have liked and the NFP demonstrated its opposition to it by boycotting the session at which it was adopted.

Murayama stepped down in January 1996, his place being taken by Hashimoto as head of the coalition cabinet. Had he achieved anything that would not otherwise have been possible? The expression of regret for the war was one thing. Also during his time as prime minister, government intervened to ensure a final and almost comprehensive conclusion to the fight for compensation for the victims of industrial pollution in Minamata. This campaign had been going since the 1960s, failing to get very far in the face of official indifference or hostility. Murayama seems to have made the difference in enabling a final solution by 1996. It is also significant that in December 1995 a bill was passed which set up a committee to report on human rights protection. There were a number of factors which contributed to government's interest in rights issues in the 1990s after several decades of disinterest, but the creation of a committee located in the PMO, nominally chaired by the PM himself, is probably an indication of the commitment of the socialist party and Murayama to this issue.

Hashimoto became prime minister in the run up to a lower house election which had to be held before June 1997. He is of the same generation as Ozawa and they had been rivals for power when the Tanaka/Takeshita faction collapsed in the early 1990s, but their political views were very similar. The previous December the NFP membership (i.e., anyone who paid the ¥1,000 membership fee) had elected its leader and Ozawa won with more than twice as many votes as his rival, Hata.

Throughout 1995 plans were made to form a new centre-left party. A planned announcement was aborted following news of the earthquake. Discussions were resumed in the summer, but not until September 1996, only weeks before the general election, was agreement reached to form a Democratic Party of Japan (Minshutō; DPJ). It included some defectors from the NFP, some former members of the JSP and the Sakigake. It boasted three 'stars'. Two were brothers, Hatoyama Kunio (b. 1948) and Hatoyama Yukio (b. 1947), grandsons of Hatoyama Ichirō who had been prime minister in 1954–6 and both formerly members of the LDP Tanaka faction. The other, Kan Naoto (b. 1946), had been a member of the Shaminren, a group that had splintered off from the JSP in 1977 but never had more than four elected members. Kan had been Minister of Health and Welfare (MHW) in 1996 as a Sakigake appointment. In that position, he had insisted on a thorough investigation of accusations that senior MHW officials had knowingly allowed blood products contaminated with the HIV virus to remain on the market, resulting in the death from AIDS of several hundred haemophiliacs. Kan not only demanded full disclosure, he also publicly apologized to the victims on behalf of the ministry (Inoguchi 1997: 96–8). Despite the wave of publicity which accompanied the launch of the DPJ, with only weeks to go before the election it seemed unlikely that it could make much impact.

Elections and reforms

The 1996 general election was the first to be held under the 'new rules' and its results have been analysed with more than usual care to see if there were any signs that it was creating a system with the features that had been desired by the reformers: were policies more important than personalities? Was less money required? Was it encouraging the formation of a two-party system? On the first point it is the impression of this observer that there was little to distinguish the policy platforms of the main parties, which seemed agreed on the need for some kind of reform of the government structure, the need to increase the consumption tax (with some disagreement about when and by just how much) and that policies should not imperil the faint signs of economic recovery. At the constituency level, one detailed set of studies concluded that 'networks of personal connections between candidates and influential local people were as influential as in the past' (Otake 1998: xvi). A two-party system seemed to be developing: 79 per cent of the seats were won either by the LDP or the NFP. On costs, the evidence suggested that candidates spent more than in previous elections, some as much as twice as much. It may be, however, that these were the one-off costs of reorganizing the electoral base and that in subsequent elections campaign costs will drop, at least for the candidates who only stand in the single member districts (Otake 1998: xx–xxi; see also McKean and Scheiner 2000).

Immediately after the election the LDP was the largest party, but it lacked an overall majority and was substantially short of the 265 seats needed to control all the committees in the lower house. The NFP was indisputably the largest opposition party and seemed likely to develop into a rival to the LDP. The DPJ did better than it might have expected given that it was formed only just before the election and seems to have benefited from people 'splitting' their vote – voting for a candidate from one party in the SMD but for a different party in the PR constituency. The JCP did well, while the JSP, now trading as the SDP (Social Democratic Party), and led once again by Doi Takako, did poorly, as did Sakigake (see table 6.2).

Although he did not have an overall majority, Hashimoto decided against renewing the formal coalition with the SDP and Sakigake, preferring instead an informal arrangement, consulting with them on policy initiatives to ensure their support. This lasted until the following summer, by which time sufficient members had drifted back into the LDP to give it an overall majority. In January 1997 Hashimoto announced his agenda for reform, comprising six principal policies:

* downsizing the number of ministries and agencies and their personnel through an organizational reshuffle and strengthening the leadership role of the PMO;

Table 6.2   Election results, House of Representatives, 1996

	SMD voting			PR voting		
	% votes cast	% seats won	seats won	% votes cast	% seats won	seats won
LDP	38.6	56.3	169	32.76	70	239
NFP	28.0	32.0	96	28.04	60	156
DPJ	10.6	5.7	17	16.10	35	52
JCP	12.6	0.7	2	13.08	24	26
SDP	2.2	1.3	4	6.38	11	15
Sakigake	1.3	0.7	2	1.05	0	2
Other parties	2.4	0.3	1	2.58	0	1
Independent	4.4	3.0	9			9
TOTAL	100.0	100.0	300	100.00	200	500

Turnout 59.6%
Source: adapted from Otake 1998: 179

- 'structural' fiscal reform, reduction of the budget deficit and reforms of the budget structures and budget-making process;
- reform of the social security systems, health insurance and pensions;
- economic reform revitalizing the Japanese economy and recovering international competitiveness through deregulation;
- financial reform through the liberalization of the financial system (a Japanese 'Big Bang');
- educational reform, liberalization and decentralization, emphasizing elite education and individuality in place of egalitarianism and collectivity. (Otake 1999: 374–5)

This programme adopted the main points of the reform agenda put forward by the Hosokawa government in late 1993, most of which in turn derived from Ozawa's 'Blueprint for a New Japan', whose roots could be found in Nakasone's proposals of the mid-1980s. But the LDP and Hashimoto were putting forward this radical and ambitious reform agenda three months *after* the general election. For whatever reason, the LDP leadership decided against setting out its policies before or during the election campaign in a way that might have made discussion of policy more central to it.

Meanwhile, the NFP was having difficulty hanging together. In December 1996 Hata defected from the party and with a few others set up the Taiyōtō (Sun Party) and before long another small group left to form the 21 Seiki (21st Century). Throughout this time there was a slow leakage of former LDP members who went back to their old party. Finally, in December 1997 the NFP formally dissolved into six mini-parties. Those close to Ozawa formed the Liberal Party (Jiyūtō). Several grouplets joined the DPJ in March 1998 to make a party of more than 100 members in the lower house. As figure 6.2 demonstrates, the period between December 1996 and December 1998 saw

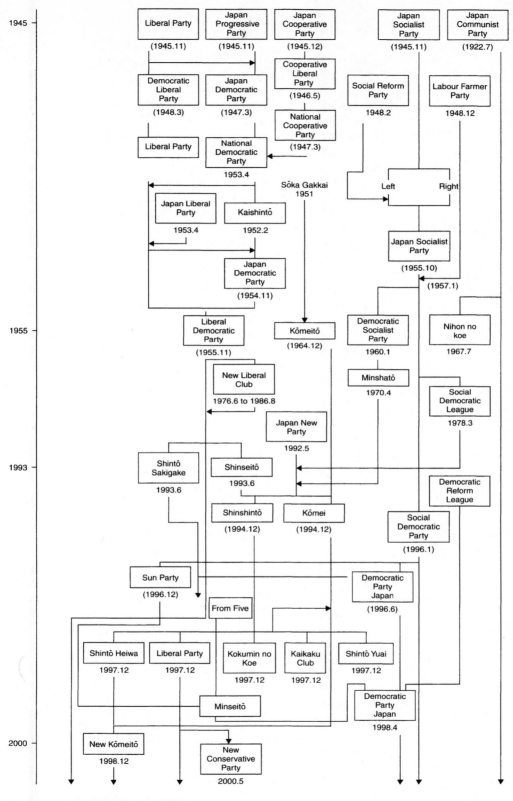

Source: adapted from Fukuoka 2001: 31

Figure 6.2   Principal parties in postwar Japan

the creation and dissolution of a number of mini-parties, demonstrating that Ozawa's attempt to create a new conservative party to oppose the LDP had failed.

Looking at political developments from the time of the 1996 election through into summer 1998, there was no reason to conclude that changing the electoral system was making elections cost less, emphasizing policy more or leading to a stable two-party system.

The next test of the government and opposition parties' performance was the House of Councillors election of 1998. The LDP went into the campaign confident that it could defend all its 60 seats and win a few more besides. Only half the members of the upper house face election each time (see below, p. 139, for more details), so had the LDP won 64 seats, it would have had 120 seats in the 252-seat assembly – not quite a majority but enough for them to get most of their legislation approved with the support of the 'independents'. In the event, they won just 45 seats, giving them a total of 103. The DPJ gained 9 seats (47 all told), as did the JCP, whose vote went up from just under four million to just over eight million. The Kōmeitō lost 2 seats and the SDP lost 7, leaving them with only one more seat than Ozawa's Liberal Party.

Hashimoto had never had a strong base within the LDP and soon after the election he resigned, taking responsibility for his party's 'defeat'. Obuchi Keizō, also from the Takeshita faction, became prime minister, a politician with a reputation for conciliation but little interest in reform. From the start it was clear that he faced problems. At the first meeting of parliament, the lower house selected Obuchi as its candidate for prime minister but the upper house selected Kan Naoto of the DPJ, who had support even from the JCP. Obuchi became prime minister, but this vote made clear that he would not be able to rely on the cooperation of the Councillors. He needed to win the support of one or more of the other parties. Obuchi's weakness was confirmed when opposition party criticism forced the government to drop its plan to bail out the Long Term Credit Bank and adopt the proposals of the DPJ leader, Kan Naoto (Sasaki 2000: 21).

Ozawa's Liberal Party had twelve seats in the upper house. His support plus the occasional help from the conservative independents might have been enough to enable the LDP to enact their policies. They entered a coalition in January 1999 exacting the price that the size of the cabinet should be reduced from 20 to 18 and that the number of PR seats in the lower house go down from 200 to 150. The former request could be implemented immediately, but the latter required legislation. It was also unpopular among the smaller parties, since this was where they got most of their seats. Kōmeitō would be badly affected and indeed it retaliated by suggesting a partial reversion to the former system in which there would be 450 seats elected from 150 multi-member constituencies. Kōmeitō's views were important because the LDP also needed their support to be certain of getting bills approved by the House of Councillors. In the end a compromise was reached: the number of lower house PR seats was reduced to just 180. Kōmeitō was reassured and was made a formal member of the coalition with two cabinet seats in October 1999.

Finally, it seemed that there was a stable base for the Obuchi government, and during the next few months a raft of major reforms were approved. The budget for fiscal 1999 was passed by 17 March, earlier than any budget since 1945, guidelines enabling greater cooperation between the USA and Japan in regional security were approved with little fuss, along with laws reforming the central bureaucracy, officially recognizing *Hinomaru* and *Kimigayo* as the national flag and anthem, reforming parliamentary procedure and permitting the use of wiretapping to monitor criminal activity. Many of these were controversial proposals that only a few years before would have gridlocked parliamentary business. Obuchi's success was in part no doubt due to his skills as a political fixer, skilfully dealing with his coalition partners. However, we should note that opposition to his proposals was no longer as powerful as it had been – there was broad agreement amongst the opposition parties, with the exception of the JCP. So the speed with which these proposals were approved owes less to Obuchi's power than to opposition weakness. Moreover, Obuchi's wider popularity was based on the abandoning of Hashimoto's commitment to fiscal reconstruction and the launch of a massive supplementary budget in an effort to stimulate economic growth.

However, in April 2000 Obuchi collapsed, and died two weeks later without regaining consciousness. The party had quickly to find a successor. Within a few days it chose Mori Yoshirō (b. 1937), LDP secretary general with experience in MITI, the MoE and the MoC. Early in his career Mori had been a member of the Seirankai which advocated rearmament and revision of the pacifist constitution. Soon after taking over as prime minister he was reported as having referred to Japan as a 'divine nation' (*kami no kuni*), a phrase redolent of pre-war nationalism. This was not a good omen for leading the LDP into the general election of June 2000.

The general election of 25 June 2000

In that it did not result in a change of government and left them with an 'absolute stable majority', the election can be regarded as a victory for the ruling coalition even though all three parties lost seats: the LDP 37, Kōmeitō 11 and the Conservatives 11. Meanwhile, the opposition parties improved their position: DPJ from 95 to 127, the Liberal Party 18 to 22 and SDP 14 to 19. Only the JCP lost seats: down from 26 to 20. The LDP did slightly better in the single member constituencies than in the previous election, with votes up from 38.6 to 41.1 per cent and seats from 169 to 177. However, support in the PR constituencies, considered to be a better reflection of party popularity, was only 28.3 per cent and the comparative success in the single seat elections was due to the electoral pacts with Kōmeitō not to run competing candidates (see table 6.3).

Although he claimed success in the general election, Mori was not popular within the LDP or the country at large. From the start of 2001 criticism of his regime grew, until he finally agreed to step down once a successor was chosen. The two main contenders were Hashimoto Ryūtarō and Koizumi Junichirō,

Table 6.3 Election results, House of Representatives, 2000

	SMD voting		PR voting		
	% votes cast	seats won (300)	% votes cast	seats won (180)	total seats won
LDP	41.1	177	28.3	56	233
DPJ	27.6	80	25.2	47	127
JCP	12.1	0	11.2	20	20
SDP	3.8	4	9.4	15	19
New Conservative	2.0	7	0.4	0	7
New Kōmeitō	2.0	7	13.0	24	31
Liberal	3.4	4	11.0	18	22
Other	8.1	21	1.5	0	21
TOTAL	100.0	300	100.0	180	480

Turnout 62.5%
Source: http://www.ifes.org/eguide/resultsum/japanres.htm

but as a total of four candidates stood the two-stage electoral process took place. Hashimoto, as leader of the biggest faction, was expected to win, but there were some indications that all was not following the usual script when twenty members did not turn up to the meeting to announce his candidacy. Moreover, Koizumi, though the inheritor of the leadership of Mori's faction, ostentatiously resigned from that faction prior to the election and criticized faction-based politics. The first stage of the electoral process selected the representatives of each prefecture who would attend a party congress in Tokyo at which the final selection would be made. In most prefectures, whichever candidate received a majority of support from the membership would get all that prefecture's votes on a winner-take-all basis. It was expected to be fairly close in the country at large, but that the faction system would ensure that the position of leader would pass to Hashimoto. However, to everyone's surprise, Koizumi won an overwhelming majority of support in the country at large, which meant that the party had no choice but to let him succeed Mori.

He appointed a cabinet which retained seven ministers in the same posts, including a total of five women, two of whom were in the senior posts of Minister of Justice and Foreign Affairs, and three non-politicians. The process of the formation of this so-called 'national salvation' government broke most of the unwritten rules that previously had guided the selection of cabinet ministers, and may turn out to be an important turning point.

Though viewed with suspicion within the LDP, Koizumi was massively popular with the general public, with support in opinion polls as high as 90 per cent. He sustained his popularity during the 2001 House of Councillors election in which the LDP won a total of 65 seats: 45 in the electoral districts and 20 in the national PR constituency. This was a substantial improvement on the result in 1995 when the same cohort stood for election and the LDP only won 46 seats. Kōmeitō maintained its strength at 23, while the NCP was down from 7 to 5. The largest opposition party, the DPJ, increased its total number to 59, much less than it had hoped, while the SDP was down 4 seats to 8 and the JCP down 3 to 20. The Liberal Party increased its holding from 5 to 8. This was the first time the 'open list' system was used and it was expected that it would benefit the LDP, which would fill its list with media and sports stars. The LDP did indeed do this, but the overwhelming popularity of Koizumi was such that it is hard to assess just what impact the new arrangements had. Nevertheless, even after this undoubted success the LDP still only had 111 upper house seats (out of 247). It will need its coalition partners until 2004 at least.

Political parties at the start of the twenty-first century

In autumn 2001 the LDP (with 232 representatives and 111 councillors) had a clear majority in the lower house, but needed its coalition partners to ensure the passage of bills through the upper house. Although factions were officially disbanded (again) in 1995, they remained the main feature of LDP organization and their activity the most plausible explanation of developments within the party. However, the election of Koizumi Junichirō to the post of party president in May 2001 may indicate that change is imminent. The party had endorsed most of the elements of the six-point programme put forward by Hashimoto in 1997. His successors abandoned the commitment to reduce the budget deficit, but the massive public spending programmes of 1999 and 2000 had little impact on economic recovery, and increased the total national debt to 130 per cent of GDP at the start of 2001. This presents a serious problem, as it can only be paid off by increasing taxes, but such a move is liable to snuff out whatever embers of economic revival might be present. Koizumi, however, pledged to increase the national debt no more even if this should create short-term problems for the economy. He faces serious opposition from within his own party which he has promised to ignore in order to give priority to the national interest. Can Koizumi implement his reforms and keep the LDP united?

The Liberal Party (with 22 representatives and 8 councillors) split in May 2000 when Ozawa took his followers out of the coalition leaving behind a small group of 'conservatives' (made up of 7 representatives and 5 councillors), who called themselves the New Conservative Party and were led by Ogi Chikage. This was not a split caused by differences in policy but simply about whether the policies could best be pursued in government or outside it. There followed an acrimonious debate about access to the state-provided funds which will probably make reconciliation difficult. This left the Liberal Party as very much a one-man party. Only four of the lower house members were elected in single seats, three from Iwate prefecture, Ozawa's power base. The remaining eighteen were elected in the PR constituencies where people vote in support of Ozawa's policies and attitude, rather than for the party as such. Liberal Party gains in 2001, too, were in the PR constituency and around Iwate. While this gives Ozawa personal endorsement to continue to push a neo-liberal agenda, it does not suggest that a stable party has been created which will survive his political demise. Meanwhile, one expects that the 'new conservatives' will be reabsorbed into the LDP.

The other coalition partner, Kōmeitō (with 31 representatives and 23 councillors), had apparently dismantled its national organization when it merged with others to form the NFP in 1994, although the grassroots organization that overlapped with the Sōka Gakkai structure remained intact and was very effective in getting its supporters to the polls. When the NFP collapsed in December 1997, it formed the 'New Party Peace' (Shintō Heiwa) from lower house members, but the 'New' Kōmeitō was set up in December 1998 restoring the pre-1993 structure. The promise of a seat in cabinet, and presumably some more material rewards, persuaded the party to become a member of the coalition cabinet from October 1999. Even before this its leader Kanzaki Takenori was boasting that the party had the power of veto over all bills proposed to cabinet, but it is hard to ascertain whether this power of veto has increased or been reduced by formal cabinet membership. During the election of 2000 there was a degree of cooperation with the LDP to prevent competition between the coalition partners in SMDs, although complaints from New Kōmeitō suggested that while its supporters obediently voted for the LDP candidate, LDP voters did not always reciprocate. For the foreseeable future the Kōmeitō seems likely to remain locked in an embrace with the LDP with which it has been cooperating since the late 1990s.

The DPJ (with 129 representatives and 58 councillors) is now the main opposition party. It has a centre-left platform: 'popular sovereignty', 'respect for fundamental human rights and pacifism', free market principles should 'permeate economic life' but individuals should be guaranteed social security and safety, while government should become more transparent and less centralized. Although rarely openly discussed, there are reported to be five factional groupings within the party: those with a JSP background (30–40), those who came into the party through Sakigake (15), those who came from the DSP (25), those who came with Hata Tsutomu from the NFP (20) and, earlier, the Takeshita faction, and the largest group composed mainly of those elected in 2000 and 2001 who support Hatoyama Yukio ('NHK Ohayō Nippon', 28 September 1999; personal communication, Sarah Hyde, 25 September 2001). The unresolved lack of unity in the party became apparent during the summer of 1999 when bills passed through the parliament on the national anthem and flag. Half the party voted with the government, the other half with the opposition. Rengō formally supports the DPJ, which gives it potentially eight million votes, but only 20 per cent of them actually vote for it. It is unclear how stable this party can be.

The SDP (with 19 representatives and 13 councillors) policy positions are similar to those of the DPJ except that it has slightly less faith in market mechanisms and more principled opposition to nationalism. Led by Doi Takako, it has a higher media profile than its size would normally merit and, judging from the performance in the 2000 and 2001 elections, it seems likely to linger on the fringes of political life. Its main source of support is the local government workers' union Jichirō, which is fearful that the reforms proposed by both the LDP and the DPJ will lead to a loss of jobs for its members. Doi has tried to make a positive feature of the fact that around half the national-level representatives are women and that it can offer a feminine approach to politics. It unlikely to be attractive to ambitious young politicians and it is difficult to see how it could be rejuvenated.

Despite (or in an odd way perhaps because of) the collapse of the international communist movement, the JCP increased its influence in the 1990s (20 representatives and 20 councillors). At its peak in the early 1980s it could credibly claim a membership of 480,000 (each subscribing 1 per cent of their annual income) and a readership of 3.5 million for its newspaper. This had dropped to 360,000 and 2.3 million by the late 1990s, although it has managed to increase its support at elections. The JCP was one of the first communist parties to become a national party and since 1966 has been committed to a 'Japanese path to communism' which later has been elaborated into a process of 'democratic change within the framework of capitalism' composed of three stages: democratic coalition government, democratic revolution and socialist revolution. New leaders Fuwa Tetsuzō (chairman) and Shii Kazuo (party secretary) have devised more pragmatic readings of policies that might enable agreement on a democratic coalition to replace the LDP. They no longer implacably oppose the US–Japan Security Treaty, the sending of SDF overseas or even the adoption of the national flag and anthem. Much of the electoral support in national and local elections has no doubt come from former supporters of the SDP who find the DPJ too right wing. Shii performs well; he often broadcasts on television and has succeeded in reducing the hostile image. There has been further moderation of the basic policy with the target of 'establishment of a democratic coalition government' being consigned to the medium-term future and the creation of a 'not as bad' government made first priority. One could imagine the JCP as a coalition partner of the DPJ were it to emerge as the largest party but without a majority.

Results of the 2000 and 2001 elections were not promising. Support from voters with no party allegiance dropped dramatically and there are limits to the extent the party can trim its radical programme. Already there is an opposition group within the party that, through its internet homepage, is critical of the leadership. Moreover, the party is ageing. The average party member is now in his or her fifties and it seems difficult to see how the party can attract the younger generation by these trimming policies, particularly as younger voters are becoming more conservative (Katō 2000: 38–40; Lam 1996; *Daily Yomiuri*, 17 July 1997).

Conclusion

It seems that Stockwin's prediction of summer 1991 was eerily accurate and that after a couple of twists and turns the DPJ has indeed emerged as the 'new party of opposition, combining elements of the old opposition parties, together . . . with centrist elements from the LDP' (Stockwin 1991: 6). On the other hand, there has been at least one 'false start' as the NFP emerged as a neo-liberal alternative to the traditionally conservative LDP. This conservative/conservative political structure did not last long because the LDP painlessly took on board the Ozawa reform agenda in 1997. Once that crumbled, the opportunity arose to create a centre-left party that could offer the electorate an alternative to the LDP. While there is still no guarantee that the DPJ will be able to remain a coherent party, there seems to have been a settling down of the political spectrum so that on the right there are the parties in government – the New Conservative Party, the Liberal Democratic Party and the Kōmeitō – facing the parties of opposition – the Democratic Party, the Social Democratic Party and the Communist Party – with the Liberal Party retaining a role as a gadfly, critical of the LDP but with contacts within it, occasionally cooperating with the opposition.

Textbooks are no place for predictions, but if I were to speculate on the likely direction of change I would have to point out that the only two dynamic parties in this list are the LDP and the DPJ and, as such, only these two parties are likely to recruit ambitious young politicians. Only they have the potential to increase their electoral support to become majority parties, although, equally, there is a chance that either might split. The Liberal Party's future depends entirely on Ozawa. Meanwhile, the Kōmeitō on the centre right and the JCP on the left have such substantial core support that they will not disappear even if they are equally unlikely to grow. For the foreseeable future the electoral systems are likely to generate coalitions but it is round the LDP and DPJ that these will form.

Part III

Structures

7

Bureaucratic Structures and their Reform

At the end of the 1990s Japanese bureaucracy underwent major reform. The number of ministries was reduced from twenty-three to thirteen and the authority of the prime minister substantially increased. There was a feeling that government was too big, both in the sense that it employed too many people and that its influence was too pervasive. Reform, it was thought, was needed to slim down central government and to reduce its ability to regulate society and the economy. Critics also argued that elected politicians had insufficient control and that reform was needed to increase their influence and thus improve democratic accountability.

In the final section of this chapter we will explain the reforms implemented in 2000–1 and attempt to assess their impact, but we begin with a general description of the executive: the prime minister, the cabinet and the bureaucracy, as they developed in the second half of the twentieth century.

The prime minister

In a presidential system such as the USA the head of state is typically elected by the population at large and selects a cabinet which is independent of the legislative assembly. In a parliamentary system, as described in the Japanese constitution, the prime minister is a member of parliament, selected by and responsible to that parliament, and he or she chooses a cabinet most or all of whom are members of parliament.

Between 1945 and 2000 the USA had ten presidents, the UK eleven prime ministers and Japan twenty-five prime ministers. Some have served for longer than average – Yoshida Shigeru for six years, 1948–54; Satō Eisaku, between 1964 and 1972; and Nakasone Yasuhiro from 1982 to 1987. These three apart, though, most have been in office for less than two years, some much less. It is tempting to think that this might reflect a cultural preference for rule by consensus and a dislike of strong leaders, except that in the same period there were only six governors of Tokyo, and many prefectures and major cities have had governors or mayors who have served for several consecutive four-year terms. The brief careers of Japanese prime ministers may just be another manifestation of the unstable factionalized structure of the LDP.

Although there is no constitutional or legal limit on the length of time a prime minister may serve, since the 1970s the LDP has had a rule that its leader may only serve a maximum of two two-year terms of office. (Nakasone was 'rewarded' with an extra year after his success in the 1986 'double election'.) This means that a prime minister has to remain very attentive to the factional balances in his party, with an eye on the forthcoming party selection process. Changing the LDP's rules to permit a four-year or unlimited term in office would do more than any one thing to strengthen the power of the prime minister, but that is likely to be opposed by the faction leaders who are out of power at any one time.

After a prime minister has resigned, or after a general election, the first item of business of parliament is to elect a new one. The candidates are the leaders of the main political parties and since 1955 the successful candidate has usually been the leader of the Liberal Democratic Party (LDP). Most LDP members of parliament belong to one of five or six factions, each of which at any one time will have between 40 and 100 members. The leader of the LDP will usually be the leader of one of the largest factions and have the support of two or more, such that he can command a majority in his party. When he selects his cabinet, a prime minister has to ensure that each of these factions is represented in the cabinet to ensure party unity. Indeed, it became common practice for faction leaders to put forward the names of their followers who they believe deserve a seat in the forthcoming cabinet when a reshuffle is imminent. The most senior posts, ministers of finance or foreign affairs, will be given to senior members of the parliamentary party who the PM trusts and who have some cabinet experience. Less prestigious posts will be given to those whose only qualification is an ability to be re-elected (usually a minimum of five times for a cabinet post). For some, this will be a stepping stone to a ministerial career, for others it will be their one and only experience of government.

Until 2001 a prime minister was nominally in charge of the Prime Minister's Office (PMO), which served him directly as well as twelve agencies and auxiliary organs. Between 1952 and 2000, while the number of ministries remained the same (apart from the upgrading from agency status of the Ministry of Home Affairs in 1960), government acquired a number of new functions such as economic planning, defence and environmental protection. When these tasks were taken on, the newly created agency was usually attached to the PMO either because it was felt that it was so important that it should formally be under the prime minister's control – for example, the Defence Agency – or because it would have disrupted the delicate balance between existing ministries, as was the case with the Environment Agency. Some of these agencies carried out functions that in other political systems would be done by fully fledged ministries, and many of the anomalies in the system have been eliminated by the reforms implemented in January 2001. Similarly, a large number of commissions and councils on topics as varied as nuclear safety, pets and gender equality have come to be attached to the PMO. The location of the Bureau for Gender Equality in the PMO was intended to symbolize the importance being given to the issue, but in other cases, such as the Council for the Protection of Animals, it was because no ministry wanted responsibility for pets.

A Japanese prime minister has extensive authority. He decides on all the main appointments and dismissals of cabinet ministers, other political appointments in government and to senior posts in the LDP. It is he who nominates the Chief Justice of the Supreme Court, although the appointment is made in the name of the emperor. He appoints the chairs of the most important advisory councils – *shingikai* – and some of them will submit their reports directly to him. The Chief Secretary to the Cabinet, a cabinet-level post since 1966, is usually occupied by someone close to the prime minister, often in the same faction, and he assists the prime minister in cabinet, ensuring a steady flow of paperwork. It is he who faces the press conferences following cabinet meetings and who makes announcements in emergencies. Some prime ministers have tried to create bodies outside the constitutional structure. Ohira created a number of 'think tanks' and Nakasone set up an advisory body on educational reform. Mori had a group of five or six academics and senior businessmen who met with him once or twice a month. Within cabinet the prime minister sets the agenda and as decisions are made by consensus this may give him the opportunity to summarize the 'feeling of the meeting' and finesse any opposition. Media attention is focused on him, which enables him to exercise considerable influence on the party and other ministers. Through these channels, a prime minister can exert broad influence on policy direction.

There are limitations to his authority though. First, and crucially, until 2001 he had no legal power to initiate policy or to insist that his ministers initiate policy – his was essentially a coordinating role. Secondly, the Cabinet Secretariat/PMO was small compared to most ministries and composed mainly of individuals seconded from elsewhere and whose loyalty remained with their ministry of origin. Only three or four appointments were made by the prime minister personally. Reforms to cabinet law made in June 1996 allowed the prime minister to make three special appointments giving him advisers who had no ties either to the ministries, the party or factions, but this did not greatly increase his power base. Thirdly, there are weaknesses that derive from the nature of the LDP. The shifting sands of interfactional relationships have been an unreliable basis for the exercise of prime ministerial power particularly since the enforcement of the rule on two-year terms for the party leader. Finally, he is responsible to parliament, which he and his party may not always control. The LDP has not had a majority in the upper house since 1989. This became such a problem for Obuchi in 1999 that he felt obliged to enter into a coalition with first the Liberal Party and then the Kōmeitō in order to ensure his policies were approved. Coalition cabinets in 1993–6 and then since 1999 have forced prime ministers to be even more circumspect about policy-making as they have to win over all the parties before proposing bills to parliament. Moreover, the fact that a Japanese prime minister has only rarely been in power for more than two years has prevented any of them from introducing a policy programme with a personal stamp on it. There are, of course, many states where coalition government is the norm and it is not necessarily associated with an inability to govern effectively. However, when comparing the powers of the Japanese prime minister with those of the US president or the UK prime minister critics and politicians have often concluded that the Japanese leader is weak. Nakasone advocated constitutional reform to create a directly elected prime minister as a way of enhancing his personal authority, a call endorsed by Koizumi.

Cabinet

Constitutionally, the cabinet is responsible to parliament and can be forced to resign if the lower house passes a motion of no confidence (Article 69). At least half of its members must be members of parliament, although in fact only rarely have non-elected politicians been appointed to cabinet posts. Where they have, it has usually been because they have special skills believed to be important for the resolution of pressing problems. All members of the cabinet must be civilians (Article 66).

At the end of the occupation there were eleven ministries, plus the PMO. Apart from the elevation of the Ministry of Home Affairs from agency status in 1960, there was no change in the framework of central government until 2001, except for the creation of agencies within the PMO. Some of these were placed under the control of a director with cabinet rank. Cabinet law was periodically revised to allow an increase in size up to a maximum of twenty.

Before 2000 most ministries had one *seimu jikan* (parliamentary vice-minister), the more important ministries – MAFF, MoF, MITI – had two. They took part in planning and would perform the minister's functions in his absence. They are typically younger politicians who have been elected a couple of times. They are appointed by the prime minister and, like ministers, they lose their post when he resigns or reshuffles his pack. In the late 1990s attempts were made to develop the role of the parliamentary vice-ministers and as part of the wider reforms of 2000–1 they may acquire a new significance.

A newly elected LDP politician in the later twentieth century could expect to acquire some experience of government as a *seimu jikan* after being elected two or three times, followed by a lesser cabinet post in their fifth or sixth term in elected office (Stockwin 1999: 101). If his performance was deemed successful, he might be selected to head one of the more influential ministries which in turn might enable him to establish a reputation so that he could be considered a possible prime minister. However, success in this promotion game depends not only on an individual's performance in government but also on his ability to negotiate the LDP's internal structure.

Alert readers will have noted that we have referred to ministers and prime ministers as 'he'. Women were rarely appointed to ministerial positions before the 1980s. In the late 1980s when Doi Takako was leader of the JSP and voters appeared to be responding to her encouragement of women to become involved in politics, there seemed to be a deliberate attempt made to include women. Kaifu included two in his cabinet. Usually, women occupy only a token role within cabinet, but Koizumi included five among his seventeen-strong team and appointed one, Tanaka Makiko, to foreign affairs.

Cabinet itself meets at least twice a week on Tuesdays and Fridays, rarely for more than two hours, sometimes for only fifteen minutes, which causes some to doubt whether it really does play a central role in decision-making. At lunch time on the day before cabinet meets, the administrative vice-ministers, the most senior civil servants in each ministry, gather in the presence of the Chief Cabinet Secretary to go through the items on the agenda. While some suggest that this is just concerned with fine tuning and the coordination of items that concern more than one department, others argue that it plays a more significant role and can prevent items from being discussed by cabinet (Gotoda 1994: 114, 237).

The bureaucracy

The two most commented-on features of the Japanese bureaucracy are that it is small but possesses considerable authority. There has been constant pressure since at least the 1960s to restrict the size of the civil service, which in part explains why in 1994 there were only 40 government workers for every 1,000 people in Japan, compared to 68 in Germany and 86 in the USA (Schwartz 1998: 26).

Entrance into the civil service is by examination taken after university graduation. Competition is intense. In 1992 more than 30,000 took the higher civil service examination, of whom only 2,075 passed. The ministries then select from those who pass the exam; not all who pass are hired – only 41.1 per cent of those who passed the exam in 1986 got a civil service job (Koh 1989: 91). The most prestigious ministries get first pick of the successful candidates. Apart from the fact that, for example, MAFF will want some agriculture specialists and MHW people with medical knowledge, there is a preference for generalists, particularly graduates of the law faculties of the highest ranked universities, preferably Tokyo University. Not all ministries will be after the same kind of recruit. Kasumigaseki lore has it that the MoF seeks out those who are dour and dependable, MFA looks for international-ists and MITI the trendies.

Once recruited, there is virtually no movement between the ministries, except that those in the main ministries may be seconded temporarily to one of the agencies. Within the ministry, individuals are constantly being moved round, serving no more than two years in any one post. By the time they become a section chief, typically after fifteen years, they will be familiar with most of their ministry's activities. There is an unwritten rule that no one who enters a ministry in one year will serve in a position junior to someone recruited later. People retire rather than serve under a 'junior'. So as people reach the peak of the promotion pyramid, fewer of their peers will be left in the ministry. Of the twenty-seven who join the MoF from university, there will only be sixteen left after twenty-five years, eight remaining after thirty years and three to five after thirty-two. In the end there will be only one representative of that cohort when an appointment is made to the post of administrative vice-minister. Even he will only serve two years before retiring at the age of fifty-five (Inoki 1995: 230).

This system has several strengths. It creates a permanent civil service composed of relatively young people who are in constant circulation, a system that allows new ideas to percolate swiftly through the structure. A strong *esprit de corps* exists among the younger officials who know they will be together for a considerable period, and this produces a loyalty to the organization, a willingness to work long hours and a preference for long-term planning. At lower levels, committed work is rewarded with better training and more interesting jobs which ultimately may mean 'real' promotion to the more senior levels where the pay increases dramatically. Moreover, the more senior the final post occupied before retirement, the more senior and better paid post the individual is likely to be offered in his second career (Inoki 1995: 230–2).

Competition between ministries can be healthy but may result in activities which duplicate or even contradict policies being pursued elsewhere. Ministries are particularly eager to develop policies that might extend their areas of interest. In the 1980s several ministries – MAFF, MHW, MoE, MITI, STA – each established research projects or administrative sub-sections to develop 'biotechnology'. This was in part in order to create the basis for a claim on any new funds, but it was also intended to maintain influence over their traditional clients. Thus, for example, MHW developed a biotechnology promotion policy partly in order to dissuade the pharmaceutical companies from becoming involved in the research projects funded by MITI. Not all such competition is wasteful, but the sectionalism within Japanese bureaucracy as a whole was criticized in the 1990s and one aim of the reorganization project was to facilitate coordination and reduce waste.

Even the most talented members of a ministry retire at 55, and most of their colleagues will have left before then. Given the life expectancy of Japanese males, they can expect another 20–5 years of active life, during which time most will seek *amakudari* (descent from heaven), or to 'parachute down', as many bureaucrats more prosaically refer to it. There are four main options before them: to enter politics in either central or local government, or to find employment in the public or private sector.

Between 1955 and 1983, 21 per cent of the LDP members of the lower house had worked in the higher civil service. Moreover, between 1957 and 1972, 50 per cent of cabinet posts were occupied by former bureaucrats (Pempel 1998: 183). Since then the proportion has declined, as seniority within a faction became more important than status to qualify for a ministerial post. Of the 480 representatives elected to the lower house in 2000, 86 were former bureaucrats. A growing number of prefectural vice-ministers (a non-elected post) are filled by retired bureaucrats, many, though not all, from MHA. For some, this may be a stepping stone towards standing as a candidate for governor. In 1995 27 of the 47 prefectures had a governor who had formerly been in the national bureaucracy, 16 of whom were from MHA (Fujioka 1997: 106). There are no restrictions on transfers into local government or into public corporations or non-profit organizations established by national government. As of April 1992 there were 92 of these, employing 784 managing directors and more than 600,000 people in total, including JETRO (Japan External Trade Organization, MITI), the Japan Highways Corporation (MoC) and the Pension Service Public Corporation (MHW). More than half of those in middle management and 60 per cent of the managing directors of these corporations have transferred from the related ministry (Inoki 1995: 217). It is sometimes alleged that the main reason for the existence of these bodies is to provide jobs for ex-bureaucrats.

There are some restrictions on retired bureaucrats moving directly into executive positions in industries that they have regulated. However, they are not policed too scrupulously, in part for fear of breach of an individual's constitutional right to freedom of occupation. A common pattern would be for an individual to spend two years working in a public corporation before taking up a post in industry. Former employees of the MoF often end up in financial institutions, former MHW officials in pharmaceutical companies, MITI OBs ('old boys') find their way into many companies.

There are some flows in the opposite direction in the form of the temporary transfer (1–2 years) of employees from outside government into posts in central government, bank employees into the Economic Planning Agency, local government officers into the MoL or Keidanren officials into MITI (Inoki 1995: 217). This is a rather different phenomenon, in that it involves people early in their careers, usually when they are in their twenties or thirties, and the aim is to create a number of individuals with knowledge of how government works and a set of contacts that they will maintain throughout their careers.

The effect of both kinds of personnel exchange is to create a network of linkages that cut across and blur the boundaries of state and society. This might be thought of as a way in which the state has been able to extend its control while remaining fairly 'small', or it can be seen as creating a structure of interdependence between the state and some of the main actors in society that improves the nature of policy-making and the effectiveness of policy-implementation.

On the other hand, there are many critics of *amakudari* and related practices who argue that it protects the interests of the powerful from effective democratic surveillance and promotes 'cronyism' in public life. Overt criticism of central government officials used to be rare, but during the 1990s there was a series of well-documented cases of corruption which caused public confidence in the bureaucracy to decline (see below, pp. 119–21).

Administrative guidance

These close connections between the public and private spheres have enabled the bureaucracy to exert influence over society and economy in ways that go well beyond its legal authority using 'administrative guidance' (*gyōsei shidō*). The ministry most renowned for its use of this strategy was MITI, which would, for example, use its influence to insist that all within a business sector reduce production by a certain amount to avoid over-production and 'excessive competition', or limit exports to a particular market if there was a possibility of adverse reaction. However, many other ministries and even local governments have been able to make demands of their clients that go beyond their formal power. They are able to exact compliance mainly because of the way Japan is so extensively regulated. Even if companies or clients know that they have no obligation to comply in a specific case, they will be aware that the next time they need a permit in a situation where the agency does have full authority, obstacles may emerge.

This policy strategy was cheap, flexible and accepted by industry and society in the 1950s and 1960s. However, it seemed to operate unfairly against non-Japanese companies and there were domestic critics too who disliked the lack of transparency it brought to the policy process. As Japan opened up its domestic market and as Japanese companies became transnational organizations, it became difficult for MITI to use administrative guidance to get its way. Moreover, from the early 1990s demands grew for an overall reduction in regulation and an increase in democratic accountability. A law introduced in 1994 sought to reduce the arbitrary nature of administrative guidance by insisting that any requests be put in writing and that non-compliance would not be penalized. Nevertheless, close links continue to exist between bureaucrats and client groups, which give them greater scope to exert extra-legal influence than their counterparts in many European or American states.

Advisory councils

As part of its policy for democratizing Japan's administration in the 1940s, the USA insisted on the creation of advisory councils (*shingikai*) in as many areas as possible. By 1991 there were 214 such councils plus another 400 'panels' appointed by ministers or bureaux to advise on specific matters. Some questioned the value of these councils, and there was a drive to reduce their number, so that by July 1996 only 164 remained. The number of 'panels' is harder to estimate, as they are less open to public scrutiny, but there are probably fewer than there were. Whatever the aims of the occupation reformers, there is real doubt about the contribution of these councils to the democratic control of the policy process. Critics point to the way the appropriate ministry decides on the remit of the council (which it may not exceed): it decides the membership, provides most of the data for the deliberations and even drafts the final report. They may be used simply to legitimate decisions already made in the ministry. At other times they are used by politicians to introduce a policy that is likely to be unpopular. In this way a prime minister or minister can disown responsibility for a measure (such as the consumption tax in 1989, for example) by claiming he is only acting on the advice of a council of experts.

Some *shingikai* are examining bodies, ensuring the fair application of law or endorsing reports made by specialists, for example on the licensing of pharmaceutical products. Their activity is relatively uncontroversial except that some actors in the sector affected by these decisions may feel unjustly excluded from participation in the *shingikai* – a complaint made by representatives of the pharmaceutical industry who are rarely found on any of the committees set up by the MHW, in contrast to the ubiquity of the medical profession. Other kinds of *shingikai* (occasionally the same ones operating in a different mode) play more of a planning role, producing long-term policy recommendations that are sometimes called 'visions'. Thus the Industrial Structure Council in MITI produced sets of suggestions for the overall development of Japanese industry for each of the final decades of the twentieth century, and there were sometimes 'visions' developed for specific industries.

A typical *shingikai* will be composed of between 30 and 100 members; some will be academics, some from the media, some from the industry and professions affected by the decisions and some representatives of organized labour. What is often not clear is how many of a committee are former members of the ministry now into their second career – old boys, OBs. Some suspect that by appointing a high proportion of OBs the ministry will be able to ensure that the councils come to the required conclusions. On the other hand, OBs may be in a better position to criticize or even reject the policy proposals of their former juniors and less willing to be railroaded to a set of decisions by them (Schwartz 1998: 66–9).

It is not clear, then, whether *shingikai* do contribute to the democratic control of policy-making, as there are severe limits on their independence. They act as arenas in which the various actors in a policy network can be brought together in the presence of (and usually the building of) the related ministry officials. In other words, they enable interaction between a ministry and its clients which can still further blur the boundary between state and society.

The budget and the FILP

Government spending as a proportion of the GNP looks relatively low in comparison to other advanced capitalist countries. It increased in the 1980s, but the government was able to keep it under control in the 1990s (see table 7.1).

According to the constitution, the authority to compile the budget rests with the cabinet (Article 73), but budget formulation was done by the Budget Bureau in the Ministry of Finance. There is a cycle of budget preparation which follows a regular pattern in the Japanese political year. It begins in July when the budgeting policy is announced for the next financial year. This might

Table 7.1 Government current disbursement as a percentage of GDP

	1976	1988	1999
Canada	35.8	40.1	42.5*
France	41.8	46.8	48.5
Germany	44.0	43.8	44.8
Japan	**23.6**	**34.3**	**30.0***
UK	39.7	40.2	37.8
USA	29.5	31.6	32.7**

* 1998
** 1997
Source: Muramatsu 1994: 29 and OECD

be a decision to try to reduce the overall size of the budget, to set a zero ceiling or to permit increases of 1–2 per cent or more.

Over the summer and early autumn the requests of the various ministries are reviewed and attempts made to bring the total within the parameters announced in July. Budgets from some of the ministries are difficult to control – for example, expenditure on pensions or health care increases as the population ages. MoF examiners will try to remove items they consider unnecessary. Around 20 December a final draft is prepared by the MoF and presented to the ministries and agencies, having first been accepted at a cabinet meeting. At this stage the ministry may turn to its friends within the LDP asking them to use their influence to have certain items that were rejected by the MoF restored to the budget estimates. If sufficient support for an item can be found within the ruling party, it may be reinstated. However, in any one year the number of such items may be more than the budget could stand, in which case a final ruling may have to be made through negotiation between the senior leaders of the LDP. This process is usually completed and approved by cabinet by 30 December. Thus by the early new year a Budget Bill can be drawn up to be presented to parliament. This bill needs to be approved by both houses, but in case of a dispute the decision of the lower house stands. Little of the content of the bill is changed in the course of its passage through parliament, but if it contains controversial items or if there are other items in the session's timetable to which the opposition parties strongly object, they may try to delay the passage of the bill. If delayed for too long, it may become difficult for government to carry out its business. Normally a government will hope to have the budget bill approved by the end of February, allowing good time for implementation at the start of the new financial year on 1 April. Thereafter, the MoF supervises the expenditure process and a Board of Audit checks the settlement of accounts. However, this part of the process has very little political salience.

As described above, the budget process that decides what taxes will be spent on which projects is formally supervised by the elected assemblies and subject to the demands of the political process. However, there is another source of money to support government spending: the Fiscal Investment and Loan Programme (FILP). This consists of funds that are deposited with government agencies such as the postal savings system, surpluses from welfare insurance accounts or pensions schemes, which are made available to government to spend through, for example, the Government Housing Loan Corporation or the Development Bank of Japan. There has been much less political control over the way these funds have been used, although from fiscal year 1973 FILP proposals have been presented for parliamentary approval along with the rest of the national budget. In the mid-1950s FILP made up 3.4 per cent of the GNP, but by 1990 it had grown to an estimated 8.2 per cent. During the 1950s and 1960s most of FILP funds were used to support four basic industries – electric power, shipping, coal, iron and steel – and the general improvement of infrastructure – mainly roads and ports. From the late 1960s the FILP contribution to support big business declined and the amount spent on supporting small and medium-sized enterprises, on housing loans and protecting or improving the environment, has increased. Priority was initially placed on giving assistance to industrial growth when industry was in an 'infant' stage, but since the 1980s 'the role of FILP shifted to the adjustment of social tensions by providing financing to low productivity sectors' (Noguchi 1995: 287). In the 1990s the supplementary budgets that have tried to stimulate the economy by increasing spending on social infrastructure have been provided through the FILP system (Miyawaki 1993: 22).

Whereas the general account budget is largely funded by taxation, the FILP is funded mainly from market sources and, as such, will need to be repaid. Although it was known as a 'second budget', by the early 1990s its size exceeded that of the general account and during the late 1990s it continued to grow as the government launched massive public works, spending in order to stimulate economic growth. Demands have emerged for the overhaul of government finances and the integration of the FILP into the general budget structure. This may be possible following reform of the central government system.

Public distrust of bureaucrats

It used to be said that although there was widespread distrust of party politicians, there was broad respect for the bureaucracy which appeared to be above corruption. While the image of politicians has not improved during the 1990s, evidence of government officials' involvement in corrupt practices has accumulated, resulting in a clear decline in public trust in government as a whole. Let us briefly mention two examples of this.

HIV-infected blood

For a number of years Japan was unable domestically to generate sufficient blood products for medical use such as the clotting factor needed by haemophiliacs, so supplies were imported from the USA. Between 1982 and 1986 untreated batches of this clotting agent were imported from the USA at a time when it was known that it might be infected by the HIV virus and when supplies of heat-treated (and therefore safe) clotting agents were available. As a result 40 per cent of haemophiliacs in Japan – 1,800 people – became infected with HIV, of whom, by 1997, 400 had died. The MHW refused to accept any responsibility for the patients' suffering until 1996, when Kan Naoto, a social democrat, was appointed minister at MHW by Hashimoto. Kan launched a full investigation which demonstrated that the ministry had sought to hide its responsibility.

The company that imported and sold the blood product was Green Cross, an employer of many retired officials from the MHW Pharmaceutical Affairs Bureau (PAB). The chief of the PAB at the time the issue first emerged was keen that any disclosures should not cause problems for his former colleagues at Green Cross where he too may have hoped to find employment after leaving the ministry. As a result, he ignored the advice from the MHW's AIDS research group which said that untreated blood products should not be licensed for use (Inoguchi 1997: 97–8). When the truth was revealed, Kan issued a full-scale apology and promised compensation to the infected patients. Later, criminal prosecutions were launched on those in Green Cross deemed to have been responsible.

Three points emerge from this. The untreated blood remained available because of the close connection with Green Cross, not because of any direct corruption such as bribes from the company. Second, the generalists who usually occupy the most senior posts can, and in this case did, overlook the recommendations of the specialists who, it was said, did not understand the 'big picture'. Third, the incident would not have been brought to public attention if it had not been for the appointment of Kan Naoto, who insisted on a full investigation in the face of strong internal resistance. It is unlikely that the links between business and bureaucrat would have been investigated by an LDP politician; indeed, LDP ministers in charge of MHW had been satisfied with the explanations that were later shown to have been at best untruthful. A couple of years later there were further revelations that a MHW permanent vice-minister had received a bribe of ¥60 million to give permission for the construction of an old person's care facility (Fujioka 1997: 159). This had a major impact because of the distrust generated at the time of the HIV incident.

Bureaucratic entertainment expenses

Before 1945 the relationship between central and local government was one in which central government imposed various duties on the regional authorities and, periodically, inspectors were sent out to make sure they were being carried out. To help ensure that they did not receive a negative report, local authorities would provide the best possible entertainment for the inspectors (*Kan-kan settai*). The post-occupation reforms changed the balance of power between central and local authorities. Most local government activity is now either funded by local taxation or by money that comes directly from central government to pay for the various services that are provided locally. However, about 15 per cent of a local authority's income derives from sub-sidies of various kinds and these can contribute significantly to the region's infrastructure. They may also improve the electability of local politicians and, by attracting industry, increase the local tax base. Naturally, all local author-ities want at least their fair share of such subsidies, and the best way to get them is to ensure that ministry officials are well treated when they visit the region or when local officials visit Tokyo. In 1993 Nagasaki prefecture spent ¥117 million (around $1 million) on such entertainment (Inoguchi 1997: 99). This kind of expenditure went unchecked until 1994, when groups of lawyers and citizen movement activists started to demand freedom of information about local government activity. Initial awareness about how much civil servants were spending on entertaining each other came just at a time when the recession was forcing cuts in expenditure on travel and entertainment by private companies. By 1995 it had become a major issue and public pressure had forced some prefectures to cut entertainment budgets by half.

These cuts are likely to continue. First, there has been some decentraliza-tion, some relaxation of central control that has enabled local authorities to take the initiative in areas where central subsidies are not needed. Secondly, when the consumption tax was increased from 3 to 5 per cent in 1997 half the increase (i.e. one of the 2 per cent) was allocated for local government. This too should make it less important to get central government finance (Inoguchi 1997: 99–101, 105–6).

These were not the only scandals to have increased public distrust of the bureaucracy, which surveys of the mid-1990s suggested was shared by 65 per cent of the population. The use of taxpayers' money to bail out the home finance institutions, inadequate provision of information amounting to a cover-up following an accident at the Monju nuclear power plant, revelations about the excessive 'entertainment' provided for MoF officials by financial institutions: all have further contributed to a feeling that the bureaucracy can no longer be trusted. Distrust of politicians is nothing new and of course not unique to Japan. The reforms of the electoral system discussed in chapter 8 were aimed at reducing this. Reforms proposed for the bureaucracy which emerged in the later 1990s were aimed to reduce the 'excessive' competition between ministries, to strengthen power and authority at the centre of government, but also to 'modernize' the administrative structure so it could recapture lost respect.

Administrative reform

Background

Each of the major political parties announced their support for administra-tive reform during the 1996 election campaign, and Hashimoto Ryūtarō, LDP prime minister after the election, committed himself to ensuring that it was carried out. Few believed at the time that reform would take place, or if it did, that it would amount to radical change. Nevertheless, fundamental changes have been made in the structure. In this section we will review the process of reform and describe the system of government that has been created.

It is usual to divide the process of administrative reform into three phases. The main impact of the first round of reform in the 1960s was to place limits on the size of central government. A law enacted in 1964 abolished one bureau in each ministry and created a rule that no new bureau could be established in any ministry unless a comparable bureau was abolished – a principle known as 'scrap and build'. Some flexibility was introduced into the system in 1969 when it became possible to reallocate personnel according to need at the same time as fixing the overall maximum number of government employees. This is said to have resulted in the total number of bureaucrats dropping from 899,333 in 1967 to 887,022 in 1983 (Fujioka 1997: 156).

The second phase of reform started in the early 1980s, a time of revival of interest in neo-liberalism; Ronald Reagan was in the White House, Margaret Thatcher was the UK prime minister. The assumption behind these reforms was that government in Japan too should aim to do less. In the short term government spending should either not grow or be cut back; in the medium term the public corporations should be privatized so they ceased to be a drain on the public purse; and in the longer term a programme of deregulation should be introduced to stimulate economic growth and thus increase government revenue without increasing tax rates. Nakasone Yasuhiro, prime minister from 1982 to 1987, sought to restructure Japanese politics, and he adopted this agenda with some enthusiasm. A tight 'ceiling' was imposed on growth of the overall budget in the 1980s. NTT and Japan Tobacco were privatized in 1985 and the national railway system was privatized in 1987. A recommendation to create a Comprehensive Planning Agency was resisted by the bureaucrats, but in 1984 parts of the PMO and the Administrative Management Agency were consolidated into the Management and Coordination Agency, whose director was given cabinet status. However, the proposals to reduce the number of items that were subject to administrative regulation failed; between 1981 and 1988 it actually increased from 10,045 to 10,169. Nevertheless, the economic growth of the late 1980s did generate sufficient revenue to eliminate the budget deficit by 1990 (Fujioka 1997: 156–8).

However, the boom conditions of the 1980s soon turned to bust in the early 1990s as the 'bubble economy' collapsed. The economy entered a decade of slow to no growth, which, for the first time since the war, was caused by internal problems rather than the impact of changes in the world economy. This was accompanied by growing budget deficits which once more formed the context for discussion of administrative reform. The third round of reform was based on the assumption that proposals would have to come from party politicians. This was in the heady days when the LDP was out of power for the first time since 1955 and almost anything seemed possible. The project of administrative reform was entering a new phase, where it concerned not just the effectiveness of reform but how to exert democratic control over it (Namikawa 1997: 16).

The LDP was out of power for less than a year (July 1993–June 1994), during which time the electoral system was radically reformed. It returned to power in coalition with the JSP. Proposals for the decentralization of government and the deregulation of the economy were coming from the new parties and from private think tanks. These ideas were taken up by party politicians at the time of the general election of 1996 and, when Hashimoto became leader of an exclusively LDP cabinet following that election, he set up an administrative reform council with himself in the chair. This produced a final report in December 1997, and early in 1998 the basic enabling legislation was passed, aiming to create new government structures to be in place by January 2001.

The basic premise of the report is that government in Japan has grown 'extremely large and rigid'; it suggests ways 'to realize a streamlined, efficient and transparent government that permits effective execution of important state functions' (Final Report, Executive Summary, http://www.kantei.go.jp/foreign/central_government/index.html). The report focused on three areas.

First, it sought to reform the functions of the cabinet and increase the leadership role of the prime minister. It suggested the use of cabinet committees to focus on specific issues, the reduction of the number of ministers to 15–17 and the need for cabinet authorization of appointments to the most senior positions in ministries and bureaux. Cabinet law should be revised or reinterpreted to enable the prime minister to initiate policy. The confusing PMO/Cabinet Secretariat system should be abolished and replaced by a Cabinet Secretariat operating mainly through politically appointed staff empowered to plan and draft 'basic policies' including external affairs and security, crisis management, economic policy and budget formation. The Cabinet Office should combine the functions of the PMO with those of the Economic Planning Agency (EPA) and the Okinawa Development Agency. A Defence Agency should be created with ministry status and a Ministry of General Affairs set up to take over the roles of the Management and Coordination Agency (MCA), the Ministry of Posts and Telecommunications (MPT) and the Ministry of Home Affairs (MHA).

Secondly, the other functions of government should be reorganized to create nine ministries. There was extensive debate about the details of these reforms, most of which need not concern us. The renaming of the Ministry of Finance from Okurashō (the *Okura* refers to the imperial storehouse and was associated with government for more than 1,000 years) to Zaimushō met with some resistance. More significant were the proposals to transfer some budgetary powers to the Cabinet Office and to strip the Zaimushō of its crisis management functions. Loosely modelled on the reforms of the British civil service, it was suggested that 'agencies' be created either at ministerial level to be headed by a minister of state, at the executive level under the control of the Cabinet Office or a ministry, or as policy agencies with a degree of independence. *Shingikai* are to be kept to a minimum and their operations made more transparent.

Thirdly, government should cut back its activity, cease its 'excessive' intervention in the private sector and local government and re-examine its use of regulations and subsidies. The report proposed a drastic cut in personnel. The number of secretariats and bureaux should be reduced from 128 to 90 and during the first ten years of the operations of the new structure the number on the central government payroll should go down 10 per cent. Hashimoto's successor, Obuchi, revised this target to 20 per cent.

The report's other aims include reform of the civil service system, introduction of a legal right to obtain government information and endorsement of the idea of rapid decentralization.

Implementation

Hashimoto was clearly committed to these reform proposals, but it was feared that if and when he ceased to be prime minister enthusiasm for them would wane in the face of bureaucratic resistance. Hashimoto took responsibility for the LDP's poor electoral performance in the upper house elections of July 1998 and was replaced by Obuchi Keizō who had less personal interest in administrative reform – but the reform process continued. On 8 July 1999, 17 related bills were passed which would reduce the number of central agencies from 23 to 14 by 2001 and thus reduce the size of the cabinet to 14 (plus 3 additional ministers that a PM can appoint at his discretion).

In January 2001 the new central government structure came into operation with 13 cabinet-level organs replacing the previous 23 with the functions combined, as in figure 7.1, to create the new structure described in figure 7.2.

Assessment

Some are sceptical about the likely impact of these reforms. The reduction in the size of government could be made without affecting the central bureaucracy. In 1995, 26 per cent of government employees worked in postal services and 4.4 per cent in hospitals. Simply making the post office an 'agency', planned for 2003, and changing the status of national hospitals would cut the central government payroll by 30 per cent. Any cuts in the size of the defence establishment, too, would reduce the size of government. There is plenty of room for fudging these figures.

There has been a real reduction in the number of secretariats, from 128 to 96, and the number of 'offices' from 1,200 to 1,000, which may represent some economies of scale. *Shingikai* have been abolished or amalgamated to reduce their total number to 29. However, most bureaux have simply been shifted round into different and bigger ministries with the process of policy formation within them remaining largely undisturbed. Reorganization of the central government offices alone will have almost no impact on changing the system of vested interests. In the late 1980s the relationship between the MHW and the pharmaceutical industry was still being explained in terms of

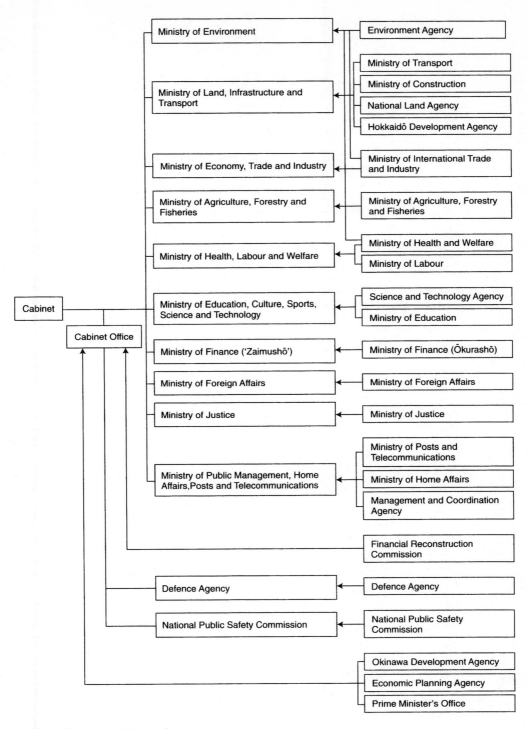

Note: Shows only cabinet-level organs
Source: *Japan Echo*, 28 (1) February 2001: 58. Reproduced by permission of the publisher

Figure 7.1   Streamlining of the central government structure

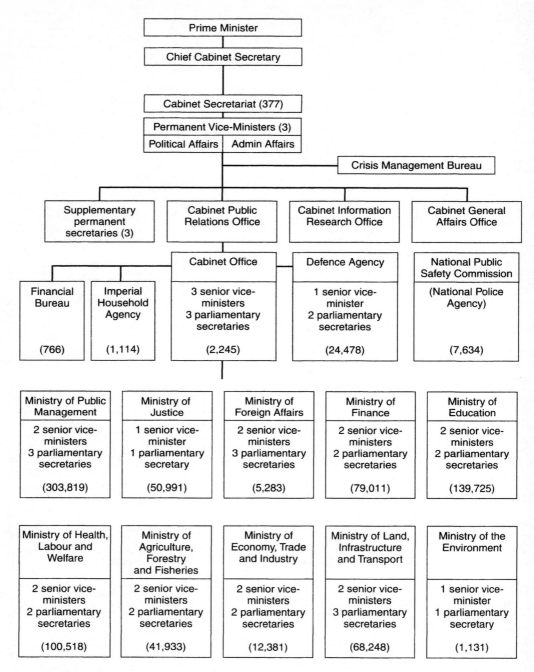

Prime Minister

Chief Cabinet Secretary

Cabinet Secretariat (377)

Permanent Vice-Ministers (3)

| Political Affairs | Admin Affairs |

Crisis Management Bureau

| Supplementary permanent secretaries (3) | Cabinet Public Relations Office | Cabinet Information Research Office | Cabinet General Affairs Office |

| Cabinet Office | Defence Agency | National Public Safety Commission |

Financial Bureau	Imperial Household Agency	3 senior vice-ministers 3 parliamentary secretaries	1 senior vice-minister 2 parliamentary secretaries	(National Police Agency)
(766)	(1,114)	(2,245)	(24,478)	(7,634)

Ministry of Public Management	Ministry of Justice	Ministry of Foreign Affairs	Ministry of Finance	Ministry of Education
2 senior vice-ministers 3 parliamentary secretaries	1 senior vice-minister 1 parliamentary secretary	2 senior vice-ministers 3 parliamentary secretaries	2 senior vice-ministers 2 parliamentary secretaries	2 senior vice-ministers 2 parliamentary secretaries
(303,819)	(50,991)	(5,283)	(79,011)	(139,725)

Ministry of Health, Labour and Welfare	Ministry of Agriculture, Forestry and Fisheries	Ministry of Economy, Trade and Industry	Ministry of Land, Infrastructure and Transport	Ministry of the Environment
2 senior vice-ministers 2 parliamentary secretaries	2 senior vice-ministers 2 parliamentary secretaries	2 senior vice-ministers 2 parliamentary secretaries	2 senior vice-ministers 3 parliamentary secretaries	1 senior vice-minister 1 parliamentary secretary
(100,518)	(41,933)	(12,381)	(68,248)	(1,131)

Note: The figures indicate number of employees
Source: Takizawa 2001: 199

Figure 7.2   The new government structure

a tradition of government industry links established when the pre-war Naimushō controlled the industry before the formation of MHW in 1938. Will it take forty or more years, or will we at least need to wait for a completely new set of bureaucrats to be recruited, before the pre-2001 patterns are eliminated?

On the other hand, the reforms in ministry structure plus the strengthening of the role of the prime minister and cabinet could change the balance between the bureaucracy and elected politicians. A prime minister is now able to appoint up to five assistants: Koizumi formed a 'foreign policy task force' of four scholars, industrialists and ex-bureaucrats. Hitherto, cabinet discussion was largely restricted to dealing with the policy issues pre-approved at the vice-ministerial meeting held the previous day, but the revised Cabinet law authorizes the Cabinet Secretariat to develop concrete policy plans under the direction of the prime minister and cabinet, if necessary independent of the relevant ministry. The prime minister is also authorized to form a Council on Economic and Fiscal Policy as part of the aim to ensure the Cabinet Secretariat coordinates policy at the highest level. Based on recommendations from this Council, the prime minister will initiate the budget process by proposing the total size of the budget and prioritizing major spending items. This shifts the essential function of budget formation from the MoF to the Cabinet Secretariat. In late 2000 around a hundred people were recruited from outside the bureaucracy to form a high-quality core staff with loyalty direct to the Cabinet Office. The new Cabinet Office absorbed the PMO, the EPA and the Okinawa Development Agency and is empowered to order ministries to provide the prime minister with information. This enables him to express his opinion directly to a ministry.

Not directly related to cabinet reform, but in the same spirit of strengthening the role of the prime minister, in 2000 a National Basic Policy Committee was set up in both houses. It meets every week that parliament is in session. The prime minister is required to attend, and for forty minutes there is debate on current issues between him and the leaders of the opposition parties, with time being allocated between them roughly in proportion to their parliamentary support. Modelled on the British 'Question Time' in the House of Commons, the aim is to provide an opportunity to make important policy announcements and for government policy to be criticized. It is also intended to increase the transparency of government and to enable greater display of leadership. The first session took place on 23 February 2000 and began with a question about what the prime minister had had for breakfast (answer: a pizza).

In July 1999 bureaucrats had been prohibited from answering questions in parliament. Later it was decided to appoint twenty-two senior vice-ministers and twenty-six parliamentary secretaries, placing between one and three of each in every ministry, distributed as shown in figure 7.2. Senior vice-ministers can deputize for the minister in his absence either within the department or, for example, by answering questions in parliament. Some have been given special areas of responsibility within their ministries. Doubling the number of elected politicians within the bureaucracy could be the first step towards increasing their control over policy-making. However, the fact that the bureaucracy has successfully resisted demands that the committee of administrative vice-ministers no longer meet suggests that it will not be easy to reduce their power. In an era of coalition cabinets, it is no doubt helpful for a prime minister to have the number of positions he can distribute increase from just over thirty to sixty-five.

Conclusion

Little of what was proposed in the late 1990s was new; for example, the transfer of the budget function from the MoF to the PMO appears in the 1964 report. In the past, the bureaucracy had been able to prevent any significant change that threatened its authority. Why were things different in the 1990s? First, the scandals of the mid-1990s had reduced the prestige of several key ministries in the eyes of the electorate. Secondly, the economic ministries (MoF, MITI, EPA), which had claimed much of the credit for economic growth, appeared incapable of doing anything about the recession. Politicians who may have feared tinkering with a machine that was able to deliver growth were less reluctant to try to improve the effectiveness of institutions that seemed unable to have a positive impact. There was a feeling that something had to be done. Even though by international comparison Japanese government is not particularly 'big', limiting its size has been a constant theme since the 1960s and, given the huge budget deficit of the 1990s, it is not surprising that it should re-emerge. Most major companies have responded to the successive years of economic stagnation by restructuring their businesses, some almost abandoning their commitment to lifetime employment. When most of industry is involved in radical reform, it is hard for bureaucrats to argue that they should be an exception.

Also significant, although perhaps less crucial, are the proposals to move the political and administrative capital away from Tokyo. This idea has been around since the time of the devastating Great Kantō earthquake in 1923, but it re-emerged following the earthquake in Kōbe in 1995. Transferring the capital to a site less prone to earthquakes would reduce the disruption that will occur when the next major earthquake hits Tokyo. Separating the political/administrative capital from the financial/industrial centre might also reduce the scope for improper business influence over political and administrative decisions. Although a site had not yet been chosen, the government was committed in the late 1990s to moving some or all government functions out of Tokyo. Enthusiasm for this project ebbs and flows. When the idea of decentralizing the functions of government is being emphasized, the topic of moving the capital seems less important. On the other hand, if the ministries are to be relocated it makes sense to reform the organizational structure before plans are made to construct a new set of government buildings. Many still doubt whether the capital will move, but in the early 1990s few envisaged the radical reform of the structure of government that has now been completed.

These reforms could make fundamental changes to the relationship between the bureaucracy and elected institutions and even the nature of the state in Japan. The balance between the various institutions of government, big business, the parties and pressure groups that has been maintained since the 1950s has created a system of 'governed interdependence' that some argue has enabled Japan to react more effectively than many other states to changes in domestic circumstances and the international environment (Weiss 1998). On the other hand, analysts such as Stockwin have been more impressed by immobility within the decision-making process even when there has been widespread support for a change (Stockwin et al. 1988). The agreement about the need for deregulation and the evidence of increased use of permits by bureaucracy to regulate industry and society in the 1980s was one example of this. From Weiss's perspective, these reforms threaten the pattern of 'governed interdependence', perhaps weakening the ability of the state to make and implement policy and thus jeopardizing the possibilities for economic growth. However, they are likely to eliminate the 'bottle-necks' in the policy-making process, so that when government decides on a course of action it will be possible to carry it out.

The reforms have not only altered the structure of the government ministries, but also the balance between them and the elected part of the political system. Both ministers and the prime minister must now defend their actions and policies before an elected body. They can no longer rely on senior civil servants.

However, the reforms of the late 1990s only create the possibility for change, they do not guarantee it. It remains to be seen, for example, whether prime ministers will be able to develop the functions of the Cabinet Secretariat and Cabinet Office. Will a prime minister be able to insist on policy changes in the face of opposition from factions within his party or alliances of special interest politicians and bureaucrats? Will cabinet ministers and their deputies be able to exert an influence over their ministries? Will they be allowed to remain in office long enough to master their briefs? Will faction leaders continue to be able to insist on the appointment of incompetent members of their factions? The reforms that we have described in this chapter only deal with the sources of weakness of the prime minister as the head of the executive branch of government. They do not affect at all his weaknesses as leader of the LDP. And for as long as the opposition parties remain divided and weak, this is crucially important.

8

Parliament

If reform of the bureaucracy was a major theme of politics in the later 1990s, reform of the electoral system was the key item on the agenda in the first half of the 1990s. Disputes on the issue split the LDP in 1993, precipitating an election that forced it into opposition for the first time since its formation in 1955. Moreover, the legislation of 1995 did not end the debate. Further reforms have been implemented in the later 1990s, often amid great controversy, and more may follow.

Meanwhile, there have also been some changes made in the way parliament works. As we saw towards the end of the previous chapter, one consequence and probably one aim of the reform of the bureaucracy was to increase the significance of the two houses of parliament within the decision-making process, enhancing the role of elected politicians – for example, by ending the practice whereby senior bureaucrats would answer questions in parliament. There is a broad consensus among the reformers, both politicians and academics, that the aim is to create something like the strong two-party system operating in Britain (Otake 1998: ix). This would, it is argued, increase the significance of the political parties within the policy-making process. And it is reform of the electoral system that was thought likely to be most significant in changing the balance between the political parties within the parliamentary institutions. Quite fundamental change was made in the way representatives are elected to the lower house and this appears to have had an impact on the relations between the parties.

We will focus mainly on the role played by the *Kokkai* – parliament – and its two constituent houses: the House of Representatives (HR) and the House of Councillors (HC). First we will outline their structure and membership, then their changing role within the policy-making process and finally their electoral systems. Elections also select the members of the local government assemblies, and in chapter 9 we will look at electoral systems there and at the relationship between central and local government. A common question in both of these areas is what role elected assemblies play in contemporary Japanese politics – which is to enquire about the nature of democracy in Japan.

Kokkai: *structure and membership*

The 1947 constitution provides for a two-chamber parliament – the House of Representatives (Shūgiin) and House of Councillors (Sangiin). Together, they are considered to be 'representative of all the people' (Article 43), 'the highest organ of state power and . . . the sole law-making organ of the state' (Article 41). The size of the lower house grew slowly from 464 in 1946 to 511 at the time of the 1993 election. It stood at 500 in 1996. Though not large by international standards, there were demands that it be made smaller and it was reduced to 480 after the 2000 election; some want it to be further reduced to 450. The House of Councillors had 250 members until Okinawa was returned to Japanese sovereignty in 1972, when two more seats were added. Its size went down to 247 in 2001 and will be reduced to 242 in 2004. Representatives serve for a maximum term of four years which can be ended at any time by a dissolution of the house. Councillors serve for a fixed term of six years with half of them facing election every three.

The powers of the two chambers are very similar except that decisions in the HR take precedence in three crucial areas: the budget, approval of treaties and the designation of a prime minister. In the case of ordinary legislation, when the Councillors amend or reject a bill that is sent to them by the lower house, it will nevertheless become law if passed a second time by the HR on a two-thirds majority. Alternatively, a joint committee of both houses may be called to resolve the issue. The business of government was not greatly affected by conflict between the two houses until 1989. However, following the LDP's loss of control in the HC in that year, the opposition parties began to try to exert some influence, not only voting for the leader of the JSP to be prime minister but also presenting a budget bill of their own. Both were rejected by the lower house. The government's budget bill and the LDP candidate, Kaifu Toshiki, were adopted. Nevertheless, the lack of a majority in the upper house proved inconvenient to the LDP during the 1990s and caused it to enter into coalition agreements with the Kōmeitō and Liberal/Conservative parties in 1999–2000, despite having a majority in the lower house.

Each house has jurisdiction over its members' qualifications, publishes records of its proceedings, selects its president/speaker, controls its own proceedings and conducts its 'investigations in relation to government'. This latter provision is the legal basis for the committee system in each house. A distinction is sometimes made between the British style of parliamentary democracy in which the deliberations of the whole house have prime importance, and the US system, where the proceedings of various committees have most significance. Despite being a parliamentary system, Japan is closer to the US model. There are two kinds of committee: standing committees and special committees. As of September 2001 each house has seventeen standing committees and a number of special committees, usually five or six. Each elected member of a house is obliged to serve on at least one committee (except for the speaker, his deputy and serving government ministers) and some serve on three or four (Mulgan 2000: 543). The activities of each of the ministries and agencies represented in cabinet are overseen by a committee that will consider bills presented to the house. Any bill can be supported, rejected or simply not acted upon, but a resolution of only twenty members of the house is sufficient to insist that it be submitted to a plenary session. Two committees are concerned with internal business – the Discipline Committee and the Committee on House Management. This latter deals with important decisions such as the order of business in plenary sessions and who will be called to speak or ask questions. A Committee of Audit exists with powers to review how well government money has been used, but this is pretty ineffectual. More important is the Budget Committee, not so much for the control it exerts over the process of budget formation but rather because it is the forum within which members of the house can directly question cabinet ministers on any aspect of policy supported by government funding (which leaves out very little). These sessions, which are broadcast on radio and television, were the closest the Japanese parliamentary system got to 'Question Time'-type political confrontation until the reforms of 2000.

The make-up of the committees is allocated in proportion to total house membership, and while the LDP had a secure majority it provided the chair and most of the members for each standing committee. As its majority dwindled in the 1970s, it lost its overall control of many committees. When the electoral tide ran in the LDP's favour once more in the double election of 1986, it could reassert control over all committees, but since 1989 it has had no overall control in the upper house and has struggled to control the lower house even when it had a nominal majority. In 1997, for example, when the LDP had a small majority in the lower house, it provided chairs for only eight of the twenty standing committees (Jiji Tsushinsha 1997: 140–8).

The legislature and legislation

Most legislation originates in proposals generated within a ministry which are then approved by the policy committee of the ruling party (usually the LDP) and cabinet before their submission to one of the houses. Figures 8.1 and 8.2 illustrate the process from the original idea up to submission of the bill and the process of approval in each house.

Policy tribes

During the 1980s it became clear that groups were being formed of LDP politicians who, having taken a serious interest in a particular sphere of

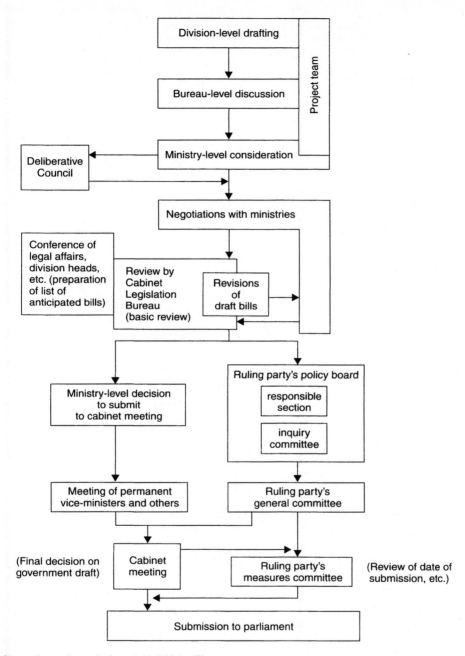

Division-level drafting

Project team

Bureau-level discussion

Ministry-level consideration

Deliberative Council

Negotiations with ministries

Conference of legal affairs, division heads, etc. (preparation of list of anticipated bills)

Review by Cabinet Legislation Bureau (basic review)

Revisions of draft bills

Ministry-level decision to submit to cabinet meeting

Ruling party's policy board

responsible section

inquiry committee

Meeting of permanent vice-ministers and others

Ruling party's general committee

(Final decision on government draft)

Cabinet meeting

Ruling party's measures committee

(Review of date of submission, etc.)

Submission to parliament

Source: *Law in Japan: An Annual*, 19 (1986): 173

Figure 8.1 The drafting process of cabinet bills

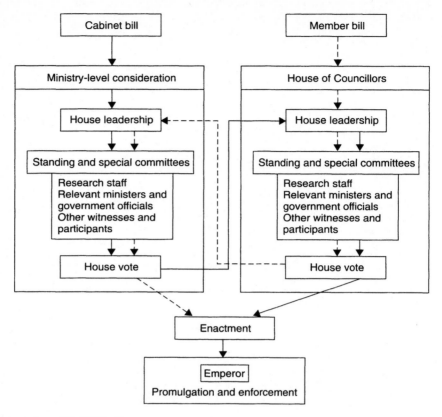

Source: *Jurisuto*, 805 (1984): 19

Figure 8.2 Parliamentary deliberation and action

policy-making following service on one of the house committees and/or one of the subcommittees of the party's policy board, had acquired a degree of policy expertise that matched that of some of the senior members of the ministry. On the one hand, they had a policy agenda that they wished to see implemented, while the members of the bureaucracy realized that if their proposals were to pass smoothly through the system it was helpful to have the senior LDP politicians well briefed and on their side. This might be particularly important if there was likely to be resistance to the proposal from another ministry or within the LDP. Meanwhile, members of the LDP could benefit not only from the increased prestige of direct involvement in the policy process but also because they could use their position to make sure that the benefits of the policy were felt by their constituents, thus improving their chances of re-election. Involvement in transport and construction policy was particularly attractive for this reason.

Thus the custom emerged of having middle-ranking bureaucrats discuss proposals informally with LDP members of parliament or present policy ideas to a subcommittee of the LDP. In this way the strength of opinion within the party could be assessed and, if unfavourable to the proposal, it could be dropped or amended. The activities of these 'tribes' (*zoku*) of LDP members with clearly identifiable policy interests were documented in the 1980s by journalists and academics (Inoguchi and Iwai 1987). At any one time there are ten *zoku*, which vary in size from around ten to more than fifty, with the largest being those that facilitate access to resources such as roads or building work which can be channelled towards their constituents. At their core there will be a small group of senior LDP politicians who have held cabinet posts, often in the ministry in charge of the policy area. Not only will bureaucrats routinely consult the *zoku* when they are formulating legislation, they may also persuade them to intervene in the budget approval process if one of their favourite projects is in danger of being cut.

However the proposal originates within a ministry, if it has any implications for other ministries (and most do) it will then be discussed by a group composed of representatives of all concerned before it proceeds to the overtly political part of the process. At more or less the same time the bill will also be passing through the party policy review process. Within the LDP the key committee is the PARC (Policy Affairs Research Council), which has to give its formal approval to all major bills. It is served by a number of subcommittees whose members may have experience working on one of the relevant parliamentary committees, may have worked in the ministry prior to entering politics or may even have served as a minister or political vice-minister there.

It is said that at one time, in the 1950s and 1960s, PARC was simply a forum where senior ministry officials would explain their policy plans to senior LDP officers prior to their submission. By the 1980s, however, PARC was playing a more active role in the policy process and could not be relied on to 'rubber stamp' suggestions from the bureaucracy. This is part of the process that led to the rise of the *zoku* already mentioned. Once the bill has the support of PARC, it may be submitted to cabinet. This already rather complex process was made still more difficult to follow in the late 1990s when the LDP could only rule with the support of first the JSP/Sakigake (1994–6) and then the Liberal/Conservative Party/Kōmeitō (1999–). Somewhere along the path of getting PARC approval, the agreement of the coalition partners had also to be negotiated.

Meanwhile, and in parallel to this, the bill is assessed by the appropriate section of the PM/Cabinet Office prior to formal consideration by the meeting of permanent vice-ministers on the day before the cabinet meeting, which will endorse the proposal.

It is only at this point that the bill enters the parliamentary process. Here, there are two important stages. First is the decision made by the House Management Committee about when the bill will be considered in the forthcoming session. The ruling party has usually controlled this committee and it will need to assess how important it is and how much opposition it will provoke. An important but controversial bill considered early in a session may mean that there is no time to get less important measures approved.

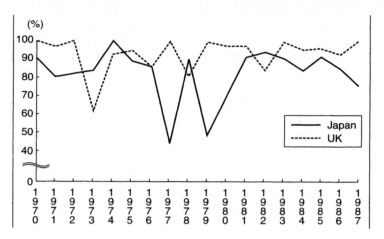

Source: Mabuchi et al. 1997: 125

Figure 8.3 Proportion of cabinet-proposed bills approved by the British and Japanese parliaments, 1970–87

The LDP has usually been able to control parliamentary affairs by virtue of a substantial majority, which has given it control of all committees in both houses. But there have been times in the 1970s, 1980s and, of course, the 1990s when it has not controlled all the committees. These committees are not as powerful, for example, as those in the US Congress. Should a committee decide to 'kill' a bill referred to it, a resolution supported by twenty or more members is sufficient to ensure it is submitted to the house plenary session (Stockwin 1999: 118). When a bill is approved by one house it is then considered by the other (where it may face similar delays) before final promulgation in the name of the emperor.

Writing in 1974, Baerwald noted that many members viewed the committees as essentially 'ornamental' and thought their deliberations were largely a waste of time (1974: 94). However, as it became clear that LDP politicians could exert influence through their *zoku* at various stages of the process, there has been a reconsideration of the role played by the house committees, if only as part of a system that 'trains' these politicians and gives them access to those involved in policy formulation and implementation.

Many commentators, both domestic and foreign, still doubt whether parliament plays a significant role in the policy process. Certainly, it is not as important as the US Congress, but if we compare it with the British parliament a rather different picture emerges. Figure 8.3 compares the proportions of bills submitted by cabinet that were approved by parliament in the UK and Japan. While there were some years when the Japanese parliament accepted less than half of the bills proposed to it, in some years the British parliament approved all of them. This suggests that the executive cannot depend on the compliant approval of the legislature. Moreover, we might note that the LDP was in power throughout this time and that on two occasions, in 1979 and 1986, it failed to get approval for two key measures that would have raised taxes. What is the cause of this apparent inability of the prime minister and cabinet to control parliamentary proceedings?

One major point of leverage is that, with a few exceptions, 'any matter not decided in a session shall not be carried over into the following session'. There are three types of parliamentary session: the ordinary session (*tsūjō kokkai*) is normally convened in January, lasts 150 days and may only be extended once; an extraordinary session (*rinji kokkai*) which can be called by the cabinet or when requested by 25 per cent or more of the members of either house; and a special session (*tokubetsu kokkai*) which must be convened within thirty days of a general election and whose first business is to elect a prime minister. Apart from in emergencies, the HC can only sit while the HR is in session (Constitution Article 54) and when the two houses disagree over extensions to the session the will of the HR prevails.

Rarely, if ever, is a government bill rejected by one of the houses. More common is for obstacles to be put in the way of the smooth passage of a bill such that it runs out of time. In the USA a session of the House of Representatives runs for two years, the UK House of Commons is in session for a year, but in Japan the longest session is only 150 days with perhaps some extension. In these circumstances the decisions of the house management committees are crucial in determining the order in which bills are considered. It will have to allow ample time for the passage of a controversial measure, but if the business of the house becomes dominated by that issue opposition parties may be able to drag out discussion so that not only does the contested issue fail to pass on to the statute book but so do many other less disputed bills. Alternatively, opposition parties may delay the passage of an important piece of legislation, such as the budget, so that there is no time to consider a bill they are opposed to.

The most spectacular and time-consuming way of delaying a decision occurs when an opposition party tables a series of amendments to a bill and then insists on voting on them by casting ballots in the boxes located by the Speaker's chair. No time limits govern this process and what can take as little as 15–20 minutes can be stretched out to several hours by the 'cow walk' strategy (*gyūho senjutsu*) when opposition party members move to and from the ballot box at a snail's pace. A no confidence motion in the cabinet, a minister or chair of a committee may be submitted by twenty members and normally takes precedence over other business. These may also be voted on at a 'snail's pace'. Voting can last all night. Such delaying tactics can be used to force a government to make concessions. If time starts to run short, the opposition may agree to permit passage of (say) the budget in exchange for the modification or abandonment of a measure it dislikes. The relative brevity of the parliamentary sessions gives opposition parties the ability to influence policy-making even when the LDP is firmly in power.

Since 1989, and particularly since 1993, there has been much closer attention paid to parliamentary affairs. And yet, as befits its position within a parliamentary system, the main role of parliament is less as an independent body that is powerful in itself, but, rather, an arena which attempts to curb the power of the executive, forcing it to think again about proposals of major import.

Zoku politicians experienced a decline in influence during the coalition cabinets of the mid-1990s while the LDP was out of power. The tight three-way link between bureaucrats, politicians and elite interest group leaders was broken. In its place 'project teams' were created of members of parliament of the parties in the ruling coalition. Indeed, there was some optimism at the time that not only was a new method of policy-making being formed but that this would create an opening for radically new policies. Such hopes were confounded by the creation of an LDP–JSP coalition which not only brought the LDP back in power but also forced the JSP to divest itself of its more radical policy commitments. Nevertheless, under Murayama it seemed as though there was a more open, democratic discussion of policy in the Policy Adjustment Council and related committees, although some observers suggest that real power returned to the LDP's PARC.

Even after Hashimoto ended the formal coalition with the JSP and Sakigake in 1996, he still maintained consultative links with them because he lacked a majority in the lower house. By 1998 enough former LDP members had defected back to give them a HR majority but they still lacked a majority in the HC following the election of that year. New coalition arrangements, this time with the Liberals and the Kōmeitō, have meant that the LDP still has to consult with others when formulating policy agenda both in and out of parliament.

Moreover, the decline in the involvement of bureaucrats in parliamentary politics reached the point in autumn 1999 where they were forbidden from answering questions in place of ministers in all except the most specialist of areas. This might make parliament more of a forum for active debate of current issues but, on the other hand, given the delicate coalition arrangements, it may be that individual, 'back bench' members are less free to speak their minds because they need to take care to transmit the party viewpoint. More may still be decided in closed negotiations between coalition party leaders than as a result of parliamentary debate.

The changes that have taken place in the way that the parliamentary system deals with legislation demonstrate the way in which the political process in Japan is constantly evolving. In the 'tentative' assessment that Baerwald made of Japan's parliament in the early 1970s, he suggested that its two main roles were as legitimizer of decisions made by the government and the training ground or finishing school for Japan's political leaders (Baerwald 1974: 141). In the twenty-five years since then the importance of the elected representatives has increased; at least some *zoku* members of the ruling party can exert influence on the policy process even though this is rarely done through the institutions of the houses. Since 1993 the LDP has not been the sole party in power and the role of *zoku* has declined, but the overall influence of the elected politicians may be increasing. It is not likely that the influence of the houses or their committees will grow to rival that of their equivalents in the US Congress, but there are signs that there will be increased attention paid to their deliberations as the parliamentary institutions become a more important arena for party politics in an era when coalition government is the norm.

Election systems

House of Councillors

Elections are held for half of the House of Councillors seats every three years in July. Until 2001, 100 of the councillors were elected by the national constituency (50 each time), the remaining 152 (76 each time) were elected from constituencies whose boundaries are the same as the 47 prefectural local governments. The least populous elect 2 (1 each time), the most populous 8 (4 each time). Since 1983, on HC election day an elector has had two votes, one which he or she casts for a person in the local constituency and one for a party in the national constituency. The local constituencies are single or multi-member constituencies, with the elector casting a non-transferable vote. In the national constituency, prior to the elections the parties put forward a list of candidates, and votes were allocated to the party using the D'Hondt system, with the decision about who the seat is allocated to depending on ranking on the list. This results in the preferences of voters being translated into seats roughly in proportion to the percentage of seats won. Thus a party winning 20 per cent of the total vote in the national constituency will be allotted ten seats and the first ten candidates on the party's list become Councillors. Should a Councillor die or resign there will either be a by-election, in the case of the local constituency, or, in the case of the national constituency, the next person on the list submitted by the party is declared elected as long as he or she is still a member of that party.

Controversial reforms introduced in autumn 2000 changed the voting system in the national constituency from a 'closed list' to an 'open list' system. Whereas previously voters had cast ballots just for a party, from July 2001 they are able to vote for either a party or a candidate. The number of seats for each party is decided by how many votes it and its affiliated candidates receive; who gets the seats is decided by the number of votes won by each candidate. This means that the parties do not need to rank their candidates and that there is competition between candidates of the same party. At the same time, as already stated, the number of seats was reduced to 247 in 2001 and will go down again in 2004 to 242 (146 in local constituencies and 96 in the national constituencies).

This works to the advantage of the LDP, which has always failed to win as many votes in the name of the party as for its candidates (indeed, this is precisely why it was introduced). For instance, in the HR election of 2000, LDP candidates won 24.9 million votes but only 16.9 million voters supported the party in the PR bloc elections. It also saves them the troublesome task of ranking their candidates.

House of Representatives

Between 1947 and 1993 members of the HR were selected by a process that can be summarized as a 'single non-transferable vote in multi-member constituencies'. It changed slightly over the half century but at the time it was last used there were 511 representatives from 129 districts, each of which returned 2–6 members in proportion to the size of its population.

The system originated in the 1920s as a result of a compromise between the three parties in the ruling coalition at the time universal manhood suffrage was introduced. The large constituencies gave each party the opportunity to be represented in each district. The system attracted much criticism by the 1980s, but it had several merits. The number of 'dead votes' – votes cast for losing candidates – was very small: only 15 million out of an electorate of more than 80 million in 1993. Secondly, even small parties had a chance to win, since the maximum number of votes needed to win a seat was:

$$\text{No. of votes to win} = \frac{\text{Total vote}}{\text{No. of seats} + 1} + 1$$

And, where one or two candidates attracted more votes than they needed, it was possible for small parties to have their candidate elected with as little as 10 per cent of the total votes. Although not a system of proportional representation, it permitted wider representation of parties than is possible in an Anglo-American, 'first-past-the-post' system. Thirdly, LDP-supporting candidates who did not receive official endorsement could still stand as independents maintaining a dynamic system within the party, despite the fact that it was the party in power for more than thirty-five years.

However, despite these positive features the electoral system was regarded as the main, and sometimes sole, cause of political corruption in Japan. If a party were to succeed in winning a majority, it was necessary to have two or more candidates returned from each constituency. This meant that candidates from the same party were competing against each other to some extent. In order to ensure that voters were loyal to him (only rarely her) he had to establish a personal support group – a *kōenkai* – which is very expensive to create and maintain. To keep followers loyal, it is necessary to send gifts, flowers or cards on births, marriages and deaths, and cards at New Year and mid-summer to members of the *kōenkai* and their families, and also to attend and sometimes pay for parties in the constituency or for constituents' visits to Tokyo. The candidate had to demonstrate to them how his presence in Tokyo would directly benefit the constituency in general and his supporters in particular. Even in a year in which no election is held it is reported that politicians spend around ¥1 million ($10,000) on mailings, constituency gifts and donations (*Tokyo Shimbun* 29 August 1989, quoted in Richardson 1997: 27–8). This would be a significant part of an elected politician's salary of ¥16,550,000. Some politicians have personal fortunes, but few are able to sustain such a constant drain on their wealth. In practice they need to be able to attract supporters.

There will be some support from local sources, from small and medium-sized enterprises or the local branch of Nōkyō (farmers' cooperative). The national party will be able to supply some funds and an individual politician may have personal access to national-level resources, big businesses or industrial associations, although not usually early in their careers. However, a major source of funding, and one that will give him an edge over rivals from the same party, is the amount he receives from one of the factions within the LDP. At any one time since 1955 there have been four to six key factions within the LDP, each with 40–100 members who owe personal loyalty to the faction leader. Size is crucially important and each faction leader constantly seeks new recruits. During the 1980s *kōenkai* established links with the factions. Where there was more than one LDP representative in a constituency each would be linked to a different faction and rivalry between them would often be as fierce as with candidates from rival parties. The whole system depended on the faction leader being able to raise large amounts of money and channel it to his followers. This sometimes forced the politicians into compromising situations with businessmen.

Political bribery, 'an inducement improperly influencing the performance of a public function meant to be gratuitously exercised', is neither peculiar to Japan nor a modern phenomenon there (definition in Mitchell 1996: xiii). Before the war, exposure of serious political bribery led to the resignation of cabinets in 1914 and 1934 and a bribery scandal in October 1948 destroyed the Ashida administration. However, by the 1970s it was widely believed that the underlying problem, the reason, for example, that had led to Tanaka Kakuei becoming involved in the Lockheed scandal, was that the electoral system required large amounts of cash to lubricate its mechanism. There were two possible solutions: to prevent supply of the funds or cut off demand for it. Miki Takeo, who replaced Tanaka as prime minister in 1974, tried to cut off the supply by imposing radical reforms to curb money politics and restrict the amount that any organization could give a party or individual politician. As the bill passed through the party and parliamentary system, its content was watered down until the Act, which became law in January 1976, 'essentially made legal and legitimate various practices that had received heavy criticism during the previous year' (Mitchell 1996: 119).

At the end of the 1980s many politicians were shown to have been involved in the Recruit scandal, including virtually all senior members of the LDP and several members of the opposition parties (although no members of the JCP). No senior politicians were indicted, no politicians were found guilty and all were re-elected at the next general election. In 1992 Sagawa Express was shown to have made semi-legal 'donations' to 130 members of parliament, including ¥500,000 to Kanemaru Shin which he had not declared. He did go to court, but faced only a small fine. In March 1993 Kanemaru was arrested again, this time on charges of tax evasion, and a televised search of his home found tens of millions of dollars worth of gold bars, cash and bonds (Mitchell 1996: 127). This formed part of the background to the crisis within the LDP in summer 1993 which split the party and led to its loss of power following the general election of June that year.

Previous attempts to prevent the supply of money had failed, so attention turned to reducing demand for it, which meant reform of the electoral system. Since the mid-1950s there had been suggestions that a first-past-the-post single member constituency should be introduced and the idea surfaced once more while Tanaka Kakuei was prime minister in 1972–4. However, this would have resulted in a massive majority for the LDP and the smaller parties would be wiped out. A computer simulation using the election data of 1986 showed that if that election had used a single member constituency system with 500 seats available, the LDP would have won 453 seats, and even if the opposition parties had cooperated and only put up one candidate against the LDP, they would still have won 372 seats (Horie 1989: 142). The 1986 election was a 'double election' in that both the upper and lower houses were elected on the same day and the LDP did exceptionally well. Even so, the LDP only got 38.6 per cent of the vote in the national constituency of the House of Councillors election. A fully proportional system would have left the LDP with no overall control and forced it to enter into coalitions with the smaller parties. Gradually, a consensus developed that any new system would have to contain elements of both systems – some single member seats with an element of proportionality. The electoral reform package introduced in 1994 was based on such a compromise.

The main characteristics of the new system were as follows. The number of seats in the lower house was reduced from 511 to 500, of which 300 would be elected from single seat constituencies and 200 from eleven regions that would select members of parliament by a D'Hondt list system (as in the upper house national constituency). The number of representatives from each bloc would be in proportion to its population: the largest, Kinki (Osaka area) was allocated 33 seats, the smallest, Shikoku, 7. Each elector votes for a person in the single member constituency and a party in the regional bloc. Thus far the system was similar to that used in Germany and fairly straightforward. Peculiarly Japanese complications resulted from the following apparently minor additions: candidates can stand in either the single seat district or as part of the regional bloc, *or both* (dual candidacy). Parties can list the candidates in order of preference or list some or all as equal – e.g., 1,2,3,4 or 1,2,3,3 or 1,1,1,1. Dual candidates are removed from the list if they are elected by the constituency. Where more than one un-successful 'dual candidacy' candidate is ranked equally in the party list, and one seat is available, the winner is determined by the 'close loser rate', i.e. the candidate who lost by the closest margin (number of votes for losing candidate divided by the number of votes for the winning candidate). What at first glance looked like a fairly straightforward, if two-level, system is greatly complicated by the possibility of dual candidacy. The key point is that this enables the parties to avoid making a possibly divisive decision on an order of preference.

Electoral reform preoccupied parliament in 1994–5, with extensive debate over details such as whether the split between the number of seats be 250:250 or 274:226 or 300:200. The more single seats, the greater the LDP advantage. Originally it was suggested that voters should indicate their

Table 8.1   Distribution of public subsidies in 1999 (¥ million)

LDP	14,896.75
DPJ	6,927.50
Kōmeitō	3,332.15
Liberal Party	2,796.53
SDP	2,113.67
Kaikaku Club	586.76
Sakigake	346.44
Niin Club	146.95
Jiyu Rengō	130.23
Mushozoku no kai	115.58
TOTAL	31,392.56

Source: Fukuoka 2001: 171

choice by putting a cross against the name of the candidate or party, but at a later stage, when the LDP was back in power, this was changed back to the old system whereby voters must write their selection on the ballot paper, which gives a marginal advantage to the LDP.

The new system was used for the first time in 1996. However, there were soon more demands for reforms. The Liberal Party, which was pressing for a reduction in the size of the bureaucracy, also wanted to reduce the number of PR seats in the House of Representatives from 200 to 150, which would have a disproportional impact on smaller parties such as the Kōmeitō. Meanwhile, the Kōmeitō proposed the introduction of 150 multi-member constituencies, each returning three members. The LDP agreed to cut the number of PR seats to 180 immediately and promised to consider ways to reduce the total number of seats to 450 in the near future. This brought the Liberal Party into coalition in January 1999. One can anticipate further reforms of the electoral system over the next ten years or so; even the reintroduction of the multi-member constituency system cannot be ruled out.

Electoral reform was accompanied by a fresh round of legislation aiming at reducing the demand for money in politics. First, a system of public subsidies to political parties was introduced (see table 8.1). To qualify, a party must have at least five members in parliament, have won 2 per cent of the vote in an upper or lower house election and submit reports to the Ministry of Home Affairs listing party members, votes received at previous elections and other details. The total annual subsidy is ¥250 per head, about ¥30.9 billion. Of the main parties, the JCP receives nothing, as it objects to supplying the required information, particularly about its membership. Its share of the money is distributed among the other parties (Wada 1998: 176). Secondly, attempts have been made to restrict donations by forcing politicians to designate a single political fund and setting a maximum contribution of any person or corporation at ¥500,000 (half the previous maximum), prohibiting donations to factions and insisting on the disclosure of the names of those who contribute over ¥50,000. Thirdly, there were heavy penalties imposed for violations of the election law which makes candidates responsible for the actions of their supporters. Now, if any of the relations or employees of a successful candidate are found guilty of violations of the election law, that candidate must forfeit his or her seat in parliament. Kikuchi Fukujiro, an LDP member in the House of Representatives, resigned in October 1997 after his son and secretary were convicted of buying votes in the election of October 1996. There have been other examples of this. The law had more teeth than previous attempts.

Malapportionment was a problem prior to the reforms of the 1990s. No redrawing of constituency boundaries had taken place between 1947 and 1994, even though there had been massive migration from rural to urban areas in the era of rapid economic growth. In July 1985 the Supreme Court ruled the 1983 lower house election to have been unlawful because the seats were distributed so disproportionately that it contravened the constitutional guarantee of equality under the law. Moreover, the Court threatened to nullify the next election if there was no revision of the seat allocation. Some tinkering with the system had taken place in the past, and the court ruling persuaded the government to remove seven seats from the most depopulated areas and add eight to the metropolitan constituencies. This was implemented prior to the 1986 election and there was more shuffling of seats in 1993. The disparity between the most and least populated constituencies was reduced from 5.12:1 to 2.81:1, just below the threshold of fairness that the Supreme Court set at 3:1. Introduction of the single member constituency system pushed this down to 2.14:1 but it has recently started to creep up. It remains to be seen whether it will be easier to revise the boundaries of the new single member constituencies.

Disproportionality was a problem in the House of Councillors, too, reaching a peak of 6.59:1 in 1995. Readjustment prior to the 1995 election changed this to 4.97:1, still significantly above the 3:1 guideline figure. The upper house problem will remain intractable as long as the principle of using the prefectures as the constituency is retained with at least one representative to be elected every three years (Mulgan 2000: 330–2).

Conclusion

At the start of the twenty-first century Japan's parliament has recently revised the way its members are selected and has acquired greater authority within the policy-making process. Changes within the bureaucracy discussed in the previous chapter will increase the number of political appointments within its top echelons and enable political influence over the promotion of senior officials. Meanwhile, the exclusive domination of LDP as ruling party has been broken, and as long as it is necessary for the majority party to rule with the support of minor parties, party politics will continue to be more important than before the 1990s and this should mean that the focus remains fixed on parliament. An Anglo-American system in which two parties alternate in power has not yet emerged, and there is no certainty that it will.

Nevertheless, the prospects for increased democratic control, an increase in the influence of elected politicians over the policy-making process, are better now than at any time in the previous half century.

9

Local Government

The Meiji government saw the decentralized nature of the Japanese state as a major source of weakness and created an administrative structure that permitted only minimal local autonomy. The 1947 constitution sought fundamental change in the central–local balance and made the 'principle of local autonomy' a core theme (Articles 92–5). This enabled the development of a Local Autonomy Law, which defined the structure, composition and powers of locally elected assemblies and bureaucracies. Local government is often considered a backwater of political life and yet on a day-to-day basis its functions are as important to citizens as those of central government, especially when they go wrong. Moreover, the relation between central and local government can tell us a great deal about the overall character of a state. One thinks, for example, of the confederal nature of Switzerland, the regionalism of Spain and Italy or the division of power between state and federal government in the USA, Canada or Australia.

Despite the constitutional change, there has been a strong presumption of the pre-eminent power of the 'centre' – Tokyo – linked to the transcendent authority of the emperor. It was not obvious that the localities would be able to assert themselves. Indeed, the Japanese discourse of *Nihonjinron* – Japanese telling themselves and others who and what they are – which emerged in the 1960s emphasized the homogeneity of Japanese culture and de-emphasized regional differences, thus serving the dynamic of centralism that remained from the pre-war political structure. This, however, changed and is still changing. Industrialization was accompanied by migration to the cities, but this process has slowed almost to a halt. Some evidence exists, if not for a U-turn, by which people returned to their town or village of origin, then at least for a J-turn, in which people leave the metropolitan areas to live in cities or towns near where they were born. Villages and rural areas have tried hard to invigorate their local economies, reviving folk festivals and inventing cultural events or traditional local industries. New brands of dried mushrooms or shrimps are created, *shōyu* and *miso* are produced using old techniques, new varieties of citrus fruit are grown for sale to the tourists or in nearby cities. All of this has been accompanied by a new interest in local government and its relations with the centre.

The powerful Ministry of the Interior (Naimushō) was dismantled during the occupation, but in 1960 the Ministry of Home Affairs (MHA) was created and by the end of the decade was said to exert a pervasive influence over the formally independent local public entities. On the other hand, in the late 1960s and 1970s several of the larger metropolitan authorities, including Tokyo and Kyoto, were controlled by left-wing parties which came into conflict with the conservative central government. This pushed the topic of the proper scope of authority of local governments to the fore.

In the 1990s an enthusiasm for reform also embraced the structure of local government. On the one hand, there was considerable interest in decentralization, moving power away from the centre and towards local government. At the same time, the desire to reduce the size of government also included local government, and there were proposals that would result in a significant reduction in the number of local government units and swingeing cuts in personnel. There is no necessary contradiction between these two sets of policy. Reducing the number of units of government could be accompanied by the remaining ones being granted more power vis-à-vis central government. Nevertheless, the implementation of this policy would require decisive action by central government which would be portrayed by those authorities about to be abolished as weakening the spirit of local autonomy. Local government reform is likely to be a significant political issue for the foreseeable future for both cultural and political reasons.

In this brief sketch of local government in Japan, we will begin with an outline of the structure of local administrations and discuss the main functions currently carried out by them. Then we will turn to the crucial area of finance – who funds what? Since local government as an arena of political competition is not often commented on in English-language works, we will consider some aspects of this. Finally, we will comment on the reforms of the 1990s.

The structure of local government

The Local Autonomy Law of 1947 created a two-tier system of local administration: prefectures and municipalities. There are forty-seven prefectural authorities, forty-three of which are similar to counties in the UK, plus the metropolitan areas of Tokyo, Osaka and Kyoto, and the island of Hokkaido. Each has a single chamber elected council and a directly elected governor whose relation to the elected assembly is similar to that of the US President to Congress. Governors submit a high proportion of the proposals passed by the council each year, including the budget, and they have a power of veto over council resolutions which the assembly may override by a two-thirds

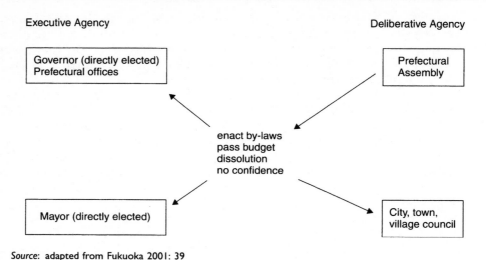

Executive Agency

Deliberative Agency

Governor (directly elected)
Prefectural offices

Prefectural
Assembly

enact by-laws
pass budget
dissolution
no confidence

Mayor (directly elected)

City, town,
village council

Source: adapted from Fukuoka 2001: 39

Figure 9.1   Balance of powers in Japanese local government

majority. An assembly may dismiss a governor by a vote of 'no confidence', a governor may dissolve the council and force an election (see figure 9.1).

At the local level are the cities, towns and villages, whose voters elect an assembly and a mayor whose relation to the council is similar to that of the prefectural assembly to governor. This relatively straightforward structure was made slightly more complicated by the designation of 'special cities' – in theory, cities with a population of more than 500,000, but in practice most of the twelve special cities have more than a million residents – Osaka, Kyoto, Nagoya, Yokohama, Kōbe, Kita-Kyūshū, Sapporo, Kawasaki, Fukuoka, Hiroshima, Sendai, Chiba. These have powers somewhat broader than those of other cities, similar to the prefectures, and for most purposes they are responsible directly to central government not through the prefectural administration. These big cities are divided up into wards (*ku*) for administrative purposes, each of which has an office/town hall which provides municipal services for the local residents.

Tokyo is an exception. There is a council of 127 members and a directly elected governor which is responsible for the twenty-three *ku* each of which has its own council, a number of 'new towns' on the edge of Tokyo proper and a group of Pacific islands to the south of Tokyo. The Tokyo metropolis serves twelve million people.

Ordinary cities, towns and villages (*shi, chō, son*) are defined entirely according to the size of population: cities have more than 50,000 residents, towns 10–50,000 and villages fewer than 10,000. As soon as the population of a town exceeds 50,000 it will apply for recognition as a city, which will give the local authority significantly more power vis-à-vis the prefecture, for example. There seems to be no process of 'demotion' if a city drops below the population threshold.

Table 9.1 Changes in the numbers of cities, towns and villages, 1953–2001

Date	Cities	Towns	Villages	Total
April 1953	280	1,953	7,808	10,041
October 1960	555	1,925	1,030	3,510
April 1970	564	2,027	689	3,280
April 1985	651	2,001	601	3,253
April 1996	666	1,990	576	3,232
May 2001	670	1,988	566	3,224

Source: Namikawa 1997: 106; updated Nov 2001

Local government has responded with remarkable flexibility to the rapid urbanization that has occurred since the 1960s and which concentrated the population around Tokyo, Osaka and Nagoya. As the spaces between towns and villages have been filled in by housing, it has been relatively easy to persuade local government units to combine to create new towns and cities, and in this process the number of towns and villages has declined. Consolidation of local government units creates a larger tax base, which enables the new local authority to perform its tasks more effectively. For example, a large authority may be able to afford to support welfare facilities for more than twice as many old people as the two smaller ones because of economies of scale.

Some propose to accelerate this process to reduce the number of local government units to 250–300. This would remove a whole tier of local government – the prefectures – while also eliminating the villages and small towns where per capita cost of government is highest, thus improving the efficiency of local government. On the other hand, it would also reduce the democratic accountability of local government and, perhaps more significantly, it would arouse the opposition of the 60,000 plus locally elected politicians, most of whom would lose their posts (see table 9.1).

Functions of local government

There is significant variation in the precise range of activities that local authorities undertake, with those of the prefecture being more extensive than the towns and villages. However, we can identify six general areas in which local government plays an important role:

1 *Provision and supervision of local infrastructure*: roads and rivers, tap water provision and sewage disposal, port facilities. Functions important in the monitoring of existing industry and attracting new industry which both provides employment for local residents and increases the tax revenue of the authority.

2   *Welfare facilities for the elderly, the handicapped and children*: care of the
    elderly has become an increasing concern in rural areas as many younger
    people have left for jobs in the city leaving no one to care for their
    parents. Provision of home helpers, day care centres and communal
    facilities has become a priority and in some areas towns may compete to
    make the best provision. At the same time high quality child care may
    help to slow down migration to the cities although this is less attractive
    to politicians as children cannot vote (unlike the elderly).
3   *Education and cultural services*: not only the provision of compulsory edu-
    cation, but also facilities for adult education, libraries, swimming pools,
    museums and art galleries, and halls for public performances.
4   *Public health and environment administration*: supervision of public health
    standards (licensing restaurants etc.), collection and treatment of garbage,
    consumer protection.
5   *Administration and promotion of local industry, forestry, agriculture
    and/or fishing*: the promotion and sale of local produce in the town,
    prefectural capital or further afield, and the creation of plans for the
    development of local industry.
6   *'Citizen services'*: the supervision of the family register system, registra-
    tion of residents and foreigners, issuing certificates relating to national
    insurance and pension entitlement, and, as a result of these activities, pro-
    ducing statistics for central government.

Many of the activities of local government listed above are carried out under
instruction from central government and subject to strict regulations. Social
welfare or agriculture policy, for example, is decided centrally, funded at least
in part from central sources and implemented under the watchful eye of a
MAFF or MHW official seconded to the prefectural office for a two- or three-
year period. In such cases the local government unit is doing little more than
acting as an agent of central government.

   Prefectural authorities are responsible for planning and coordinating
large-scale construction projects, broader plans for welfare, education or
public health promotion. Most prefectures run a university and will usually
have a museum. There may well be some rivalry, duplication or, in some eyes,
waste as (say) Fukuoka city operates a museum, international office or industry promotion policy at the same time as the prefecture. Not only is there
rivalry or lack of cooperation between levels of local government, but there
is a similar lack of communication between the local representatives of
central government. Thus one finds towns where the MoE has constructed a
'Cultural Centre', the MHW a 'Social Welfare Centre' and the MoL a 'Worker
Communication Hall': three buildings when one would have sufficed (Fujioka
1997: 44). Of course this is not simply bureaucratic inefficiency. In such a
situation the local and national politicians have three times as much to claim
credit for if three buildings go up; local builders, architects, cleaners etc. have
three times as much work.

   Nevertheless, in the 1990s this duplication or rivalry persuaded some of
the necessity for radical reform. Usually the demands have been for an

increase in the power of local government at the expense of central government. Hosokawa Morihiro, prime minister from August 1993 to April 1994, famously commented that while he was governor of Kumamoto it was not possible to relocate even a bus stop without authorization from Tokyo. A 'Local Decentralization Promotion Law' and a 'Decentralization Package Law' were passed in May 1995 and July 1999 respectively to promote a shift in authority and resources from the centre into the hands of local government. There have also been some pilot projects launched which allow some municipal governments to use certain central funds more freely or to take on some of the functions reserved for 'special cities'. How far central government is prepared to go in loosening the reins of control remains to be seen, but at the start of the new century some change is clearly under way.

Local government finance

The financing of local government activity is a complex matter, the details of which need not concern us, but unless we have a grasp of the overall pattern of where the money comes from we will not be able to assess how much autonomy local governments have. Broadly speaking, there are four sources of local government income: money raised by local taxes, money transferred from central government, money raised by public loans and revenues from charges levied for the provision of goods and services. This last category is self-explanatory and accounts for 5–10 per cent of the income of a prefecture or municipality. A degree of deficit financing is permitted through the issuing of bonds redeemable after two or more years. Until the 1980s this accounted for around 10 per cent of revenues, but in the 1990s it increased to 15 per cent (Namikawa 1997: 100).

Funds come from central government in two main ways. First, local authorities are reimbursed for the performance of functions delegated to them as defined in national law. Most of these must be used for the specified purpose, for example the maintenance of the family records. Secondly, the local allocation tax is a fixed percentage of some national taxes which are distributed to local government for it to use as it sees fit. A fixed percentage of individual and corporate income taxes (around 32 per cent) and taxes on alcoholic beverages are reallocated in this way. Similarly, a proportion of the sales tax is distributed to local authorities and when it was increased from 3 to 5 per cent in 1997 half the increase went to local government. Local taxes are imposed on incomes both individual and corporate, fixed assets (mainly municipal) and enterprises (mainly prefectural) and on automobiles, tobacco consumption, restaurants and hotels.

Overall, between a third and a half of local government spending money is raised by local taxes, with up to two-thirds coming from central government. The exact balance will vary according to region. If a local government's basic financial revenue exceeds its basic financial needs, it will receive no local grant tax at all – four prefectures and 170 municipalities were in this category in 1990 (Akizuki 1995: 345). In 1996 Tokyo Metropolitan Council received no local allocation tax money and central government subsidy made up only 6 per cent of its income, while in the same year Okinawa prefecture got 31 per cent of its income from the local allocation tax and 35.5 per cent from central subsidy. Meanwhile, the proportion of money coming from central and local sources also varies considerably according to category: expenditure on social welfare being divided roughly 60:40, while the central government pays a much bigger proportion of the education bill – closer to 90 per cent.

Reformers would like to see the proportion raised from local sources increased and the dependency on central government reduced. However, they recognize that the uneven distribution of wealth across the country would make this difficult. There was a trend for the amount raised locally to increase as the economy grew up to 1990, but there is no indication about how this was affected by the recession of the 1990s. There is reported to be considerable waste in local government administration. This includes not only the duplication of effort mentioned above, but also over-manning – the number of local government employees steadily increased from 2.5 million to 2.8 million between 1974 and 1990, while the number employed in national government went down from 1.6 million to 1.1 million – and local government employees are, on average, paid better than their central government equivalent with the same qualifications.

Central–local relations

Before the war, control over local government was exercised by the Ministry of the Interior (Naimushō). The occupation regarded this ministry to have been a bastion of ultra-nationalism and it was dismantled in 1947. A Local Autonomy Agency was created in 1949, which in 1950 took control of election administration and local finance and was renamed the Home Affairs Agency, becoming a full ministry (the MHA) in 1960. It was the smallest of all the ministries with, in 1997, only three bureaux and 587 employees compared to more than 12,000 in MITI or 46,000 in MAFF (Institute of Administrative Management 1997: 18, 20, 26). In 2001 it became part of the Ministry of Public Management but its three bureaux remained intact. However, the importance of the MHA within the structure of government belies its size because of the close links it has with local government.

Officials in central ministries are often seconded to local government; an official from MAFF may serve in the agricultural division of a prefecture or someone from the MoE may spend a couple of years in a prefectural university. However, MHA officials can expect to spend around half of their careers working in local government, alternating two to three years in local government with a similar period spent back in Tokyo. At any one time, twenty-five of the forty-seven Chief Financial Officers in prefectural government have been MHA officials on secondment and almost as many have served as deputy governors. It is not unusual for former senior MHA bureaucrats to stand for election to posts of governors – in 1996 thirteen governors were ex-MHA officials, although it should also be noted that twelve other governors had served in central government earlier in their careers (Namikawa 1997: 103). Akizuki notes that whereas in other ministries senior bureaucrats might compete for the top posts of bureau chief or administrative vice-minister, or seek a 'soft landing' in a public corporation related to the work of the ministry after retirement, senior MHA officials aim at prefectural governorships as a second career goal. Where ex-bureaucrats are successfully elected they will often have served in that prefecture at least once and may even have been vice-governor immediately before election (Akizuki 1995: 348).

While the MHA has a raft of disciplinary powers and constantly puts pressure on local governments to balance their budgets, the relationship between the ministry and local authorities is generally less control of one by the other and more pursuit of mutual benefit. Local government sees the MHA as a conduit for access to central government and a useful source of expert manpower which it can use in negotiations with ministries such as the MoF or MAFF. Meanwhile, the MHA needs the local authorities as allies in its struggles with other ministries. The MHA is small and weak if it has to stand alone, but powerful if it has the support of the millions of local government officers behind it. Indeed, given the background of the MHA it is unlikely it could have developed in any other way: until 1960 it was not even a ministry. It engineered a system of local government finance that is decided not by negotiation but by a simple formula that redistributes resources to rural areas, not coincidentally important areas of LDP support. Its activities are thereby largely depoliticized even if there is scope for political intervention in raising subsidies for projects financed and administered by other ministries. Within this system there is a strong element of reciprocal dependency between MHA and local authorities such that it is not really appropriate to ask if this set of arrangements means that the central state is strong – as in pre-war Japan – or the local governments have increased their power. The MHA is a central agency in charge of controlling local government through financial and administrative methods. However, this control is not inconsistent with enabling local initiatives. Senior MHA officials located in Tokyo hope both to work for central government – for example, preventing local government deficits – and at the same time be seen to advocate local autonomy, first as a means of seeming successful in their present career and, secondly, in order to establish credibility for a future career within the political structure of local government. It is unlikely that absorption into the Ministry of Public Management will disturb this pattern.

Local government as a political arena

Americans involved in occupation policy took the idea of local government as being the schoolroom for democracy very seriously. Not only are the governors and mayors and assemblies directly elected but the local electorate can also exercise the power of 'recall' over the governor/mayor, a councillor

Table 9.2 Members of local assemblies (31 December 1999)

	Prefecture	Special ward (Tokyo)	City	Town and village
LDP	1,389	320	1,598	231
DPJ	187	83	497	56
JCP	185	166	1,900	2,182
New Kōmeitō	169	184	1,439	626
SDP	100	25	529	219
Kōmei*	25	11	432	309
LP	20	9	9	2
Other	96	32	246	62
Independents	727	142	11,900	36,389
Total	2,898	972	18,550	40,076

* This table lists assembly representatives by the party name used when they were elected. Before the formation of the New Kōmeitō in December 1998 local politicians associated with what had been the Kōmeitō stood using the label, Kōmei.
Source: Election Department, Local Administration Bureau, Ministry of Home Affairs

or indeed the whole assembly (by election following receipt of a petition of one-third of the electorate) or even the creation/revision/abolition of a by-law (following a petition of 2 per cent of the electorate and the approval of the council), or order an audit of the local authority's affairs (by a petition of 2 per cent of the electorate) (Fujioka 1997: 52). It has to be said that not a great deal of use has been made of these powers, and the thresholds for implementing them are rather high, but there have been occasions when a threat to resort to them has been used as part of a strategy by citizens' movements to have their demands taken seriously.

Election to the House of Representatives by a single non-transferable vote in multi-member constituencies was used for the last time in 1993, but it continues to be used in local government. Prefectures, cities, towns and villages are divided into administrative areas which serve as constituencies in local elections, with representatives in proportion to the size of the population. In a prefecture such as Fukuoka, for example, the prefectural assembly is composed of ninety-one members elected from forty-seven constituencies each returning from one to four representatives. Meanwhile, Fukuoka city council has a total of sixty-three representatives elected from the seven *ku*, each of which is an administrative area of the city.

As table 9.2 suggests, a large majority of local government politicians are not formally linked to any party. A two-party system seemed to be emerging at the national level in the mid-1950s as the two conservative parties combined to form the LDP and the socialist parties reunited in the JSP. However, most local politics was dominated by conservatives, with any interesting political conflict taking place within their ranks. Few of those running for the chief executive posts had open party endorsement, though many had ties to a faction of the LDP. Rapid economic growth benefited most people, but it also generated urban problems and environmental pollution. Opposition parties recognized this dissatisfaction and articulated demands for a cleaner environment and improved social infrastructure. Local government chief executives supported by the JSP, and sometimes the JCP, were elected in the late 1960s and early 1970s such that at one time there were 'progressive' mayors in 131 cities which, combined with the population of prefectures run by 'progressive' governors, meant that 45 per cent of the population was governed by the 'opposition' at local level. Not only did they initiate policies to control industrially generated pollution, they also introduced social welfare measures such as free health care for the elderly. This put pressure on central government to adopt similar policies and it also gave opposition parties a degree of credibility in the eyes of the electorate. Some even suggested that its record in local government might be translated into power at the national level. And, indeed, the LDP grip on parliament did slip in the 1970s.

However, the opposition party control of local government was not consolidated. The first phase of the oil shocks of the 1970s reduced the rate of growth of taxation revenue available to local government, which meant that there was less scope for policy innovation at the local level. Secondly, the LDP took on board the main elements of opposition party policy – implementation of strict pollution regulation – and, in 1973, adopted a more generous welfare programme, thus undermining their distinctive appeal. Thirdly, the 'anti-LDP' coalitions of support that previously had been composed of just the JSP and the JCP from 1974 onwards expanded to include the centre-left parties and on occasion even the LDP. By the 1980s coalitions supporting an incumbent would more often include both the LDP and the JSP, but seek deliberately to exclude the JCP. This did not mean there was no party politics in local government. In 1993 just as the '1955 system' was about to collapse the prefectural assembly in particular contained many members who belonged to political parties, though parties were less evident at lower levels. At the prefectural levels LDP politicians are often connected to one of the factions, and activity in local politics has been a route to national politics within the JSP too. Former prime minister Murayama rose to prominence within the Oita prefectural assembly before standing for a seat in the national parliament. In the general election of 2000, 304 candidates had a background in local government of whom 128 were elected – 26.7 per cent of the lower house. Local LDP politicians can channel support upwards and act as conduits through which largesse can flow downwards, whether in terms of favours for electors or construction projects for the region. Prefectural assembly members will often be key figures in the *kōenkai* of a national level politician.

The split in the LDP in 1993 caused serious problems for many assembly members. Should they remain loyal to the party even if this meant cutting their ties to their patron, the national politician who had deserted the LDP? Or should they stick with the patron and sever links with the LDP? To choose the former would cut direct links to national power; to do the latter might reduce influence locally. This choice was even more complicated because the reform of the electoral system required new links between local and national politicians. Most local politicians deferred their decisions as long as possible and coalition strategies adopted by the LDP throughout the 1990s did not make these choices any easier. The patterns of loyalty remain in flux.

To return to the prefectural elections. Immediately before 1993, in only five prefectures was the LDP *not* part of the coalition supporting the governors, but between June 1993 and April 1995 the LDP lost seven governorships, mostly to candidates supported by the Shinseitō/Shinshintō. The grand coalitions that have been formed to support a particular candidate for a governorship usually result in very predictable elections where one candidate wins an overwhelming share of the vote. So, for example, of the ninety-four elections held at this level in the 1980s only twenty-three can be regarded as 'competitive' in the sense that the top loser won more than half the votes of the winner. In effect, then, the choice of chief executive was made more by bargaining between leaders of the local parties than by the electorate. Not surprisingly, turn-out in these elections dropped below 50 per cent.

Voter dissatisfaction with this became apparent in 1995 when a grand coalition of the SDP, DSP, LDP and Kōmeitō jointly supported Ishihara Nobuo for the post of governor of Tokyo and a similar coalition backed the incumbent for a second term in Osaka. Two '*tarento*' (celebrity) candidates, Aoshima Yukio and Yokoyama Nokku, both of them with a background in show business but also with considerable experience in the upper house, decided to run against the parties' candidates. They won by considerable margins. In 1999 Yokoyama ran for a second term and was re-elected; Aoshima did not run but was not replaced by a tame party candidate. Rather, in a close-fought election, Ishihara Shintarō, formerly of the LDP but standing in this election as an independent, was elected. An election in Chiba in March 2001 returned another non-party governor in what may be the start of a trend for local voters to reject the LDP candidates as well as those put forward by the opposition parties.

Nevertheless, despite the control exerted by the MHA and the lack of genuine competition in the election of chief executives in many areas, it is clear that local governments *can* make a difference even if not always. The governor of Oita prefecture, Hiramatsu Morihiko, who had an earlier career in MITI, is generally considered to have been responsible for policies that have promoted the development of local industry, reducing the rate of depopulation without creating environmental pollution or urban congestion (Broadbent 1998: 322). Kanagawa prefecture in general and Kawasaki city in particular have sought to develop policies that support the promotion of human rights by disseminating ideas of children's rights within schools and opening positions within local government to all permanent residents.

As a final example, the attitude taken by the governor of Okinawa in 1995 showed that local government policies can even have a foreign policy dimension. There are several US military bases on Okinawa, some of which occupy land that has been compulsorily leased from the landowners. Early in 1995 two American soldiers were arrested for the rape of a young girl and this reignited opposition to the US presence. Some of the leases were up for renewal, but the owners of the land refused to sign new ones. US occupation

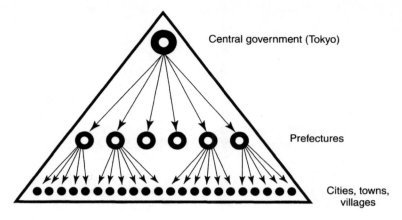

Central government (Tokyo)

Prefectures

Cities, towns,
villages

Source: Namikawa 1997: 87

Figure 9.2   State and society centred on Tokyo

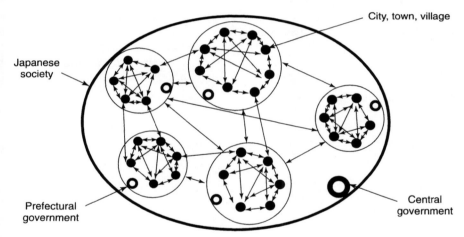

City, town, village

Japanese
society

Prefectural
government

Central
government

Source: Namikawa 1997: 87

Figure 9.3   Devolved government system

of the land could nevertheless be legalized if the local mayor or, failing that, the governor were to sign the leases. When both the mayors and the governor refused to sign, the prime minister, on behalf of the government, had to take the governor to court and have the court rule that his refusal was illegal. This is perhaps the most dramatic example of an attempt by a local authority to resist central government control and we should note that in the end the government not only got its way but at the next election the uncooperative governor was voted out. Nevertheless, he had extensive support for his action. This final example does show that there is no aspect of central government policy that might not form part of a local government's remit and, moreover, that there is a growth of interest in politics at the local level.

Conclusion

The change we have seen working its way through Japanese politics at the national level is also present in local politics. The most ambitious reformers' plans would reconstruct the relation between government and society such that the state would cease to dominate society and, instead, work as one component of it. In place of the pyramidal structure with government based in Tokyo (see figure 9.2), there would be a decentralized system in which central and prefectural government would still play a role but where there would be greater autonomy for the lowest levels of government. The vertical patterns of control and information flow would be replaced by 'random access' systems (see figure 9.3).

At the start of the twenty-first century, a time when central government is undergoing significant structural change, we can expect reform of local government too. Demands for change are coming not only from within government and academia, but also from the electorate. The kind of 'random access' structure is one that sociologists might consider uncongenial to Japanese people, but old patterns are breaking down in the workplace and this may be the prelude to radical change in local government too.

Part IV
Policies

10

Foreign and Defence Policy

While there may be debate about whether a state should have an industrial or social welfare policy and how actively such a policy should be supported, there is no doubt that an ability to defend itself and conduct an independent foreign policy are key features of any definition of a modern state. Indeed, a state that is unable to assert its sovereignty in either of these two areas may be regarded as lacking the basic qualities of a normal state. Critics of Japanese government on both left and right have questioned whether it has been able to conduct an autonomous foreign and defence policy since 1952. Some conclude that it has not and that it must reacquire the ability to do so in order to become what Ozawa Ichirō called a 'normal' state.

Before 1994 the two sides of the debate were fairly clearly marked. On the one hand, there were those who sought basic reform: abolition or radical revision of Article 9 of the constitution, reinforcement of the USA–Japan partnership and participation of the Social-Defence Forces (SDF) in the international system. On this side of the debate were the LDP, Kōmeitō and the DSP. The socialist opposition (JSP and JCP) sought a policy guided by single country pacifism, the dissolution of the SDF and the abrogation of the Security Treaty with the USA. The JSP abandoned 'constitutional pacifism' in summer 1994 when Murayama became prime minister in the LDP/JSP coalition cabinet. The DPJ has taken its place as the main opposition party, but it is composed of individuals whose origins range from the LDP to the JSP, including those who both support and oppose the retention of the 'peace clause'. Meanwhile, even the JCP has moderated its opposition to the USA–Japan alliance and to the overseas use of the SDF. The party politics of foreign and defence policy are now unclear, but the basic issues remain the same and centre on Japan's relations with the USA and the constitutional nature of the SDF.

Foreign and defence policies are vast and complex areas, and all that we can do here is to sketch out some of the parameters within which Japan acts.

We will start by discussing the Yoshida doctrine and its development since the 1970s. Next we will look at the relationship between Japan and the USA from the end of the occupation until the Gulf War. For much of the postwar era Japan has looked east across the Pacific for leadership, but since the 1970s the country has also been aware of the need to create or restore links with its neighbours in Asia. The nature of these links will provide a third theme. Fourthly, we will briefly consider the domestic issue of the size, nature and constitutionality of the SDF. Finally, we will summarize the main themes of foreign and defence policy in the 1990s and consider the prospects for the twenty-first century.

Yoshida doctrine

Japan was one of the major powers of the pre-war world. Recognized as a dominant power within Asia after 1919, Japan was a permanent member of the Security Council of the League of Nations from 1920 until withdrawing in 1933. Postwar Japan has not sought to regain that position. The country was not allowed to join the UN until 1956 and until the 1990s did not seem interested in playing a major role within it. Meanwhile, although the Japanese economy had grown to become the second biggest in the world, there was no attempt to translate that economic power into strategic influence backed up by military might. The Yoshida doctrine and its lingering influence go a long way to account for this.

Yoshida Shigeru was prime minister for seven of the first eight and a half years of the postwar period. Not only did he dominate domestic politics during this time but his close followers, Ikeda Hayato and Satō Eisaku, ensured that the influence of his ideas flowed into the 1970s and, some would say, beyond. Yoshida's approach to foreign policy was based on the idea that by focusing on economic growth and political passivity Japan might be able to win the peace after losing the war. Crucial to this strategy was a refusal to be drawn into Cold War rivalries that would have meant that scarce resources were used for militarization. John Foster Dulles, of the US State Department, arrived in Japan in 1950 to urge Japan to rearm. Yoshida refused, arguing that to do so would delay economic recovery and this would permit the growth of the socialist and communist movements. Moreover, it would alarm Japan's Asian neighbours, who had suffered at the hands of the militarists. Some concessions were made to the American demands. Limited rearmament took place after the outbreak of the Korean War, and Japan consented to the continued presence of US bases on Japanese soil. For the most part, though, Yoshida argued that Japan would allocate only a bare minimum to self-defence, relying instead on the USA for security guarantees. The USA had 210,000 troops in Japan in 1954, although the numbers were down to 21,000 by March 2000 (Kawai and Suzuki 2000: 72).

In the second half of the 1950s prime minister Kishi supported revision of the constitution to enable rearmament and provoked massive popular opposition in the anti-*Ampo* demonstrations of 1959–60. As soon as the Security Treaty was ratified Kishi was replaced by Ikeda, who quickly dropped the divisive issues and returned the focus to economic growth. His successor, Satō Eisaku, faced China's acquisition of nuclear weapons, US involvement in Vietnam and the prospect of a second round of protests as the Security Treaty came up for renegotiation in 1970. His response was to elaborate the Yoshida doctrine in the form of the four pillars of Japan's nuclear policy:

- reliance on the US nuclear umbrella;
- commitment to three non-nuclear principles (not to produce, possess or have them on Japanese soil);
- promotion of worldwide disarmament;
- development of nuclear energy for peaceful purposes.

That same year, 1967, Satō announced three principles for arms exports: not to export them to the communist bloc, or to countries covered by a UN arms embargo, or to countries involved in armed conflict. This was later extended by prime minister Miki to a ban on all arms exports.

Defence expenditure had exceeded 1 per cent GNP in the late 1950s, on average 1.45 per cent in 1954–9. In the 1960s it became practice to keep it below 1 per cent and in 1976 it became official government policy that total defence expenditure, 'shall not exceed an amount equivalent to one hundredth of the GNP of the said financial year' (National Defence Programme Outline 1976, quoted in Pyle 1988: 456).

The international situation has changed radically since the 1960s, particularly since 1989–90. Moreover, Japan's role within the world economy has been transformed. Per capita GNP in 1960 was $456 in Japan, compared to $2,308 in the USA. These figures were $36,572 and $28,422 respectively in 1996 (Keizai Kōhō Center 1998: 17). Meanwhile, not a great deal has changed in foreign policy. The concern to balance security and economic concerns remains and there continues to be a tendency to give priority to economic growth and social welfare at the expense of defence policy. Dissatisfaction with the consequences of the Yoshida doctrine came to be expressed more volubly in the 1990s and it may not be possible to sustain it for long into the new century. However, its influence has penetrated deeply into the thinking of both bureaucrats and electors. It has become the conventional wisdom, the common sense of foreign policy, against which those who would innovate must argue.

Relations with the USA

Japan's relations with the USA have been the cornerstone of its diplomacy since the early 1950s. The USA sought to develop Japan as a reliable ally in the Pacific from at least 1947–8. It was prepared to accept Yoshida's refusal to rearm since it feared 'losing' Japan to communism in the same way that it had 'lost' China only a few years earlier. Japan became a close ally of the USA under terms defined by the Security Treaty, which was initially accepted in 1951, renegotiated in 1959 and renewed in 1970.

To Yoshida, the Security Treaty provided Japan with US protection, committing Japan to maintaining only a small, lightly armed force. His critics to left and right resented three aspects of this arrangement. First, the USA retained the right to take part in the suppression of 'disturbances' within Japan, compromising Japan's sovereignty. Secondly, Japan undertook not to grant military rights to other powers without the consent of the USA, again limiting its freedom of action. Thirdly, Japan gave up its jurisdiction over the US forces based in Japan. American forces had sole jurisdiction over off-duty US military even when they committed crimes outside military bases. This reminded many Japanese of the extra-territoriality rules imposed by western powers in the unequal treaties of the 1850s (Tsuzuki 2000: 377). In the course of the 1959 negotiations the USA surrendered its right to intervene in Japan's domestic affairs, but both governments agreed on the need to 'contain communism'. Nevertheless, while the USA undertook to take primary responsibility for the defence of the Far East, Japan's only commitment was to contribute to the defence of its own borders alongside US forces. Throughout the 1960s Japan was a loyal ally of and largely dependent on the USA, and following the renewal of the treaty in 1970 this position seemed to be confirmed.

However, a series of events in the early 1970s suggested that the USA might not be a completely reliable senior partner from either a security or economic perspective. In July 1971 President Nixon announced his intention to visit Beijing with no prior consultation with Tokyo and giving them only twenty-four hours warning of the reversal in its policy. Japan had been eager to develop economic relations with China in the 1960s but had been held back by the need to adhere to US policy to support Taiwan. Only a month later, in August, Nixon announced his decision to float the dollar, abandoning the stable exchange rate framework within which the long postwar boom had been possible. This caused the revaluation of the yen, which made Japanese exports more expensive.

Then, in the aftermath of the Arab-Israeli war of 1973, OPEC cut off oil supplies to all countries with close ties to Israel, including Japan. There followed an intense flurry of diplomatic activity in which Japan persuaded OPEC that it was neutral. The Palestine Liberation Organization (PLO) was granted quasi-diplomatic status, allowed to set up an office in Tokyo and oil began to flow once more, but at prices four times the previous levels. Oil prices continued to rise throughout the next ten years, to a peak of $34.94 per barrel compared to $1.84 in 1970. In 1970 more than 70 per cent of Japan's energy came from oil, 99.7 per cent of which was imported, and most of that came from the Middle East (Kawai and Suzuki 2000: 169–71). This crisis starkly demonstrated the need for Japan to develop its own foreign policy, at least in those areas where its interests did not coincide with those of the USA. While the USA was also affected by the price increase, it was far less dependent on imported Middle East oil.

This might have been the beginning of greater independence for Japan from the USA, but the increased threat from the Soviet Union held them together. Soon after the signing of the Treaty of Friendship with China in 1978, the Soviet Union moved more troops onto the 'Northern Isles' only a few miles from Japanese territory. More generally, there was a build-up of Soviet troops in the Far East, and SS20s, Russian cruise missiles, were placed along the border with China. Japan was well within range. In 1979 the Soviet Union strengthened its alliance with Vietnam and sent troops into Afghanistan. Whatever concern there might have been about the costs of remaining closely tied to American foreign policy, fear of the Soviet threat prevented Japan from breaking loose throughout the 1980s.

Nevertheless, until 1981 the word 'alliance' was not used to describe the USA–Japan relationship because of its militarist connotations (Inoguchi 1988: 40). In 1982 Nakasone took over as prime minister with a reputation of being more nationalist than most of his generation of politicians and someone likely to move away from a foreign policy based on the Yoshida doctrine. In 1985, while Nakasone was still in office, the Plaza Accord was reached, by which the finance ministers of the USA, UK, France, Germany and Japan agreed to intervene in the currency markets to reduce the value of the dollar. The value of the yen rose rapidly from ¥260 = $1 to ¥120 = $1 by 1987. Exports of Japanese goods became difficult, but this was a period characterized by the export of capital to the USA and Europe, as well as Asia.

Trade conflict between the USA and Japan first became evident between 1968 and 1969, and culminated in the imposition of quotas for textile imports by the USA in 1971. Japan's exports to the USA increased, creating a bilateral surplus, and overall Japan was generating large annual surpluses compared to the US deficits. Conflict between the two countries about trade issues became a 'chronic disease' (Komiya and Itoh 1988: 202). Some of the issues were resolved by Japan's acceptance of voluntary exports restraints – for example, on the export of automobiles – but this did nothing to dispel the criticisms that although tariffs and quotas had been reduced or eliminated, there remained many areas where non-tariff barriers prevented US and other countries' companies from free access to the Japanese markets. MOSS (Market Oriented Sector Specific) and SII (Structural Impediments Initiative) talks were held in 1986 and 1989, aimed at addressing these issues.

Yet despite these periodic conflicts and the undercurrent of growing nationalism, particularly in the 1980s, there were constant reassertions on both sides of the Pacific of the importance of the USA–Japan alliance. Even Nakasone took great pride in being on first-name terms with 'Ron'(ald Reagan), while describing Japan in 1983 as 'an unsinkable aircraft carrier' for US forces (Tsuzuki 2000: 432). None of Nakasone's successors has played such a proactive role in foreign policy development, but there was speculation that the USA–Japan relationship might not survive the collapse of the Soviet Union. In the absence of a common enemy, was there any reason why Japan should stay so close to the USA?

Japan and its neighbours

In the 1950s Japan faced an Asia composed of former colonies, former enemies and/or currently communist states, none of which was inclined to be friendly. As Japanese companies began to reconstruct themselves in the late 1940s, some sought to re-enter Asian markets, notably China, but the USA prevented Japan from establishing diplomatic links with China which might have enabled trade to develop. When indirect trade links were developed, they were established on the basis of 'separating politics from economics'. Japan signed a treaty with the Republic of China on Taiwan in April 1952 and took part in the postwar development of the island. Negotiations with the Soviet Union resulted in a joint declaration in October 1956 ending the state of war between the two countries, but no agreement was possible on the question of the border between the two countries to the north-east of Hokkaido.

Attempts to normalize relations with South Korea during the 1950s were equally unsuccessful. Park Chung-hee, President of South Korea, who came to power following a military *coup d'état* in 1961, had been trained by the Japanese before 1945 and he was eager to get access to Japanese capital to fund the development projects being planned by his government. In 1965 the Japan–Korea Basic Treaty was signed by prime minister Satō and President Park and later ratified amid bitter criticism in both Seoul and Tokyo. Japan recognized the Republic of Korea (i.e. South Korea) as 'the only lawful government in Korea' and trade relations were revived. This encouraged Japanese investment to the extent that by 1970 Japan was South Korea's main source of capital.

Reparations paid by Japan within Asia in the 1950s were usually in the form of credits for Japanese-manufactured goods rather than simple cash transfers. As such, they established, or sometimes re-established, links with the Japanese economy. US aid in Asia was also used to develop sources of supply for Japan (Tsuzuki 2000: 378). Later, as Japan took over the role as the major contributor of overseas development aid (ODA) within the region, it continued to serve mainly the interests of the Japanese economy, developing markets and sources of raw materials. As Rix comments, 'Asian development was more a means of achieving Japanese objectives than a goal in its own right' (quoted in Preston 2000: 99). Japanese foreign direct investment (FDI) expanded relatively slowly before 1985, mainly in pursuit of raw materials, cheap labour and market access. FDI in the Pacific Asia region grew rapidly after the revaluation of the yen following the Plaza Accord in 1985. This not only facilitated entry into Asian markets by Japanese banks and companies, but it also made it necessary for them to do so as it was increasingly expensive to supply US and other western markets with goods made in Japan. The same goods assembled in Malaysia, South Korea or Singapore, where land, labour power and raw materials were cheaper, could be marketed at lower prices but still make high profits. Pacific Asian economies thus became 'production platforms' for Japanese goods, a trend that continued throughout the rest of the twentieth century.

Japanese aid to the region also increased rapidly after 1985, demonstrating the complementary nature of ODA and FDI, with ODA often funding the infrastructure that was a prerequisite for the building of factories. By the early 1990s Japan had overtaken the USA as the main source of FDI in Pacific Asia. This led to talk of the emergence of a 'yen zone' in which the Japanese economy would dominate Pacific Asia and emerge as a rival to the USA. A softer metaphor, which contains less allusion to pre-war imperialist policies, is that of the 'flying goose pattern', in which Japan takes the lead, followed by a small group made up of South Korea, Taiwan, Singapore and Hong Kong with, slightly behind them, Malaysia, Thailand and Indonesia and, some way further back, Vietnam, Cambodia and Laos.

Where China fits into either of these models is unclear. Once the USA had opened the way, the Tanaka government 'normalized' Sino-Japanese relations in 1972 and in 1978 a trade agreement and a Treaty of Peace and Friendship were signed. Thereafter, Japan played a delicate game of fostering good relations with China as a major market and source of raw materials, present and future, while maintaining good relations with Taiwan. Between 1978 and 1991 the Chinese economy grew at an average rate of 9 per cent per year (Preston 1998: 177). China rapidly became a source of imports to Japan, second only to the USA by 1994, and a little more slowly, a major market for Japanese products – again, second only to the USA. Indeed, China had become so important to the Japanese economy by 1989 that both politicians and businessmen felt that they could not afford to protest too much at the time of the Tiananmen Square incident.

The Self-Defence Forces

Four US divisions were sent from Japan to Korea following the outbreak of war in June 1950. On 10 August a government decree was issued to create a National Police Reserve of 75,000 men (i.e., four divisions), a force strong enough to deal with domestic military confrontation, rioting or large-scale political strikes. The Americans armed them at first with carbines and light machine guns, and later with heavier weaponry, including bazookas. In 1951 many military and naval officers who had been purged in 1945–6 were delisted and a large proportion of them enlisted in the police reserve, eager to maintain the traditions of the imperial army (Tsuzuki 2000: 384–5). The navy had never ceased to exist. A core group of the Maritime Security Board had been formed within the Ministry of Transport after the formal dissolution of the Navy Ministry in November 1945. This consisted, among other things, of minesweepers, which cleared Korean ports prior to the landing of US troops in 1950. In 1954 the Defence Agency was established within the PMO and defence policy was placed under a National Defence Council in order to ensure civilian control.

There was puzzlement and anger at this re-creation of an armed force only five years after the adoption of a constitution which seemed to commit Japan to pacifism. Yet both left and right could plausibly appeal to tradition in support of their position. The right could point to the centuries of samurai tradition which had generated the martial values that had been the basis of the pre-war value system. On the other hand, the left could point out that only 6 per cent of the pre-1868 population consisted of samurai and that the rest of the population was positively forbidden to bear arms. Even the samurai had largely lost touch with their military roots as they were turned into a civil bureaucracy. Indeed, many of the reforms of the late nineteenth century were intended to create a military ethos where it was either weak or non-existent. It could be argued, then, that it was the aggressive militarism of 1900–45 that was the aberration, not postwar pacifism.

Of course, Article 9 of the constitution seemed to preclude the possibility of any kind of defence force. Stockwin argues persuasively, however, that careful changes were made in the wording of the 'peace clause' as it was being ratified in the House of Representatives, deliberately to allow for the creation of some form of defence capability (1999: 167–8). Several attempts were made to test the constitutionality of the SDF. In 1952 Suzuki Mosaburō of the JSP attempted to have the Supreme Court rule on the constitutionality of the National Police Reserve. The Supreme Court declined to do so, arguing that, unlike its equivalent in West Germany, it could only rule on concrete legal disputes between two parties. Some lower courts have on occasions made rulings that have been based on a pacifist reading of the constitution, but these have always been overturned by the Supreme Court. By the 1980s the constitutional debate was largely over. Even the JSP was tied to a rather convoluted policy that regarded the SDF as unconstitutional but not illegal. Much of the debate moved on to how the SDF might be used and this developed still further in the 1990s.

Japan continued to be pressured by the USA to expand further its military, while at home members of the Defence Production Committee of the Keidanren also lobbied for more defence spending. In May 1957 the Kishi cabinet announced the Basic Policy for National Defence (see figure 10.1) which was still quoted by the Japan Defence Agency on its web site in 2001 as the 'basis for national security'. While looking forward to the creation of an effective UN peacekeeping structure, it commits Japan to both creating 'effective defense capabilities' and maintaining the Japan–USA security arrangements. The following year a three-year defence plan was launched which increased the Ground Self Defence Force (i.e. the army) to 180,000 men, providing the Naval SDF with 124,000 tonnage of vessels and the Air SDF with 1,300 aircraft. This provided welcome orders for the former munitions industry.

In the 1960s the convention arose that defence spending would be kept below 1 per cent of the GNP. This became official policy in 1976 and it has been more or less maintained, so that in the financial year 2000 it stood at 0.987 per cent of the GNP. Nevertheless, this still meant that in 1995 Japan was spending more on defence than any country apart from Russia and the USA: $50.2 billion compared to $82 billion and $277.8 billion respectively. This is substantially more than European countries such as France ($48.0 billion), Germany ($41.8 billion) or the UK ($34.2 billion) (see table 10.1). Table 10.1 needs to be interpreted with care, though. For example, the apparent increase

The objective of national defence is to prevent direct and indirect aggression, but once invaded, to repel such aggression thereby preserving the independence and peace of Japan founded on democratic principles.

To achieve this objective, the government of Japan hereby establishes the following principles:

1   To support the activities of the United Nations and promote international cooperation, thereby contributing to the realization of world peace.
2   To promote public welfare and enhance the people's love for the country, thereby establishing the sound basis essential to Japan's security.
3   To develop incrementally the effective defense capabilities necessary for self-defence, with regard to the nation's resources and the prevailing domestic situation.
4   To deal with external aggression on the basis of the Japan–US security arrangements, pending the effective functioning of the United Nations in the future in deterring and repelling such aggression.

Source: http://www.jda.go.jp/e/policy/f_work/frame21_.htm

Figure 10.1   Basic policy for national defence (Decided by the National Defence Council and by the Cabinet on 20 May 1957)

Table 10.1   Defence expenditure and military power

Defence expenditure ($US per capita)			% GDP (1995)	Numbers in armed forces (000s)	
	1985	1997		1985	1997
USA	1,537	1,018	3.8	2,151.6	1,447.6
UK	803	611	3.1	327.1	213.8
France	843	708	3.1	464.3	380.8
Russia	n/a	435	7.4	n/a	1,240
Japan	**254**	**325**	**1.1**	**243**	**235.6**
North Korea	290	246	n/a	838	1,055
South Korea	218	320	3.4	598	672
China	27	30	5.7	3,900	2,840
India	12	13	2.5	1,260	1,145
Taiwan	n/a	620	5.0	n/a	240

n/a: not available
Sources: International Institute for Strategic Studies 1999: 104; Keizai Kōhō Center 1998: 86

in the amount spent on defence by Japan between 1985 and 1997 is mostly accounted for by the increase in the value of the yen against the dollar. Had these tables been expressed in yen, there would have been little or no increase over those twelve years. The overall number of men under arms in the states neighbouring Japan can be explained by their use of conscription, something that is specifically forbidden by Article 18 of the constitution.

Japan and the world since 1990

The collapse of the Soviet Union removed the major single threat to the security of Japan, but the end of the Cold War meant more to the Europeans than

it did to East Asians. The main Cold War fault lines in Asia ran between North
and South Korea and between China and Taiwan. There was no certainty that
'hot war' would not break out across these borders throughout the 1990s.
More important for the development of Japan's foreign and defence policy
was the aftermath of the Gulf War.

Japan was completely unprepared for this. Not only was the Japanese
ambassador to Kuwait on holiday at the time of the Iraqi invasion, but the
prime minister (Kaifu) was about to go on a tour of the Middle East and
could not decide whether or not to go. In the end, he sent his foreign minister, but indecision characterized the whole of Japan's response to the crisis.
In part, the problem was that following the loss of control of the upper house
in 1989 the LDP was unable to be certain that its policies would be approved
without the support of one of the opposition parties. Until 1992 that support
was not forthcoming. Others, Ozawa Ichirō for example, concluded the
problem was rooted in the structure of the executive, which was ill-equipped
for dealing with crises. Japan would continue to be unable to function
'normally' on the international stage until the structure of government was
radically reformed. This would involve at least the reform of bureaucratic
structures and, at most, the wholesale revision of the constitution.

The initial response to the invasion of Kuwait was to talk about sending
non-military personnel plus a financial contribution to assist the UN effort.
Some suggested sending minesweepers, others proposed sending medical
teams. During October 1990 prime minister Kaifu submitted a UN Peace
Force Cooperation Bill to parliament which would have created a Peace
Cooperation Force restricted to a non-combat role. The idea would have
been distinct from, but might have included members of, the SDF. The
idea was disliked by many in the LDP and did not get the support from
Kōmeitō that was crucial for it to pass through the upper house. As a result,
it was withdrawn in early November. When the multinational force took steps
to expel Iraq from Kuwait in January 1991, the Japanese government
once more focused on the issue, but it still could not offer any military support
and could only promise financial support to a total of $13 billion – and this
only after tortuous negotiations with Kōmeitō. In April, when the war was
over, parliamentary approval was given for minesweepers to be sent to
the Gulf.

By the following year, both Kōmeitō and the DSP had been persuaded
of the need for Japan to play a more positive role in UN peacekeeping
operations and in June 1992 a Peacekeeping Operations bill was approved.
Public opinion supported this more active role. When Japan sent a contin-
gent to Cambodia to assist with peacekeeping and oversee elections, public
opinion surveys showed 52 per cent approved, compared to 36 per cent who
disapproved (Stockwin 1999: 78). Over the next few years men seconded from
the SDF would participate in UN peacekeeping operations in Rwanda, the
Golan Heights, Angola, Mozambique, El Salvador and East Timor (Hoye
1998: 192).

The Basic Policy for Defence places the UN at the heart of its defence
philosophy; even the Japan–USA security arrangements are described as only

important 'pending the effective functioning of the UN . . . in deterring and repelling such aggression'. Of course, we may legitimately doubt how far such idealism influences the attitudes of LDP politicians or the advice of MFA realists, but the UN was an important point of reference for policy-makers in the 1990s and will continue to be so in the twenty-first century. Japan is the second biggest contributor to the UN budget, second only to the USA: America contributed 25 per cent of the UN budget in 2000, Japan 20.57 per cent, Germany 9.86 per cent, France 6.55 per cent and the UK 5.09 per cent (Kawai and Suzuki 2000: 78). Japan would like a permanent seat on the Security Council, although this will only be possible in the context of wider reform of the UN, which in turn depends on the attitude of the USA. President Clinton supported the Japanese ambition, but the USA will only permit reform that will reinforce or at least not undermine its influence within the UN. Meanwhile, the majority of the UN member states want reform, in particular enlargement of the Security Council precisely to reduce American domination. This is not the place for a digression on UN internal politics; suffice it to say that a compromise between these two positions, and Japan being given a permanent seat, are unlikely in the foreseeable future.

Despite having a military force equivalent in size to that of many European countries, it is still small compared to those of its Asian neighbours, and is constrained by its interpretation of Article 9, which states that it should not acquire the military capability to project power beyond its borders. Thus it has no long-range bombers, no aircraft carriers, no nuclear submarines. It remains as important as ever to rely on the Japan–USA security arrangements. Indeed, 11 per cent of the defence budget is spent on personnel and logistic support for US forces based in Japan. In 1996 President Clinton and prime minister Hashimoto agreed to review the alliance to create a 'vision for preserving and strengthening the bilateral security partnership'. This review resulted in the production of a set of guidelines for USA–Japan defence cooperation. Official spokesmen argue that these do no more than clarify ways in which the SDF would cooperate with and support the USA in case of a 'regional contingency'. However, many of the activities mentioned in the guidelines constitute an incremental increase in the support the SDF can give to US forces, and were not permitted by the guidelines that governed USA–Japan cooperation at the time of the Gulf War, for example.

Japan responded swiftly to the terrorist attacks on the USA on 11 September 2001. That same night a new office was created under the prime minister to combat terrorism. On 19 September the cabinet approved a seven-point plan to provide support for the USA. Moreover, in the following weeks Koizumi introduced an anti-terrorist bill, passed on 29 October, which enabled the SDF to give logistic assistance to the US-led forces in the Indian Ocean. Six ships were sent, the first overseas dispatch of Japanese armed forces since 1945. In December a second law, which was passed with the support of the ruling coalition and all but three of the DPJ, significantly expanded the scope of SDF participation in UN peacekeeping operations.

Government seems resolved to extend the role of the SDF in support of Japanese diplomacy and we can expect the SDF to be used overseas more often. Opposition, though still vocal, is weak.

Both the guidelines and the 1997 Defence White Paper show that the main threats to Japan's security are posed by China and North Korea. Although China is unlikely to inflict a direct attack on Japan, it has pointedly refused to rule out the possibility of military intervention in Taiwan if that country should declare independence. References to the need to deal with refugees, to evacuate citizens who are resident overseas and to deal with mines in international waters all suggest the role Japan would play in case of such an invasion. Although Japan was reluctant to endanger its economic links with China in 1989, it presumably would not hesitate to act in case of attacks on Taiwan, a key trading partner and culturally close.

Japan's import and export trade with China in 2000 amounted to more than $10 trillion, equal to one half of that with America. It is crucially important to both China and Japan to maintain their 'partnership of friendship and cooperation for peace and development'. In 1998 a joint declaration was agreed on projects in thirty-three areas, which include almost every conceivable area of cooperation: trade, science and technology, environmental protection, youth exchange, heritage preservation. There remain some 'delicate issues', of which the most important are the 'history issue' and Japan's relationship with Taiwan, but both the underlying economic link and the value of scientific and cultural exchange are so important that the two countries can hardly not maintain friendly relations.

The potential threat to regional security posed by North Korea was apparent during the crisis over the nuclear programme in 1994 and the direct threat to Japan in September 1998 when the North Koreans launched, unannounced, a missile that flew through Japanese airspace before crashing into the Pacific. Some months later a North Korean spy ship was detected in Japanese waters, but it eluded capture by Maritime Agency boats. Even though invasion is unlikely, these incidents demonstrated the dangerous and unpredictable character of the North Korean regime. Talks between the leaders of North and South Korea in 2000 made civil war on the peninsula less likely, but attention is now focused on the ability of North Korea to survive. Some predict a collapse similar to those in the former communist states of Eastern Europe. At the moment this would not be in anyone's interest. Russia and China seem happy to have a buffer state between them and the Japanese, and would have difficulty coping with the flow of 'economic refugees' that a collapse would generate. South Korea, while notionally committed to reunification, has only just recovered from the financial crisis of 1997 and could not afford the cost of rescuing the North from economic collapse. Meanwhile, Japan is happy to provide aid that will prevent a collapse of the North and to put off the day of the reunification of a country that could develop into a serious rival economically and threat militarily. Current negotiations will probably normalize Japan–North Korea diplomatic relations, with Japan agreeing to give substantial aid, possibly described as reparations.

Meanwhile, however, relations between Japan and South Korea have improved dramatically. Despite, or perhaps because of, the crises in Asian markets in 1997 Japanese and Koreans have embraced each other at a number of levels. Bans on the import of Japanese popular culture, TV cartoons and popular music have been lifted at the same time as serious negotiations began to establish a South Korea–Japan trading area within which tariff and non-tariff barriers would be progressively eliminated. In August 1999 Japan and South Korea held their first ever joint naval exercise and agreements were made for the exchange of defence intelligence (*Japan Times International*, 1–15 August 1999). Resentment at the former colonial power remains strong within Korean culture and it will no doubt erupt from time to time. Nevertheless, the cooperation in hosting the soccer World Cup in 2002 further cemented relations between the two countries.

Japan's relations with Russia remain the most important unresolved area of foreign policy. Full diplomatic relations have not been resumed because of an inability to agree on the sovereignty of four islands to the north-east of Hokkaido which were occupied by Soviet forces shortly after the end of the Second World War. Japan wants them all returned, but Russia has refused to concede anything. Russia would like to conclude an agreement quickly in order to benefit from Japanese economic cooperation in the development of its Far Eastern provinces. However, successive Russian leaders have been reluctant to give up claims to any territory for fear of domestic criticism from the right. LDP politicians, too, have been under pressure from nationalist groups both in and outside parliament not to accept any compromise. President Yeltsin and prime minister Hashimoto agreed in 1997 that the matter should be cleared up by the end of 2000. This date has now passed with no indication that either of their successors has the desire or ability to negotiate an agreement that would be acceptable both in Moscow and Tokyo.

Defence policy deliberately avoided the acquisition of the ability to project power beyond its borders. Instead, Japan has focused on extending its influence through its overseas aid policy. Net disbursements on ODA in 1999 were $15,302 million – well ahead of the USA, in second place at $9,135 million (see table 10.2).

Although the bulk of Japanese aid still goes to Asia, the amounts channelled to Africa and Latin America have increased significantly since the 1980s. Wherever it has been directed, there has been widespread criticism that it has been heavily oriented to 'tied aid' – aid that specified purchase of Japanese products, thus assisting the penetration of Japanese companies into third world markets and often accompanying the FDI strategy of major corporations.

Japan was a founding member of the group of major industrial countries which has met every year since 1975 and is now referred to as the G8 (Japan, USA, UK, France, Italy, Germany, Canada since 1976, EU since 1977, and Russia since 1997). During the 1990s Japan pursued a policy of developing bilateral links with its neighbours at the same time as supporting moves to develop regional organizations. This meant positive engagement with the Association of South-East Asian Nations (ASEAN) and participation in the

Table 10.2　Regional distribution of Japan's bilateral ODA

	1970	1980	1990	1998
Asia	98.3	70.6	59.3	62.4
Middle East	3.3	2.5	1.5	4.6
Africa	2.3	18.9	15.4	11.0
Latin America	−4.0	6.0	8.1	6.4
Europe	−0.2	0.2	6.9	1.7
Oceania	0	0.5	1.6	1.7
Unclassifiable	0.3	1.2	7.1	12.2

Source: Kawai and Suzuki 2000: 123

ASEAN + 10 foreign ministers conference, membership of and support for the Asia Pacific Economic Cooperation (APEC – ASEAN plus thirteen countries of the Asia Pacific rim) and involvement with the Asia Europe Meeting (ASEM – ASEAN plus the fifteen member countries of the EU and China, Japan and South Korea). A new structure '10 + 3' (ASEAN, China, South Korea and Japan) emerged as an economic forum in the aftermath of the Asian financial crisis of 1997. Involvement in these multi-lateral arrangements is important, as some of the bilateral links with countries such as China and South Korea are fragile and volatile, likely to be upset by manifestations of what they perceive as a lack of 'historical awareness' on Japan's part. Periodic controversy about the content of school textbooks and prime ministerial visits to the Yasukuni shrine each August are examples of this.

Conclusion

Japan's influence in international arenas such as APEC and the G8 has hitherto depended not on 'hard power', i.e. military capability, but on 'soft power', 'derived from its economic financial and technological power' (Drifte 1996: 87). However, the prolonged recession, to which there is no end in sight in the early 2000s, suggests that the economic and financial bases of that power are being eroded. For the moment the Japanese economy remains by far the biggest in Asia, but the very size of China, with more than ten times Japan's population, suggests that this will not always be the case. If the Japanese economy does not regain its dynamism, it will not be able to exert leadership in the region, let alone in the world. We may come to conclude that Japan's international influence, such as it was, peaked in the late 1990s only to decline gradually thereafter as China's international status grew. Within such a system Japan would have a special, even unique, position. Perhaps not a 'normal' country of the kind envisaged by Ozawa, but one with a particular point of view deriving from its historical and cultural circumstances. Without being able to lead, it would nevertheless be able to play a significant role within the globalized world, making a contribution as significant (but no more) as that made by countries such as Canada or Sweden.

11

Industrial Policy

Some things that states do are uncontroversial. A state that has no independent foreign or defence policy may not be considered a state at all. However, there are other policy areas, which, one might argue, states should not become involved with and which should be left to the private sector. Industrial policy is one such area. The argument of neo-liberal economists, which had tremendous influence over policy-makers in the 1980s in the USA, UK and beyond, was that market forces can and should be relied on to allocate resources in the best possible way, and that if the state meddles with the market mechanism, resource allocation will be sub-optimal and society's resources will not be used to best effect. Ironically, it was also in the 1980s that evidence was accumulating that one reason, perhaps the main reason, why the Japanese economy had been able to develop so rapidly in the twentieth century, and particularly since 1950, was because the state had devised an industrial policy to facilitate or force changes in the economy that otherwise might not have taken place.

The seminal though contested text on Japan's industrial policy is Chalmers Johnson's *MITI and the Japanese Miracle, 1925–1975*, which not only considered the working of the Ministry of International Trade and Industry (MITI) in some detail, but also proposed a way of thinking about the developmental process that set the parameters for research about economic growth both in Japan and the rest of East Asia. In the first part of this chapter we will summarize the broad outline of Johnson's argument. His account has not won universal acceptance. There are some, mainly neo-liberals, who stick to the 'no miracle occurred' line – that nothing occurred in Japan that cannot be explained by conventional economics. This includes the assumption that even if postwar growth in Japan was rapid, it might have been even more impressive if the state had not distorted the market structure. Others, such as David Friedman (1988), argue that there was something special going on that fuelled the process of growth, but it was not a result of government policy, at least not directly. Finally, there are those who, while being persuaded by Johnson's thesis about the role of the state in Japan's economic development up to 1975 – the period of 'catch-up' – argue that it has been of decreasing significance as the traditional 'smokestack' industries have become less important and 'high-tech' industries have become more so, and leading companies in most industrial sectors have outgrown the Japanese market and become international players (Callon 1995).

But first some definitions. Johnson's account of Japanese economic growth begins with a set of distinctions between states which developed on the Anglo-American pattern, the command economies of the communist world and 'late developers' such as Japan. All pre-industrial states, he suggests, played a similar and limited economic role. However, following the industrial revolution states took on more functions, but ones that had only a marginal impact on the market. Rules and regulations were devised to protect the consumer, to ensure confidence in the banking system and to provide some basic protection for the workers. For the most part, however, the market mechanisms were left free to operate. Johnson calls this a 'market rational economy' governed by a 'regulatory state', and there is no recognition of industrial policy. Countries of the communist world, such as Russia after the 1920s or Eastern Europe after the 1940s, developed command states which dominated 'ideological rational' economies. However, where neither an industrial revolution nor a socialist revolution occurred, some states took on the task of leading the drive to industrialization, establishing a plan which set substantive economic and social goals. Thus a 'plan-rational economy' is created within a 'developmental state', in which economic policies, including industrial policy, are devised to fulfil political ends. In this latter case the basic belief is that market forces will not produce the preferred outcomes, i.e. the allocation of resources which is desired by the political leaders of the state. Japan was the first of this type, but South Korea and Taiwan would be further examples.

What is meant by 'industrial policy' differs according to the analyst, but most would accept the following as a working definition:

> Direct or indirect government intervention in the market place by a range of policy instruments, including taxation, public procurement and state subsidies, to achieve a different allocation of resources at any point in time than would occur through the normal operation of the market place. (Adapted from Patrick 1986: xiii)

This kind of intervention can take place at different levels. It might be that the state attempts to influence the industrial structure so that more (or less) investment flows into (say) mining rather than agriculture, heavy rather than light industry, high-tech manufacturing rather than the service sector. Alternatively, it may seek to promote the development (or facilitate the decline) of certain specific industrial sectors, for example, steel production, computer manufacturing or pharmaceutical drugs. It may want to do so for reasons of national security or industrial promotion or social welfare.

Building the basis for high-speed growth, 1945–70

Massive inflation hindered economic activity in the early months of the occupation; it was running at an annual rate of 1,184.5 per cent in March 1946. An Economic Stabilization Board was created to try to stabilize the production of food and coal, the two staples of the economy. In January 1947 controls were reimposed on all industries and priority was given to three sectors: coal, steel and fertilizers. Between 1946 and 1949, 30 per cent of government expenditure went on industrial subsidies, most of it to these three sectors. Some basic decisions needed to be made at this stage. Should the main emphasis be on light industry and the production of consumer goods or on heavy industry and chemicals? Should priority go to price stabilization or to industrial expansion? The choice was between options that would improve living standards in the short to medium term and those whose impact would be more effective in the long term. In each case the decision taken was to prefer the long-term strategy.

By 1948–9 around 80 per cent of Japan's industrial capacity had been restored, but inflation was still a problem and very little was being exported. At this point the emphasis of US policy towards Japan changed towards ensuring that a strong economic base was established and the influence of the left, particularly the communist party, was eliminated. Both of these objectives could be achieved, it was hoped, through the implementation of the Dodge Plan, which enforced huge cuts in government expenditure, resulting in the loss of 250,000 jobs in the public sector and at least as many in private industry. The exchange rate was fixed at $1 = ¥360, a low level aimed to assist exports. Moreover, the Supreme Commander of the Allied Powers (SCAP) was beginning to return some areas of control back into Japanese hands. Control over the allocation of foreign exchange, the import of technology and licensing of joint ventures was handed over to MITI which was created in 1949 by a merger of the Ministry of Commerce and Industry with the Board of Trade. These powers would be a crucial tool in the operation of an industrial policy in the 1950s and beyond.

Capital was scarce in the 1950s, so, rather than raising funds on the markets, companies tended to borrow money from banks. Indeed, by most western accounting practices they 'over-borrowed' (borrowed more than they could pay back) from the leading financial institutions which, in turn, 'over-borrowed' from the central bank, the Bank of Japan. As long as there was growth and inflation in the system and loans were repaid, all was well. Government banks played a key role in this process. Six were created between 1949 and 1953, of which the most important was the Japan Development Bank (JDB). The JDB got most of its capital from the Fiscal Investment and Loans Programme (FILP), which got its funds from a variety of sources – mostly public savings schemes such as pensions funds and the postal savings system. Until 1973 the JDB was completely under the control of the economic bureaucrats and was an important arm of MITI policy. For example, between 1953 and 1955, 83 per cent of JDB finance went to the electrical power, ship-building, coal and steel industries. Loan applications to the JDB were screened and funds allocated to worthy projects according to priorities that were set by MITI.

MITI's Enterprise Bureau was served by forty-five committees and eighty-one subcommittees, which not only gathered evidence to guide policy formation but also provided advice on training programmes, wages and promotion schemes, as well as creating a consensus among the key players in an industry about appropriate strategies for the future. MITI's control over access to foreign capital enabled it to monitor the purchase of both raw materials and technology. Ministry officials would even accompany company representatives to assist in negotiations to ensure that prices of raw material were low and the quality high. MITI preferred Japanese companies to import foreign technology rather than machinery, and would try to ensure that companies paid as little as possible for patents. The Economic Rationalization Promotion Law enabled government (that is, MITI) to provide companies with tax exemptions or even direct subsidies to purchase state-of-the-art machinery where necessary. Taken together, this set of policy instruments enabled economic bureaucrats to put together packages that could encourage an industry or even an individual manufacturer to make investment decisions that might not otherwise have been taken. Moreover, this policy had a wider influence. Because confidence developed in MITI's ability to 'pick winners', when one company was assisted by a MITI policy package to move in a particular direction, other companies would often decide to invest in the same area even without the benefit of the package, in anticipation that it was likely to become an important sector of the market. And the more often this was true, the more likely it was that the MITI bureaucracy was making self-fulfilling prophecies.

An important instrument used by MITI to implement its industrial policy was 'administrative guidance' (*gyōsei shidō*), 'informal guidelines issued by MITI and other ministries to help specific industries deal with vexing short term problems that threaten to harm the collective interest' (Okimoto 1989: 93). It worked particularly well when there was consensus within the industrial sector (a consensus that often would have been created by one of MITI's committees), where there were relatively few companies or a small number of market leaders (a situation that MITI might have engineered by the selective use of support) and which as a whole was dependent on MITI for some reason (for instance, access to foreign currency or technology). Administrative guidance is not backed by formal legal powers although some sanctions were available to punish non-compliant companies next time they wanted permission to embark on a new project. The key to administrative guidance is that compliance is voluntary, but that it is issued following extensive consultation with key, usually all, actors in a sector.

MITI was not infallible or always able to insist on its policies. In 1953, the ministry refused to approve access to $25,000 for the acquisition of transistor technology from the USA by a small start-up company. It went ahead anyway and signed the patent agreement which it presented to MITI as a *fait accompli*. Soon after, the company changed its name to Sony and succeeded in installing transistors in radios and televisions, making them smaller and cheaper. They sold well at home and abroad. Thus a consumer electronics industry developed outside MITI's protective embrace, suggesting that bureaucratic leadership was not the only explanation for rapid economic development. Neither, as we will see in a moment, was MITI always able to implement its plans if faced by an uncooperative industry. However, rather than attempt a description of industrial policy at a general level, it may be more helpful briefly to consider the development of policy in one industrial sector: automobile manufacture. (The following account relies heavily on Mutoh 1988.)

Towards the end of the occupation there was fierce debate within government on policy towards the automobile industry. On the one hand, the 'free marketeers' in the Bank of Japan wanted to permit the free entry of car imports, while those in MITI wanted to protect the industry from foreign competition. The industry experienced an unexpected boost following the outbreak of the Korean War in 1950. Between July 1950 and February 1951 the USA ordered 7,079 trucks worth $13 million, part of the billion dollar boost given to the Japanese economy by US requisitions during the Korean War. This not only jump-started a dormant industry; it also created a valuable stock of foreign currency that was later used to fund basic industrial growth. By this time, MITI had won the argument with the Bank of Japan and, following talks with the car industry, a basic policy stance was set out with three main elements:

1 Domestic manufacturers would be protected from direct foreign investment and imports.
2 Domestic manufacturers would be permitted to import technology on favourable terms.
3 Government would provide financial assistance.

Protection consisted of a bundle of policies which included tariffs, manipulation of the commodity tax and foreign exchange allocation, quotas to restrict imports especially of small cars, and severe restrictions on investment in Japan by foreign automobile manufacturers. Promotion included access to low interest loans from the JDB, subsidies, special depreciation allowances on equipment, exemption from tariffs for the importation of necessary machinery and relatively easy access to foreign currency to acquire foreign technology. The automobile industry was one of seventeen industries given special promotion, which lasted until 1970. Support was not only given to the automobile manufacturers themselves, but in various ways assistance on training policy, quality control and technical innovation was also provided to the small and medium-sized enterprises (SMEs) which supplied the major manufacturers with the parts that were assembled into the cars. In the case of joint-venture schemes, where Japanese companies assembled cars from parts supplied by foreign companies, MITI insisted that at least 90 per cent of the parts be made in Japan within five years of the start of the agreement. Only four of the six proposed 'assembly' agreements were approved and none survived the 1950s.

There were also broader production plans. It was realized that domestic demand for cars would not develop while the road system was inadequate, so taxes on petrol and liquid petroleum gas and funds from FILP were earmarked for road construction projects. In 1955 MITI floated a plan to produce a 'people's car', a small low-cost vehicle which could be exported. In 1961 it announced a plan to consolidate the industry into two groups that would be big enough to make a major impact on overseas markets.

Road construction was inadequate until at least the 1980s, but development of a road system no doubt contributed to the expansion of the domestic market for cars. The 'people's car' was never built, but the central idea of the need to develop small cars designed for export was adopted by the major manufacturers. The smaller car-producers resisted being forced to merge with either Toyota or Nissan because the domestic market grew more rapidly than expected, and companies such as Honda and Isuzu successfully exported their cars, contrary to MITI expectations.

During the 1960s Japan became a full member of such international bodies as the IMF, World Bank and OECD, and as a consequence became committed to policies liberalizing the economy. Much of the promotion and protection system had to be gradually dismantled, although some non-tariff barriers remained. Close relationships between manufacturers and the car dealers made it difficult to access the Japanese market. The insistence that all imported cars undergo safety checks on Japanese soil slowed down imports.

In 1965, 100,000 vehicles were exported from Japan. This had increased to 700,000 by 1970 and 3,000,000 by 1978, at which point the total output of the Japanese automobile industry was equal to that of the USA. Japanese cars by this time had a reputation for good design and high reliability. Indeed, so successful was the automobile sector as an export industry that countries such as the USA were asking for 'voluntary restraint' by Japanese exporters for fear that their own automobile manufacturers would be forced out of business by Japanese imports. By 1982 the Japanese industry faced 'restraints' in 70 per cent of the world market. At this stage MITI's role had changed from creating the domestic conditions for growth to assisting with negotiations with foreign governments and trade associations to minimize protectionism. One element of this was to use administrative guidance to coordinate 'export restraint'. The industry's response to these protection barriers was to build plant behind them. Thus, in the 1980s we see the major producers – Toyota, Nissan, Honda – building factories in North America and Europe. As these companies transformed into transnational companies, they became less susceptible to MITI guidance.

The contribution of government policy to the growth of the industry is not easy to assess. Certainly, the external circumstances were favourable. From the late 1950s there was rapid and sustained growth in the worldwide demand for cars and few restrictions on trade, at least at first. Within Japan there was fierce competition among domestic producers, which forced prices down and quality up. This meant that the array of protective policies to keep out the small European cars did not create an over-protected, 'hot-house' environment in which domestic producers could rest on their laurels. Demand for their products at home supported the development of cars that sold well overseas. All of this is what is meant when analysts talk of MITI working with (rather than against) market forces. Their supportive measures – to improve the efficiency and technological level of the secondary and tertiary suppliers or provision of export credits or an infrastructure to support export activity overseas – would have been futile if conditions in the international markets had been different or the quality of Japanese cars poor. On the other hand, it is hard to imagine that Japan's export of cars would have increased so rapidly if the Japan External Trade Organization (JETRO), which was funded initially by a tax on imported bananas, had not been present in major markets to facilitate the import of raw materials and the export of manufactured goods.

Would a Japanese automobile industry have developed, or developed as rapidly, without the protection and support from MITI? A neo-liberal economist might argue that the presence of foreign competitors would have spurred Toyota or Nissan to even greater efforts to develop their cars. On the other hand, they may have been unable to compete and left the sector. We should beware of projecting back into the 1950s the economic strength that Japan had achieved by the 1970s. Reischauer, a scholar and experienced analyst of Japan, who later became US ambassador there, remarked in 1957: 'The economic situation in Japan may be so fundamentally unsound that no policies, no matter how wise, can save her from slow economic starvation and all the concomitant political and social ills that would produce' (quoted by Duus 1988: 15).

Japan's economic bureaucrats, trained during the war years and inheriting a tradition of state involvement in the management of the economy that itself can be traced back at least to the mid-nineteenth century, were not going to remain inactive in such circumstances. The Japanese economy grew on average 10 per cent per year between 1955 and 1973 and at least some of that growth can be attributed to the role government played in protecting and promoting such industries as automobile manufacturing. But what of the rest of the twentieth century?

An industrial policy for the next generation, 1973–90

Stability and growth in the world economic system, which had helped sustain Japanese economic growth over the previous two decades, came to an end in the 1970s. This became clear following the two 'Nixon shocks' of 1971 – the floating of the dollar, which allowed the rapid appreciation of the yen, and the opening of diplomatic relations with China – and the oil shock of 1973. The situation facing Japan was by no means as serious as that in the 1870s or late 1940s, but nevertheless the economic bureaucrats remained confident that only they could ensure that the Japanese economy grew faster and/or at less social cost than if left to its own devices. As Patrick puts it, 'MITI officials apparently believe they can better anticipate the long run strategic needs of the economy than the market place which inevitably has too short a time horizon and is unwilling to assume enough risk quickly enough' (1986: 11).

Nevertheless, industrial policy in the 1970s had several new features. To start with, it was a less important part of government's overall economic policy. Secondly, it became less easy for the state to influence the investment decisions of companies, since there was more capital raised through the stock exchange and less borrowed from banks. Thirdly, the use of administrative guidance receded in importance following a court ruling in 1974 that it should be subject to strict limitations (Okimoto 1989: 95). Policy developed into three distinct areas: to promote high-technology industries, to rationalize the structurally depressed industries and to promote ways either to save energy or generate energy from sources other than oil.

Dollar-denominated oil prices increased 4.5 times between January 1973 and January 1974, converting Japan's 1972 trade surplus of $6,624m into a deficit of $4,693m for 1974 (Kawai and Suzuki 2000: 288). The economy began to contract and inflation shot to a wholesale level of 35 per cent in 1974 (Vestal 1993: 170–1). The government's first response was to impose production and price controls; its second was the creation of recession cartels, particularly in energy-intensive industries such as paper, aluminium and cement, but also in structurally depressed industries such as textiles, for which the high oil prices were just one more problem. Compared to the 1950s and 1960s, there was less emphasis on promoting infant industries and more on assisting the development of new technologies. A number of large-scale research projects were funded which were designed to develop new 'next-generation' technologies that would not have been funded by the private sector because of high cost, high risk or the length of the development period. Table 11.1 demonstrates the wide variety of projects that were funded in the 1970s and 1980s.

The funding of these projects looks impressive, but there is some doubt about their success in terms of promoting growth. Those who favour a positive assessment suggest that government funding supported 'infrastructural', 'day-after-tomorrow' research, which no commercial enterprise would back but which had a good chance of generating appropriable outcomes. Many of these research projects were carried out by teams specifically put together for the five–ten-year project and included researchers from universities, publicly funded research institutions and the private sector. This mix of researchers was intended to encourage them to look beyond the bounded vision imposed on them by their specific research environment in a way that is beneficial to all (Fransman 1990: ch. 1). More practically, companies sent researchers to participate in these projects where they could observe and learn 'best practice', which they were then able to disseminate in their own laboratories on their return. Finally, it is suggested that, in a way similar to the projects of the 1950s, this government-funded research could have a knock-on effect. Companies in the private sector may conclude that if a

Table 11.1   Principal MITI R&D projects funded in the 1980s

	Period	Total funding (¥ billion)
Large-scale projects		
Machine production using high-performance lasers	1977–85	13.5
Optical measurement control systems	1979–86	15.8
Chemical manufacturing using carbon monoxide	1980–7	10.6
Deep water manganese extraction	1981–91	6.4
Deep water oil extraction technology	1978–84	18.1
Super-computers	1981–9	13.5
Automated garment production	1982–90	5.3
Robots which function under extreme conditions	1983–90	7.5
Water recycle technology	1985–90	3.2
Database systems	1985–91	1.9
High-tech assembly systems	1986–93	1.1
Satellite sensing for resource deposits	1984–90	9.6
Energy development		
Solar power	1980–	10.7
Thermal energy	1980–	9.6
Coal liquefaction/gassification	1980–	5.3
Hydrogen manufacture, storage, transportation technology	1980–	2.7
Labour-saving/energy-saving technology		
High-efficiency gas turbines	1978–87	4.0
New battery technology	1980–5	1.4
Batteries using new fuels	1981–90	1.5
Sterling engines	1982–7	0.8
Super heat pump/energy accumulations systems	1984–91	0.5
Basic technologies for 'next generation' industries		
New materials – e.g. fine ceramics, material for efficient membrane filtration	1981–	15.9
Biotechnology – e.g. bio-reactors, recombinant DNA technology	1981–	7.6
Others – third generation circuit materials, materials unaffected by light	1981–	9.3

Between 1980 and 1990 the exchange rate changed slowly from $1 = ¥226 to $1 = ¥144
Source: adapted from Vestal 1993: 213–14

particular technology has been picked out for the receipt of government/ MITI money, there must be a good reason. Thus, major companies will often create their own project teams shadowing and competing with those that are being publicly funded.

Others are more sceptical. They argue that the successes that occur would have happened without government support. Company researchers sent out on these projects are rarely the best, and are often close to retirement. Moreover, the sums of money involved are relatively small in comparison to the overall spending on R&D in any industry. Still, these measures did not hamper the development of new technology and they almost certainly helped their diffusion throughout the economy.

Towards a more dynamic R&D policy?

MITI policy for the 1990s was aimed at further developing the promotion of technology policy. R&D policy was justified by reference to the 'ageing society': 'It is extremely important that Japan find solutions to these problems in the next decade, while it still has a strong investment capacity and before it becomes a truly aged society' (MITI 1991: 9).

Supposed backwardness in R&D, particularly in basic research, was identified as one of the main issues. Creating rather than borrowing or buying in technology was emphasized partly in acknowledgement of the fact that Japan had now more or less caught up and was close to the industrial and technological frontier, and partly in recognition of the fact that Japan had an obligation to contribute to the development of scientific knowledge 'as an international public good'. Unfortunately, MITI did not anticipate the downturn in the Japanese economy which continued through the 1990s, one result of which was that total spending on R&D, which had reached 2.75 per cent of the GNP, gradually decreased (Ijichi and Goto 1998: 25). Policies aimed at reversing this included a new programme to create centres of excellence, which started in 1993, and supplementary budgets which, funded through FILP since 1992, have made significant contributions to R&D spending. In 1996 the cabinet adopted a Science and Technology Basic Plan which aimed, among other things, to double government spending on R&D by fiscal 2000 compared to fiscal 1992 (Hemmert and Oberlander 1998: 5).

Even in the 1950s the meetings of the various industry-specific committees functioned at least as much to collate indigenous best practice as to encourage the import of ideas from abroad. These committees sought to devise 'visions' for an industry – a strategy that some consider as being the characteristic feature of Japanese industrial policy-making. The creation of a 'vision' has been a process in which MITI (and to a lesser extent the Science and Technology Agency (STA)) bureaucrats have tried to generate a consensus among the key actors within the industrial sector on where the future of that sector lay before going on to persuade the whole industry to move in that direction. The aim has been to reduce uncertainty about the future and to support movement in a particular direction by the strategic use of funds to back appropriate projects.

In 1996 much was made of the fact that the 'supplementary' budget that was implemented that year included a boost for R&D spending, but it did not do much to disturb the relationship between the sources of finance for research. What is perhaps remarkable is that despite almost a decade of no to very low growth in the economy, there continued to be a steady growth in spending on R&D by both government and industry. Recent R&D promotion policy has been characterized by the requirement of a substantial contribution from industry to support the projects. The Helix project launched in 1995 to develop new technology for genome research received 70 per cent of its funding from government and 30 per cent from industry, and the share was 33:66 in the case of a project to develop satellite technology. Such a policy seems to satisfy the two necessary features of government activity: to be interventionist and small and cheap.

In 2001 MITI became the Ministry of the Economy, Trade and Industry (METI) and announced a new mission composed of five goals:

- focusing not just on industry but more broadly on social and economic systems as a whole;
- promoting the innovation needed to open the way to new social and economic growth;
- finding solutions to global environmental problems, the strains of smaller families and the greying population and other issues;
- initiating policies appropriate for Japan and the international community in the light of increasing economic globalization; and
- being receptive to the values of the elderly, non-profit organizations, regional communities and other players (METI website: www.meti.go.jp/english/other/METIintroduction/).

In March the previous year the Industrial Structure Council had produced a report elaborating the new, broader vision that informs METI policy: 'The challenges of the new age require that economic and industrial policy develop the basic conditions necessary to promote a major encounter between supply and demand, performing a coordinating function' (2000: 6). Such a policy needs to go beyond its traditional concern with industrial competitiveness and look towards 'enhancing the competitiveness of the economic system as a whole'. The aim is to enable 'sustainable growth, participation by senior citizens, and harmony with the environment'. This will require, the report suggests, changes to immigration policy, education policy and social security policy; the creation of an 'Asian economic unit', the creation by Japan of 'its own unique technology by shifting to an open and interconnected innovation system' and radical reform of local government to create 'independent local communities supported by local residents' – all of this to be coordinated by a 'lean, effective state which provides the basic conditions for self-realization' (all quotes from Industrial Structure Council 2000).

It is difficult to know how seriously to take this document. The old assumption remains that market forces will not be able to solve Japan's economic problem, now deflation. METI is needed to act as a 'navigator' to 'propel the Japanese economy' into the twenty-first century. Does this really represent a new page in the development of an effective economic and industrial policy, or is it simply the stringing together of a number of trendy phrases in an attempt to reinvent a new role for a ministry that no longer has an important role to play?

Conclusion

Japanese industry had difficulty competing in international markets during the 1950s and the economic bureaucracy chose to concentrate the country's limited resources, especially foreign currency, on promoting a relatively small number of industrial sectors. Earlier in this chapter we saw how it was done in the case of the automobile industry. Although there is no consensus among economists, the evidence suggests that the rapid economic growth of 1953–73 was, in part at least, due to the government's policies. Some sectors would have grown with difficulty, if at all, without state promotion and protection, although some others developed successfully in the face of MITI indifference.

Interest in Japan's industrial policy was at its height in the late 1980s; as the economy remained in the doldrums during the 1990s it attracted much less attention. Even if the enthusiasm for the 'developmental state' hypothesis as an explanation of Japan's postwar growth has declined, it cannot be said that there is any evidence that the impact of the activity of MITI's committees had no effect, or a negative influence. At the very least, the policy functioned to 'encourage certain industries which were already growth industries to develop sooner than they might have otherwise' (Patrick 1986: 22). This was easier to do while Japan was further behind either in terms of industrial structure or technological sophistication. By the 1990s there were few, if any, sectors where Japan was in any sense 'behind', and, increasingly, advanced industrial states have sought to emulate their rivals' structures in pursuit of technological promotion (see Howells and Neary 1995). Nevertheless, even if the scope of industrial policy has changed and reduced since the 1980s, it will continue to play a significant role in the overall policy process in the twenty-first century.

There is still no consensus on industrial policy. The Asian economic crisis of the late 1990s was evidence for some that the developmental state is obsolete in an age of globalization, and inefficient compared to American-style market capitalism. Detailed studies of the development of companies and industries have shown that not all the 'miraculous' growth within the Japanese economy can be ascribed to government activity. However, Johnson 'never said or implied that the state was solely responsible for Japan's economic achievements' (1999: 34). Crucial to the developmental state is the relationship between the state and 'civilian enterprises'. When the developmental state is working well, 'each side uses the other in a mutually beneficial relationship to achieve developmental goals and enterprise viability' (ibid.: 60). There is no obvious reason why industrial policy could not 'work well', if differently, in an era of free trade internationally and new social goals domestically.

12

Social Welfare Policies

Social welfare provision was not a significant feature of state policy until the twentieth century. This is not to say that there was no state involvement in this area before the modern period. Most states had some kind of structure which served as a safety net for the completely destitute or at least a way of pacifying those among them who threatened to disturb the social order, but they did not usually have many resources to distribute even when they were so minded. In the contemporary context, there is a lively debate about how much the state can or should do.

It is sometimes suggested that a basic principle to guide decisions about social policy should be that a particular action should not produce greater injustice than the one it is trying to alleviate. This sounds fine, but it is difficult to put into operation given that governments are often having to balance one set of short-term consequences against those of the medium to long term. Should social policy simply be about 'safety nets', below which no citizen or human being be allowed to drop? If so, how low should the safety net hang? Or should the state regard social welfare as a tool for income redistribution, so that the wealthy are taxed in order that resources can be provided for the worst off to create a just society?

In every society welfare provision comes from a variety of sources: the home, the profit-making sector, the non-profit-making sector (i.e., volunteer groups and charities) and the state. In all societies most health care, at least primary health care, is provided in the home; in pre-modern societies the rest came from health professionals who were paid for their services with a small amount from non-profit organizations such as religious bodies. Little or nothing came from the state. The same was true of child care and food. Welfare in old age was not a major problem until the twentieth century, but it then became a responsibility that was increasingly taken on by the state, although private provision has always been important. The 'mix' – how much is provided by each sector – will differ from society to society, from one sector to another and perhaps even between social classes or groups within the same sector or society. Historically, the mix may vary over time and, indeed, it may be an object of policy to shift the balance within the mix. In this sense, each country can be said to have a social welfare system characterized by a unique mix. So what is the nature of the system in Japan? (For more on this idea of 'welfare mix', see Rose 1986.)

The aim of this chapter is to outline some features of the historical background to welfare provision in Japan and then critically to review the policy process and nature of provision in two sectors: health care and personal social services.

Some background history

Welfare policy of the late nineteenth century took on some modern aspects, but only in so far as it was devised largely as a response to, or in order to pre-empt, social unrest, and not as a desire to provide minimum standards of living for Japanese citizens. Regulation of poor relief in 1874 was a reaction to popular unrest and amounted to little more than an institutionalization of the meagre welfare structures developed in some feudal local government units. In the later 1890s journalists started to 'discover' the urban poor and, not coincidentally, there was the first glimmer of socialist ideas. The number of people involved in these embryonic socialist groups was tiny, but enough to worry the ruling elite, who feared that if left alone they would create a large social movement able to threaten the stability of the state – as had happened in several European countries including Bismarck's Germany. Therefore a 'social policy' was developed which consisted of measures to restrict the development of the socialist movement, as well as some welfare provision. The most blatant example of this policy was in 1910–11 when twenty-two socialists and anarchists were arrested and eleven executed for allegedly plotting to assassinate the emperor. Soon after these executions, some hospitals were set up to provide free health care for the poor, funded in part by a ¥1.5 million donation from the imperial family (Garon 1997: 48).

Meanwhile, some employers were starting to take an interest in their workers' welfare. Female workers recruited in rural areas would be trained to work in factories for periods of up to three years before returning home. Living in cramped conditions, they would catch tuberculosis or other communicable diseases, which might be so serious that they would be unable to serve out their contracts. It was in the employers' interest then to take care of them, and some companies sponsored mutual benefit associations to protect and promote workers' health. At about the same time factories employing mainly men started to introduce welfare provision as a way of dissuading trained workers from selling their labour power to another employer. The initial phase of industrialization and urbanization had a negative impact on health standards, as can be seen from the average life expectancies, which fell from 44.25 for males and 44.73 for females in 1900–

12 to 42.06 for males and 43.2 for females in 1920–5 (Chōchiku Kōhō Chūō Iinkai 1997: 95).

The labour union movement burst into life in 1917 with demands for higher wages and improved working and living conditions. The response of the Japanese state was the Health Insurance Law of 1922, which created a system based on insurance associations formed by a company or within a local government unit. Employer and employee jointly contributed to a fund which reimbursed in whole or in part whatever a member of the association had to pay for medical treatment. Although passed in 1922, its implementation was delayed until 1927, as the government decided that it could not afford to support the scheme until the aftermath of the major earthquake in Tokyo on 1 September 1923 had been sorted out. Even by the end of the 1920s only two of the sixteen million working people were covered by the system in a total population of sixty-two million (Leichter 1979: 243).

The economic crisis of the later 1920s had particularly severe repercussions in rural areas. Doctors who ran clinics on a fee-for-service basis outside the insurance system would often close down their practices and move to the towns, as people became too poor to pay their bills. This exodus to the cities meant that health already damaged by poverty suffered further decline. Poor health standards in rural areas came first to the attention of the armed forces. They found they were having to reject an increasing number of young men from rural areas as unsuitable for military service. Pressure from the military resulted in the passage of a national health insurance law in 1937 which brought the rural population into a health insurance network based on local government units. This was extended in 1942 so that, in theory at least, nearly all the population had access to low-cost health care. Meanwhile, the administration of welfare was reformed following the creation of the Ministry of Health and Welfare (MHW) from sections of the Ministry of Interior (Naimushō).

The postwar constitution included a reference to welfare provision in Article 25:

> All people have the right to maintain the minimum standard of wholesome and cultural living.
>   In all spheres of life the state shall use its endeavours for the promotion and extension of social welfare and security and of public health.

In practice, however, the laws passed in the occupation to provide relief for the needy deliberately excluded those who were judged to be 'neglecting work or who make no effort maintaining their living'. Moreover, the Civil Code as revised in 1948 obliged 'direct blood relatives and siblings' and 'relatives living together' to support other family members (Garon 1997: 218). In other words, within the legal structure that created the social welfare system there remained a set of assumptions about the central role of the family and the need to avoid supporting the feckless indigent that was consistent with earlier attitudes towards the poor. Nevertheless, the social security budget has expanded inexorably since the 1950s: more than ¥17 trillion was budgeted for social security in financial year 2001 – 36 per cent of the general expenditure budget (*Nikkei Weekly*, 1 Jan 2001).

Medical care

During the Pacific War almost all hospitals and doctors were placed under central control and worked within the health insurance system that covered most Japanese. This might have been the forerunner of a national health service of a British variety, and indeed there were some in the MHW who favoured such a system (Campbell and Ikegami 1998: 59; Leichter 1979: 247). However, the centrally controlled system was not liked by the practitioners and there was little enthusiasm for socialized medicine among the US authorities during the occupation. As a result, the top-down wartime system was dismantled and many features of the pre-war system re-emerged. The medical profession was divided between those who worked in small, usually 'one-man' clinics and those who worked in hospitals, either privately owned, municipally maintained or part of a university hospital system. Self-employed doctors earn more, while hospital doctors have somewhat higher status and the chance to develop specialisms. During the postwar period there has been a trend for the number of small clinic-based doctors to decline – from a majority in 1976 to less than a third in 1997.

Medical insurance developed in a patchwork way. On the one hand, there were the Employer Health Insurance (EHI) systems operated by the larger companies and which covered all their permanent workforce. These were direct descendants of the health insurance associations set up in the 1920s. As of March 1999, 25.8 per cent of the population was covered by one of these 1,800 associations, which are operated by a labour-management committee of the company. Employees of small and medium-sized enterprises were covered by a Government Managed Health Insurance (GMHI) scheme, which is administered at the national level by MHW. This was developed in the 1950s and now covers 29.8 per cent of the population. Employees in the public sector are covered by one of the Mutual Aid Associations (8 per cent of the population). With one or two minor exceptions, such as seamen who are covered by special schemes, the rest of the population, the self- or non-employed, including farmers and small shopkeepers, are covered by the National Health Insurance (NHI) system set up in 1958 and operated through local government. This became fully operational in 1961 and now covers 36.1 per cent of the population (Kawai and Suzuki 2000: 228). The three main insurance programmes are funded to different extents by the employer, the employee and the state, as is illustrated by figure 12.1.

The doctor or hospital's income is worked out from a national schedule for doctors' fees and drug costs. The cost of diagnosis and treatment is decided by MHW on the basis of a points system, which takes into account the amount of time and the cost of the equipment used. Medications are both prescribed and dispensed by 85 per cent of hospitals and 80 per cent of doctors, who sell them at prices decided by the MHW, though they often buy them from

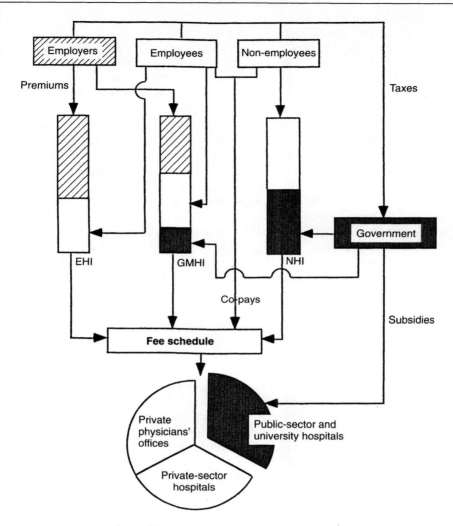

Source: adapted from Campbell and Ikegami 1998: 15

Figure 12.1   Flow of money in Japanese health care

wholesalers for considerably less. This generates significant revenue: 7 per cent of net for hospitals, 12 per cent for 'one-man' practices (Campbell and Ikegami 1998: 148). The national fee schedule applies to all patients irrespective of where they receive their treatment or which insurance scheme pays their bills. Some big companies may provide more health care in addition to the standard schemes, particularly in cases related to preventative care, which is not covered by the insurance systems, but in general an egalitarian principle guides health care provision. There used to be a difference in the amount of co-payment, with some schemes demanding only 10 per cent while others sought 30 per cent, but now all must pay 30 per cent of the cost of treatment up to a maximum (in 1997) of ¥63,000 per month (¥35,400 for low-income families) (Campbell and Ikegami 1998: 94).

Popular support for the LDP began to slip in the 1960s. The party could still win elections at the national levels, but local authorities started to fall to the opposition parties, which promised to take better care of the environment and be more generous with health care provision. The elderly were identified as the core of the nation's poorest and least healthy, a group that was bene-fiting least from the rapid economic growth. The town of Sawauchi, in Iwate prefecture, was the first to offer free medical care for the elderly in 1960 (Pempel and Muramatsu 1995: 58). The policy was adopted in several muni-cipalities and, when Minobe Ryōkichi was elected governor of Tokyo in 1967 with the support of the JCP and the JSP, he too implemented the policy. It proved popular, and in an effort to change the fortunes of the LDP it was adopted by prime minister Tanaka in 1972 as part of a package that would not only increase pensions but develop a western-style welfare state in Japan. However, to the extent that this comprehensive welfare policy had been thought through, it was premised on the Japanese economy growing at the same rate as in the previous decade. Following the oil shock of 1973, however, growth fell from the 9.8 per cent per year achieved over the period 1955–73 to 3.7 per cent in 1974–84 (Calder 1988: 173). From 1975 a serious 're-examination of welfare' began as it was realized that the state would not be able to afford its planned pension increases, particularly following the discovery of the 'ageing society' problem.

As demonstrated in table 12.1, there is no doubt that the percentage of people aged over 65 has been increasing more rapidly in Japan compared to many similar industrial countries, and that by 2050 nearly a third of Japanese citizens will be over 65. While the extent of the 'old people problem' has been exaggerated, possibly for political reasons, there is no doubt that the per capita cost of treatment of old people is high – seven times as high, for example, than for people under the age of 14 (Kawai and Suzuki 2000: 228). Moreover, during the 1980s the amount spent on the elderly increased from 18 to 29 per cent of Japan's health care budget (Campbell and Ikegami 1998: 9).

The MHW was eager to create a comprehensive welfare programme for Japan, but the MoF was reluctant to endorse a policy that would commit the state to ever-increasing amounts of expenditure. In 1979 a think-tank estab-lished by prime minister Ohira proposed a Japanese-style welfare system, in which the family would play a key role in welfare provision. At this time, Japanese government sources started to put out stories about the 'English Disease' which suggested that a major reason for that country's poor eco-nomic performance since the 1950s was the attitude to life generated by the 'cradle-to-grave' welfare system and the excessive use of government revenue for welfare purposes which might otherwise have been used to strengthen productive capacity. Whatever truth there might have been in these arguments, their main purpose in the Japanese context was to support the MoF case against those in the MHW and LDP who wanted to expand welfare provision.

Table 12.1 Proportion of people aged over 65 in selected countries

	Japan	USA	UK	Germany	France	Sweden
1970	7.1	9.8	12.9	13.7	12.9	13.7
1980	9.1	11.2	15.1	15.6	14.0	16.3
1990	12.0	12.4	15.7	15.0	14.0	17.8
2000	17.2	12.5	16.0	16.3	15.9	17.4
2010	22.0	13.2	17.1	19.2	16.6	19.5
2020	26.9	16.6	19.8	21.5	22.2	23.1
2050	32.2	21.7	24.9	28.3	25.5	26.7

Source: Chōchiku Kōhō Chūō Iinkai 1997: 99; updated Nov. 2001

Free medical care for the elderly was ended in 1983. In its place, a new law, Health Care for the Elderly, created insurance funds for the retired (but not yet over the age of 70) and the elderly (over the age of 70). Subsidies came from the three main insurance systems. The burden each of these had to bear was calculated by how much in benefits 'it would have had to pay if it had an average number of the elderly among its enrolees'. This reduced the government share of old people's health care costs from 50 per cent to 20 per cent (Campbell and Ikegami 1998: 137). For the time being, this stabilized the financing of the health care system, but the public was warned that the cost of health care would inevitably rise as the population aged. This provided the background for the introduction of a 3 per cent sales tax in 1989 and its increase to 5 per cent in April 1997. At least part of the justification for this tax was that it was needed to make sure that the state could afford the increased welfare provision.

In the 1990s a new demographic problem became apparent. To keep the Japanese population stable requires a birth rate (i.e., the number of live births per woman) of 2.07. However, over the last 30 years of the century the birth rate steadily declined to 1.34 in 1999. This will mean that Japan's population will peak in 2005 and slowly decline thereafter. So not only will the number of the elderly rise inexorably until 2025, but the number of people entering the job market will decline. Given that both the health care and pensions system are funded by those who are in work, this creates added urgency to the health funding problem. The ageing process cannot be stopped, but policy-makers have been trying to introduce policies that will persuade women to have more children – so far to no avail.

A policy review in the mid-1990s argued that it was important to improve social welfare support for old people and working parents with young children. It suggested that people over 60 should be encouraged to find work if they wanted to. Already by 1987, 36 per cent of males over 65 were working, compared to 16 per cent and 4 per cent in the USA and France (Garon 1997: 225). A survey carried out in 1992 found that whereas just over 37 per cent of workers aged 20–60 wanted to stop work before the age of 70 (and 20.9

Table 12.2   Life expectancy and neo-natal fatality in Japan and selected countries

	Male	Female	Survey date	Neo-natal fatality	Survey date
Japan	77.10	83.99	1999	3.4	1999
USA	73.60	79.40	1997	7.1	1997
UK	74.3	79.48	1996	5.9	1997
France	74.6	82.20	1998	4.8	1998
Germany	73.29	79.72	1994–6	4.6	1998
Sweden	76.18	81.39	1993–7	3.6	1997

Source: Chōchiku Kōhō Chūō Iinkai 1997: 95

per cent before 60), 54.9 per cent wanted to carry on working as long as possible (Chōchiku Kōhō Chūō Iinkai 1997: 112). If more older people choose to stay in full-time work into their 70s, the welfare crisis will not be as severe as some predict, but there seems to be no way that demands made on the medical care system will be reduced.

Japan has managed to keep the amount the state contributes to medical care well below that of comparable industrial countries, at the same time as keeping the amount spent per head below that in most European countries and less than a half that of the USA. (For detailed analysis of how it has managed to do so, see Campbell and Ikegami 1998.) Meanwhile, health care outcomes are similar to or better than those in comparable countries. Life expectancy and neo-natal fatality figures can be used as crude indicators of the success of a health care system; those shown in table 12.2 suggest that Japan can deliver health care as effectively as anywhere else.

However, the total bill for health care will inevitably rise as the population ages and there is some doubt whether the complicated system of cross-subsidization will be able to generate all the new funds needed to provide health care for the elderly. Until the early 1990s the MHW managed to keep the state share of the total social security costs, which includes the health care bill, to less than one-third, and continues to try to restrict the extent of its commitment (see table 12.3). Increases in co-payments were introduced in 1997 and increases in contributions to the company-based insurance associations have kept the problems at bay for the time being. Co-payment charges are unpopular and increases in contributions are disliked at a time when wages have been stable and they are perceived as being used to pay for other people's health care.

The most rapidly increasing cost is that of long-term care for the frail elderly. In 1994 MHW set up a Study Group on Care and Self-Reliance for the Elderly to recommend how to pay for the care of old people when they were unable to look after themselves. A *shingikai* was appointed in February 1995 which was expected to recommend MHW's preferred option of a social insurance method of finance that would be paid by all employees over the age of 20. Normally, a *shingikai* would approve the draft bill according to a scripted scenario in seven–ten sessions. However, this was the era of LDP/JSP/Sakigake coalition and the *zoku* system had broken down. Protests

Table 12.3 Sourcing of social security costs

Year	Insured persons	Employers	State participation	Other public authorities	Income from capital	Other
1970	28.5	31.2	26.4	3.6	8.8	1.6
1980	26.5	29.1	29.2	3.7	9.7	1.8
1990	27.9	31.7	20.3	4.1	12.6	3.5
1999	26.9	29.3	20.1	5.3	14.7	3.6

Source: National Institute of Population and Social Security Research

from local government, health professionals, unions and health insurance associations meant that after twenty meetings a consensus had not been reached among the committee. This alarmed LDP politicians in the run-up to the 1996 general election and so the issue was dropped. After the election a draft bill was finally agreed and passed into law in December 1997 for implementation from April 2000. Its provisions are complex, but it has two key features. The long-term care insurance premium is paid by all 'insurees' over the age of 40 – not 20, as it was thought that older people would be less likely to complain about this new 'tax' and presumably less likely to vote against those parties which introduced it. Secondly, although it is expected that most of the service providers will, in the first place, be local governments, payment of support is devised so as to encourage private sector providers to participate – both non-profit welfare organizations and for-profit companies. Currently, the market is worth $40 billion and can only grow.

Social welfare

In 2000, out of a total budget of approximately $140 billion ($1 = ¥120) about 65 per cent was spent on social insurance, mainly supporting health care, but the next two largest categories were livelihood assistance (7.3 per cent) and social welfare (21.8 per cent). The skeleton of social service provision was created between 1946 and 1964, as described in figure 12.2. We do not have the space here to consider any aspect of these services in detail, but it is important to recognize that the way they are delivered has several idio-syncratic features. For example, while there are only 15,000 welfare officials employed by local government, there are more than 190,000 *minseiiin*, unpaid volunteers who devote an average of ninety days per year to helping with the social problems being faced by the elderly, the poor, the disabled, children or single-parent families (Goodman 1998: 144–5). In other words, those who have the power to enable access to the resources described in the welfare legislation are often not paid employees of government, but volunteers. In this section, I want briefly to describe the background to this system and how it works.

The system has its origins in the period after 1918, when, in the wake of the Rice Riots, a system of district commissioners was created in Osaka to

Category	Name of law	Year of introduction
Low income	Livelihood Protection Law (*Seikatsu Hogo Hō*)	1946, revised 1950

Entitlement: assistance payments for livelihood, education, housing, medical care, childbirth, occupational needs and funerals

Children	Child Welfare Law (*Jidō Fukushihō*)	1947

Entitlement: access to facilities and playground services

Physically handicapped	Law for the Welfare of the Physically Handicapped (*Shintaishōgaisha fukushihō*)	1949, supplemented 1960, revised 1976

Entitlement: access to facilities and training; in 1960 encouraged employment; in 1976 created a fund by fining firms that failed to meet hiring quota of 1.5 per cent of all employees

Mentally retarded	Law for the Welfare of the Mentally Retarded (*Seishin hakujakusha fukushihō*)	1960

Entitlement: access to facilities

Ageing people	Law for the Welfare of Old People (*Rōjin Fukushihō*)	1963

Entitlement: physical examinations, residential care, day care, home helpers, senior citizens' clubs

Mothers with children	Law for Maternal and Child Welfare (*Bōshi fukushihō*)	1964

Entitlement: access to assistance centres, special pensions, temporary residential care

Note: The dates given indicate when the services were first introduced. All these laws have since been amended.

Figure 12.2   Six laws of welfare: Japan's categorical services

record detailed information about poor households and their living conditions and to act as intermediaries between the poor and social services, public or private. The system spread rapidly: there were 10,545 commissioners by 1925 and 74,560 in 1942, by which time the system had been adopted by practically all local government units. At the lowest level, they might help the poor to find employment, medical treatment or funds to assist their children to attend school. As a group, they lobbied for the expansion of the public relief law. Their efforts were successful and in 1932, the first year of the new system, 157,564 individuals received assistance compared to 18,111 the previous year (Garon 1997: 52–6). The commissioners were able to give advice to the not-quite-destitute about access to social services before families fell apart.

They were not, however, advocates of the poor. They were always intended to act as instruments of control and these functions became more apparent as total war approached. During the 1920s they had a key role of seeking 'to prevent the worsening of thought' – i.e. they were to prevent the political radicalization of the 'underclass'. Following introduction of the new public assistance programme in 1932, more people became eligible for relief, but this still excluded all employable persons and provided assistance 'only to those who cannot be assisted by either the family system or neighbourhood mutual assistance'. Social bureau officials frequently expressed their fears that the new law might give rise to a 'consciousness of rights' or 'the dreaded evils of excessive assistance'. In this context the role of the commissioners was to discourage the poor from applying for public assistance, offering instead moral injunctions to the poor to change their ways (all quotes from Garon 1997: 54–7).

The activities of the commissioners came under the control of the central state from 1938, as all programmes were coordinated with the plans to 'mobilize and enhance the human resources of the nation'. Their role was less to aid the poor and more to promote wartime austerity and saving. Meanwhile, more generous welfare provision was made to fatherless families (1937) and health insurance was extended to the country as a whole. Total warfare obliged the state to be concerned about the welfare of all those who were able to play a role in the military industrial mobilization, though it continued to neglect the elderly, the disabled and the mentally ill who were not.

The system survived the reforms of the occupation virtually untouched. Their name was changed to *minseiiin*, welfare commissioners, but there were no purges of their personnel and no new training was provided. Their terms of appointment were:

- to work from a position of equality with those they assist;
- to be appointed by the MHW on the recommendation of local committees;
- to serve three-year terms which could be renewed;
- to receive only out of pocket expenses.

At the end of 1946 there were 127,000 of them, mostly the 'pre-surrender generation of local notables which had little inclination to abandon the moralistic and restrictive approaches of the past' (Garon 1997: 219). It was *minseiiin* who determined eligibility for and the amounts of funds to be provided by the 1946 Livelihood Protection Law, and they routinely recommended levels of assistance well below the maxima in the belief that more generous payments would discourage self-reliance. Revisions of the law in 1950 put the task of determining eligibility into the hands of the full-time officials, but other laws of the 1950s and thereafter gave them a role in the provision of social security to the elderly, juvenile delinquents, the physically and mentally disabled and former prostitutes.

By the late 1980s there were 174,065 *minseiiin* appointed by the MHW, but they were just one of a number of welfare-related semi-official volunteer groups appointed by central or local government. Others included the mother–child health promotion commissioners (*Boshi hokenin*, of whom there were 66,114), social insurance commissioners (*Shakai hokenin* – 141,292) and elderly householders commissioners (*Rōjin Katei hokenin* – 23,555) (figures taken from Zenkoku Jinken Yōgo Iin Rengōkai 1988: 651–3). There are then several hundred thousand semi-official social workers of various kinds, although it would be a mistake to add all these figures together as one person may serve in more than one role.

By law there should be one *minseiiin* for every 120 families in the countryside and every 270 families in cities. Most are relatively old: in 1986, 83 per cent were aged 50–70, 7 per cent were over 70 and in 1992 women made up 46 per cent of the total. They are mainly retired men and women whose children have left home. Most of their work is with the elderly (56 per cent), with the rest of their time being divided between the poor (20 per cent), people with disabilities (10 per cent), children (7 per cent) and single-parent families (7 per cent). Very low rates of take-up of benefit suggest that the *minseiiin* continue actively to discourage those eligible for assistance from claiming their due or that some of those eligible for support prefer to suffer in silence rather than discuss their problems with their middle-class neighbours: less than 25 per cent of low-income families take up their entitlement to welfare benefits. Take-up rates for more specific benefits are even lower: 11 per cent of lone-mother families, 5 per cent of elderly households and 0.8 per cent of households with an elderly person (Goodman 1998: 144–8).

Beyond the *minseiiin* and similar semi-official volunteers, there is a further volunteer sector estimated at 4.5 million working within 56,000 groups which provide massive support for the formal social welfare system, particularly, though not exclusively, assisting the elderly, even though a substantial proportion of these volunteers are themselves retired. There has been considerable rhetoric from politicians and bureaucrats who praise Japan's beautiful customs and claim that practice from antiquity informs the Japanese-style welfare state. If there is anything that is unique about the current Japanese welfare system, it is the way in which the cost is kept low by the extensive use of volunteers and the way they seem to deter full use of the assistance programmes.

Conclusion

Worries about an ageing society have cast a shadow over the whole debate on social welfare since 1980 and they seem likely to continue to loom large. Special emphasis on this came out in the debate between the MHW and MoF in the 1970s on the future of welfare policy, but the bureaucracy seems to have generated a consensus within government and among the people of Japan that this is a serious problem that requires attention. There was very little opposition to the proposal that will progressively delay access to pensions from the age of 60 to 65 over the period 2001–13 which should slow down the growth in social security spending for a while. The low birth rate threatens part of the Japanese-style welfare pattern which has relied on middle-aged wives to look after their aged in-laws. The apparent reluctance of women to have children suggests that in thirty years time, possibly sooner, there will be a significant portion of the population who will have no daughter-in-law to look after them. In such circumstances, solutions to the problem of old people based on nuclear families will not work. One possible, though controversial, solution would be to allow migration, temporary or permanent, so as to bring in the workers and tax-payers needed to keep the social security system operating.

What other characteristics can we discern? First, there is the recurrent notion that poverty should not be rewarded by excessive social welfare. This was part of the philosophy of policy in the Edo era; it was also apparent in the 1920s at the time of the formation of the *minseiiin* system. In the 1970s Fukuda Takeo (who was prime minister in 1976–8) warned that 'completion of the social security system might lead to a citizenship losing its sense of independence and to the production of lazy people' (quoted in Garon 1997: 223). The low take-up of assistance programmes indicates that the *minseiiin* and others continue to discourage receipt of social security. Secondly, there is a focus on the role of the family as the ideal basis for social provision. However, it is less that there is a natural preference for family aid than that, if access to state programmes is impeded by the *minseiiin*, the poor and disadvantaged have to turn to their families for support. Thirdly, there is a strong preference to rely on large numbers of unpaid, untrained volunteers to supplement the small number of professional social workers and to avoid the need to employ large numbers of them. When the *minseiiin* system was founded in the 1920s it had many features of a system of social control rather than social welfare. At the start of the twenty-first century it and similar groups remain very important.

If we return to the notion of 'welfare mix' mentioned in the opening part of this chapter, we can see how the state in Japan became more significant in welfare provision from the 1920s, reaching a peak in 1973. However, as the cost of a comprehensive welfare policy in an ageing society became apparent, policy-makers quickly reverted to one that sought to place more of the burden back on the family, legitimated by reference to traditional customs. For-profit organizations have not played a particularly important role in social welfare so far, but new policy on the provision of long-term care mainly, though not exclusively, for the elderly will encourage private sector provision. One unusual feature is the key role played in a number of welfare areas by groups such as the *minseiiin* which do not fit easily into the welfare mix model. Although not involved to make money, nor employees of the state, these state-directed volunteers have effectively acted as its agents, and have made sure that as much as possible has been done by families.

The social welfare systems will be severely tested in the twenty-first century. Prime minister Koizumi is committed, as I write, to policies which, if ruthlessly implemented, will increase unemployment dramatically. Meanwhile, the social consequences of a low birth rate and extended longevity continue to increase demands for welfare, and the take-up rate of welfare benefits is likely to increase, putting great strain on the welfare budgets. Government is also committed to not increasing national indebtedness any further. Increasing taxation would set back whatever signs of economic recovery might be present. It is hard to see how the commitment to both current levels of welfare provision and economic policy can be maintained. On the other hand, as METI policy makes clear, it may only be possible to restore the 'virtuous cycle of supply and demand' by the re-engineering of robust safety nets that will encourage people to spend rather than save (Industrial Structure Council 2000: 7). In this case, current or even higher levels of expenditure on social welfare may be a necessary precondition to reversing the deflationary spiral.

13

Human Rights in Japan

The Japanese government has been constitutionally committed to the protection and implementation of human rights since 1947. Chapter 3 of the constitution lists in some detail the rights that are to be protected. Nevertheless, ideas of human rights were imperfectly understood by the Japanese public, and policies to implement them were not pursued with any enthusiasm, at least until the 1990s. However, the promotion and protection of human rights have not just been an issue in domestic politics. At the time that the new constitution was being drafted, a Universal Declaration of Human Rights was adopted by the United Nations General Assembly, and over the next twenty years two international covenants were devised to commit states to taking human rights seriously.

Following the US lead in this, as in other aspects of foreign policy, Japan has not been an enthusiastic supporter of the emergent international human rights regime. It was not one of the thirty-five states which were first to ratify the international covenants on civil and political rights and on economic, social and cultural rights which came into force in 1976. Japan only ratified them in 1979 at a time when the Carter administration in the USA was endorsing a human rights-based foreign policy. Even then, Japan did not ratify the first optional protocol, which would have allowed its citizens to appeal to the UN Human Rights Committee if they felt their rights had been infringed by their government.

Ratification of these covenants obliged governments to submit periodic reports on the implementation of their terms. The first report on civil and political rights submitted by Japan in October 1980 was brief – just twelve pages. Most notorious was the comment on section 27 about indigenous minorities, in which it was reported that minorities of the kind mentioned in the covenant did not exist in Japan, thus ignoring the presence of both Ainu and Koreans. A second report was submitted in 1987. Once again, there was no consultation with other groups during the process of writing the report, and non-governmental organizations (NGOs) only got to see it after it was published by the UN. By this time there was greater awareness of the reporting procedure, and twelve NGOs based in Japan submitted 'alternative' reports challenging the government version.

In the 1990s Japan produced two substantial reports on civil and political rights (1992 and 1997) and its second report on economic, social and cultural rights (1998). In the meantime, Japan ratified most of the major rights conventions adopted by the UN: on women in 1985 (CEDAW), on children in 1994 (CRC), on the elimination of racism and discrimination in 1996 (CERD) and on torture in 1999 (CAT). It has also submitted reports related to these covenants. Submission of these reports is followed by hearings held in Geneva by the relevant UN committee, when reports produced by NGOs may also be taken into consideration.

Human rights policy has been driven both by demands made of government by groups within Japan and by the changing international context within which human rights have become increasingly important. In this chapter we will look at the development of postwar policy towards some of the most significant disadvantaged groups: women, Burakumin, Koreans, Ainu and migrant workers.

Women

Patriarchal values have dominated Japanese society throughout most of recorded history. Although there were times when the society acknowledged women as legally responsible, able to own and manage property, in the Tokugawa period they had no rights of inheritance and could be divorced virtually at the whim of their husband. Confucianism, which guided Tokugawa elite thinking, decreed that a woman was subject to the three dependencies: to her father when young, to her husband after marriage and to her eldest son as a widow. Meanwhile, Buddhism offered women little consolation: 'Woman is the emissary of hell: she destroys the seed of Buddha. Her face resembles that of a saint, her heart is like that of a demon' (quoted in Ackroyd 1959: 55). Salvation was not thought to be open to women; the highest reward for practising virtue in this life was rebirth as a man.

Liberal ideas in the 1870s inspired some to argue the case for equality of opportunity and a wholesale change of attitude towards women. There were even some women who demanded the right to vote. However, to the extent that there was a change in attitude towards women in the nineteenth century, it mostly followed the example of Mori Arinori, who, as Minister of Education, supported the education of women but only because it would make them better wives and mothers and thus better able to raise the next generation.

Women's political rights were curtailed by the 1889 Peace Preservation Law, which prohibited them from attending political meetings or joining political parties. From 1925 the prohibition on attending meetings was lifted, but women could neither join parties nor vote until 1945. Schooling was co-educational at the primary level, but women who continued past compulsory education were channelled into single-sex schools where the emphasis was on the cultivation of feminine virtues. It was possible to go on from there to train as teachers, but the prestigious state-run imperial universities were only open to men. A few women were allowed entry after 1913, but in 1940 there were a mere 40 women in imperial universities compared to 29,600 men.

The Civil Code adopted in 1898 was largely unaffected by liberal ideas about women. Ann Waswo summarizes it as follows:

> Only men were legally recognised persons; women were classified in the same category as the 'deformed and mentally incompetent' and needed their father's or husband's consent before entering into a legal contract. A husband was free to dispose of his wife's property as he wished; only a wife's adultery constituted immediate grounds for divorce; in the event of divorce the husband or his parents took custody of the children. (Waswo 1996: 49)

Much changed in the occupation following the constitutional commitment to gender equality, which informed the rewriting of the legal codes of 1946–50. However, formal equality has not led to women playing equal social, political and economic roles, and government has been reluctant to encourage or enable this process. Pre-war attitudes towards women remain deep-rooted. Most women remain defined by and confined to their roles within the family as carers of children and, increasingly, the elderly. It was only at the end of the UN Decade for Women's Rights, 1985, that Japan ratified the UN Covenant on the Elimination of Discrimination Against Women (CEDAW) and passed an Equal Employment Opportunity Law (EEOL).

A Headquarters for the Promotion of Gender Equality was formed within the PMO in 1994 as the successor to a committee which was responsible for the implementation of the terms of CEDAW. This survived the reform of the PMO. National 'plans of action' for women have existed since 1977, and the current version produced in 1996 sets as a target 'to realize a gender equal society by about the year 2010' (United Nations 1997: 13). A minister for women's affairs was created in 1992, although this post has always been taken on by the (male) Chief Cabinet Secretary.

Women have not played much of a role within politics, though this may be changing. A detailed study of the background of members of Japan's lower house found that of the 2,242 individuals elected between 1946 and 1990, only 84 were women. Of these, 39 were elected in 1946, the biggest single intake of women, and 26 of these only served one term. Excluding those elected only in 1946, the breakdown of party affiliation of the 58 successful women can be seen in table 13.1. The JCP puts up more female candidates than any other party but not necessarily in winnable seats. The JSP between 1986 and 1991, when it was led by Doi Takako, the first female leader of a major party, made a concerted effort to persuade women to stand in national and local elections, and in 2000 about half of the SDP's parliamentarians were women.

Women were less successful in the multi-member constituency elections than those that employ lists, which explains why there were more women in

Table 13.1   Women elected to parliament, 1946–90

Party	Number	Percentage
LDP	11	19.0
JSP	24	41.4
JCP	14	24.1
DSP	5	8.6
Kōmeitō	3	3.4

Source: Ramsdell 1992: 180

Table 13.2   Women in national politics

	Number in both houses	Percentage of total
January 1986	27	3.6
February 1990	45	5.9
March 1994	52	6.8
March 1997	57	7.6
July 2000	78	10.7

Source: http://jinjcic.or.jp/stat/stats/18WME41.html

the upper house (13.7–15.2 per cent) than in the lower (2.4–2.8 per cent). The new electoral system seems marginally more friendly to women. The number of women in the lower house increased from 14 (2.7 per cent) to 23 (4.6 per cent) after the 1996 election and there were 35 women (7.3 per cent) elected to the lower house in June 2000. Overall the number of women elected to national parliament almost tripled between 1985 and 2000 (see table 13.2).

Meanwhile, over the same period the number of women elected to serve in local assemblies increased fourfold (see table 13.3). While this amounts to a substantial change, the absolute number remains very small. Involvement (or lack of it) in local politics is important because many national politicians who do not inherit a seat gain their first experience in politics at the local level, and if access to this level is blocked, women will not be able to progress on into national politics. In 2000 the first woman to become a prefectural governor was elected in Osaka. Gender apart, though, she was typical of many LDP-supported prefectural governors having previously had a successful career in MITI and experience working as a deputy governor in a different prefecture.

Women had five posts within Koizumi's first cabinet, two of them in the Ministries of Foreign Affairs and Justice. However, in other respects they were typical LDP ministers. Tanaka Makiko (MFA) is daughter of Tanaka Kakuei and Moriyama Mayumi (MoJ) is an ex-bureaucrat (MoL) and wife of a former LDP cabinet member. Since the early 1990s there has been a convention that no cabinet is complete without at least one woman, and we may see more women in senior posts from now on.

Following ratification of CEDAW, all remaining restrictions on women's eligibility to take examinations for the civil service were removed, but women

Table 13.3 Women in local politics

	Number of women elected to local assemblies	Percentage of total
1984	1,078	1.5
1990	1,633	2.5
1994	2,279	3.5
1997	2,954	4.6
1999	3,872	6.2

Source: http://jinjcic.or.jp/stat/stats/18WME41.html

are still rarely to be found at senior levels. In 1994 only 0.9 per cent of senior posts were filled by women (an increase from 0.3 per cent in 1975), but even this figure would be less impressive if we discounted women in top jobs in the Women and Children's Bureau (formerly MoL, now the Ministry of Health, Labour and Welfare).

Women are only slightly more common in senior management in industry. MoL figures for 1995 show that 1.5 per cent of general manager positions were filled by women (1.2 per cent in 1992) and 2.0 per cent at section chief level (2.3 per cent in 1992). The figures for 1989 suggested that women had slightly better chances of promotion in smaller companies: 3 per cent of general managers in companies with 30–99 employees were female compared to 0.1 per cent in companies with more than 500 employees. Statistics from 1997 show women filling 8.2 per cent of management positions, though one suspects that these are still mainly in the SME sector, and this does not compare well with the figures for other countries: 33 per cent in the UK, 47.7 per cent in the USA, 25.6 per cent in Germany (Akiba 1998: 6).

The EEOL has had very little impact on promotion policy and minimal impact on wages. Figure 13.1 reveals the 'M'-shaped pattern of female employment in Japan, showing how significant numbers of women leave their first employment either on marriage or first pregnancy and rejoin the workforce when their children reach the end of primary school. By the 1990s slightly more women in every age group were at work, except for those aged 15–19, most of whom were still in full-time education. Child care facilities are relatively abundant, but often not conveniently located, or they operate hours that do not allow a mother to work full time. An 'Angel Plan' was put into operation in 1995 to set up child care facilities near stations that would stay open for longer hours. This was, however, less out of any concern for women's rights than as part of a policy to prevent the birth rate from dropping any lower.

In 1985, the year the EEOL was passed, women's wages stood at 51.8 per cent of the male average. This fell to 49.6 per cent in 1990 but rose to 63.5 per cent in 1997. This compares to figures of 71.2 per cent in the UK, 75.5 per cent in the USA and 74.2 per cent in Germany (Akiba 1998: 6). At early stages of their careers, the gap between male and female pay is not large, only 91:100 in the 18–24 age group, but it widens fairly rapidly thereafter. This

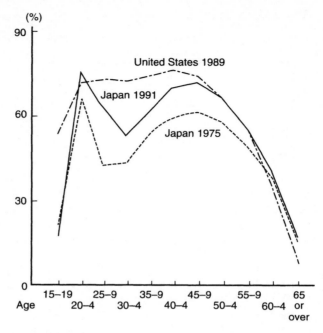

Source: *Economic Eye*, 13 (4) (1992): 10

Figure 13.1 'M'-shaped pattern of female employment

reflects two different phenomena. First, although the EEOL ostensibly forbade discrimination against women, the employers' response was to create a two-track career structure: managerial (*sōgōshoku*) and clerical (*ippanshoku*). A survey undertaken in 1995 by the MoL showed that only 4.7 per cent of companies recruited women to the management track (Watabe-Dawson 1995: 53–4). Only those on the management track can aspire to promotion to senior posts within the company, but in order to achieve this they will have to accept long working hours and extensive job rotation, including transfers within Japan or abroad at short notice. The clerical pathway is mainly for those with only manual or office skills who will rarely be asked to work late or to transfer, but who can be promoted to local management positions at best. Most Japanese women with families are not prepared to commit themselves to such service to the company and few men would sacrifice their careers to support a wife who was.

The EEOL was weak with limited applicability. It did not prohibit discriminatory practices in recruitment, job assignment or promotion, but merely exhorted companies to endeavour to provide equal opportunity. Discrimination in training employees in 'basic skills' is prohibited, but this does not cover 'on-the-job training', which is the primary mode of training in Japan (Watabe-Dawson 1995: 43). A revised EEOL was passed in 1997, effective from 1 April 1999. This changed the provision from 'endeavouring to avoid' discrimination against women to 'prohibiting' it, but there is no provision for ending the two-track system or the penalties to ensure implementation of the 'prohibition'. Government may now assist companies to take positive measures to eliminate discrimination and employers must now pay attention to issues of sexual harassment. Meanwhile, some of the restrictions on female employment on the amount of overtime and night work they can do have been lifted, and measures to 'protect motherhood' have been strengthened.

At the start of the 1990s it was predicted that the looming labour shortage would force major companies to 'feminize' the workplace in order to recruit and retain the best female workers. The prolonged recession of the 1990s meant that they no longer needed to recruit as many women as before and there was evidence of a rise in discriminatory hiring practices: recruitment brochures only sent to male applicants, not employing women who do not live with their parents, only recruiting women when insufficient men can be found. In 1995 there were 133 positions for every 100 male graduates, 45 for every 100 female graduates. Such employment statistics suggest sexist attitudes are deeply rooted and that the revised EEOL will have little effect.

Do we explain this as reflecting the continued dominance of the kind of patriarchal ideas referred to at the start of this section? Does it suggest that the state in Japan is reluctant to impose values on society, preferring instead to promote positive attitudes, teaching by example rather than by regulation? Does the lack of enforceability of the EEOL simply reflect the Japanese preference for dispute resolution by mediation rather than through the courts? Are the measures of the 1980s and 1990s just a compromise between foreign and domestic pressures to conform to CEDAW and ILO standards, without causing expensive inconvenience for major companies? Given the medium- to long-term predictions about the labour shortage in Japan, is it still likely that sooner or later demographic pressure will force employers to enact gender equality in the workplace?

Burakumin

Discrimination was part of the institutional structure of Tokugawa Japan. There were rules regulating the dress and behaviour of the four main classes – *samurai*, peasant, artisan and merchant. Intermarriage was prohibited. Not everyone fell into these four groups, however. On one hand, the nobility and imperial family existed above and beyond this status system and, on the other, in both town and country there were outcaste communities located beneath and outside it. Prejudice against such groups as leather workers, executioners and prison officers was reinforced by regulations passed in the 1720s which gave formal support to customary discrimination and included many who made a living mainly from the land.

In 1871 an Emancipation Edict was issued, freeing outcastes from all status regulations. By the end of the nineteenth century, while former status had become irrelevant in the everyday lives of most Japanese, prejudice and discrimination continued to restrict the lifestyles of former outcastes. As the economy developed, they continued to be marginal to Japanese society. Those in rural areas usually farmed the least productive land and thus had difficulty producing goods for the market economy. In towns and cities their communities became impoverished ghettoes. It should have been impossible to identify them, but when the new family registers were compiled in the 1870s local government officials in some areas marked the forms to indicate a person's former outcaste status or even insisted that all residents in a community adopt the same surname.

Some wealthier Burakumin, as they came to be known, took part in the liberal movement in the later nineteenth century, but in the twentieth century it was the more radical anarchist and socialist conceptions of equal rights that they found attractive. In 1922 Burakumin formed the Suiheisha (Leveller's Society) 'as a new collective through which we shall emancipate ourselves', which survived as an influential social movement into the late 1930s (Neary 1989).

Some expected the US reforms to be so thorough that the economic and social bases of discrimination would be eliminated and no independent social movement would be needed. However, others argued that as the capitalist economic structure was being recreated, Burakumin remained beneath or outside it. The vicious circle that runs from discrimination to poverty to images of dirt and distrust was being reproduced. State intervention, it was argued, was needed to create a virtuous, upward spiral. A successor to the Suiheisha was formed with the creation of the Buraku Liberation League (BLL) in 1955. Supported by the JSP and, to a lesser extent, the JCP, it began to formulate demands for policies to improve living conditions within the Buraku communities. In 1960 the government established a committee to recommend policy. The report, published in 1965, confirmed that Burakumin were living in ghetto-like communities and enjoying a quality of life and educational opportunity substantially poorer than those of mainstream Japanese. It recommended that the state devise policies to address the issue. This resulted in the *Dōwa* Policy Project Special Measures Law (*Dōwa Taisaku Tokubetsu Sochihō*), which had three main components: programmes to build new apartment blocs, clinics and schools; a system of grants and one-off payments to assist the poorest families; and a range of education programmes to boost the performance of Buraku children and to dispel prejudice in the majority society. These policies were initially bundled together into a ten-year plan, which began in 1969. Ten years was not long enough to complete the improvements, and the plan has been extended several times, though each time the scope of the programmes has been slightly slimmed down. By the 1990s the physical appearance of most Buraku communities had been transformed.

Even though not as virulent as before the war, prejudice and discrimination have continued. The two key occasions in a person's life when discrimination is likely to occur are when getting a job and when getting married. On both occasions, it was, and often still is, usual for the prospective employer or parents-in-law to investigate the person's family background. This used to be quite straightforward as there was easy access to family registers, including those of the 1870s which often included mention of feudal status. The BLL campaigned for access to the registers to be closed, and in 1976 the Family Register Law was revised to greatly restrict access to them. This did not deter private investigators, some of whom even published their own lists of known Buraku areas for sale to companies that wanted to avoid employing Burakumin. Osaka prefecture and some other local authorities passed by-laws making it illegal for private investigators to enquire if a person lived in a Buraku area or to pass on such information, but they have not been easy to enforce.

In the 1990s there was evidence of both improvement and continued problems. For example, 92 per cent of Buraku children enter senior high school compared to 96.5 per cent in the non-Buraku sample, but only 28.6 per cent enter higher education – up from 14.2 per cent in 1979, but still well below the national average of 40.7 per cent (*Buraku Liberation News*, May 2000: 114). This is probably related to the fact that only 10.6 per cent are employed in companies with more than 300 workers, compared to the 23.3 per cent national average.

Policies implemented up to the 1990s seem to have made real improvements in the quality of the lives of most Burakumin, but they have been quite different from those that have been implemented in the UK or USA. There, the emphasis has been on creating a framework to ensure formal legal equality in areas such as housing, education and employment. Relatively little has been done to target resources on the improvement of living standards of the minorities. In Japan very large sums – ¥13,880 billion between 1969 and 1996 – have been spent on the improvement projects, but there is still no legislation that makes discrimination illegal. The government view has been that if living conditions could be improved so that they were as good as average, there would be no need for additional legal apparatus to ensure equality of treatment.

Government resisted demands for a Basic Law for Buraku Liberation which would create precisely that kind of legal framework, but in the late 1990s it introduced a series of measures that together amount to the acceptance of the BLL case. Meanwhile, the BLL has broadened its own remit to support a wider set of demands to ensure the full realization of human rights in Japanese society.

Koreans resident in Japan

Although relatively small by international comparison, Koreans form the largest ethnic group resident in Japan, with a population of around 800,000, less than 0.7 per cent of the total population. During the period of colonial rule (1910–45) Koreans formally had the status of Japanese citizens and, indeed, measures were taken to assimilate them by discouraging the use of the Korean language or the display of Korean culture. In the Treaty of San Francisco, Japan formally gave up all claims on its former colonies and at that point the Koreans and the smaller number of Chinese and Taiwanese still in Japan formally became disenfranchised, obliged to register as foreigners at the local government office and excluded from a wide range of social and welfare benefits as well as employment in the public sector (on the Chinese community, see Vasishth 1997).

In 1945 there were about 2.3 million Koreans living in Japan, most of whom had been employed to replace Japanese workers who were fighting on the Asian continent. Although their social and political status was low, and economic situation uncertain, after Japan's surrender some of the pre-war migrants decided to stay in Japan rather than take the risk of returning to Korea, where economic, political and social conditions were even more chaotic. So, although American and Japanese authorities expected, and probably hoped, that all the Koreans would go home, in 1954 there were still 564,146 of them in Japan, of whom 2.4 per cent had been born in what was by then the 'North' (Lee 1971: 157).

Koreans in Japan remained on the margins of society, benefiting least from any economic recovery, and Japanese policy, which defined them as foreigners, helped to ensure this. Meanwhile, the DPRK (Democratic People's Republic of Korea) – i.e. North Korea – took a positive interest in its compatriots, providing funds to create an education system that ran from kindergarten to a four-year college course and subsidizing a network of credit unions that encouraged the development of 'ethnic' enterprises. Such practical support encouraged many Koreans in Japan to join the DPRK-oriented General Federation of Korean Residents in Japan (usually abbreviated to Chongryun) which by the end of the 1950s could claim the allegiance of 72 per cent of the Korean community, while its South Korean (RoK)-oriented rival – Mindan – had the support of only 26 per cent. In fact, many Koreans felt their prospects in Japan were so poor that when in the early 1960s the DPRK offered to help relocate any who wanted to move from Japan to North Korea, more than 80,000 decided to leave. This might have been an embarrassment for Japan – the first and only mass migration from a developed industrial country to a communist state – but as 75 per cent of the emigrants had been claiming livelihood assistance and it meant the reduction in size of the troublesome Korean population, it seems rather to have been welcomed by the government.

The normalization of relations between Japan and the RoK in 1965 meant that Mindan-affiliated Korean residents were granted 'permanent resident status by treaty', giving them greater security and the freedom to travel abroad. Ratification of the two major UN human rights treaties in 1979 prompted the revision of various laws and regulations which affected the Korean community, such that all became eligible to receive social welfare and have access to public housing. New regulations of 1981 granted permanent residence to all 'habitually resident Koreans', which regularized the status of the DPRK-oriented community.

Japanese policy towards the Korean minority up to and including the 1980s seems to have been based on the assumption that they were foreigners presently resident in Japan who would some day leave. They were not regarded as an ethnic minority and not mentioned in either the 1980 or the 1987 reports to the UN. It was difficult for Koreans to acquire Japanese nationality, and in any case their strong national pride discouraged this, as did the two rival organizations which claimed to represent Korean residents. Koreans had to register as foreigners at local government offices every three years, a process that involved them having their fingerprints taken, which many of them found demeaning. They were excluded from professions in the public sector, including teaching and nursing, and they remained liable to deportation for relatively minor offences, even though most had never lived anywhere other than Japan or spoke any language other than Japanese.

The influence of both Chongryun and Mindan was in decline by the 1980s and those active on behalf of Koreans in Japan were, increasingly, third-generation Koreans whose parents had been brought up in Japan. While seeking some respect for their Japanese-Korean ethnic identity, they began to demand the ending of the fingerprinting process, the end to the threat of deportation and the opening of all professions to resident Koreans. Changes were made in policy towards Koreans, but the demands of these groups probably had little impact. As had happened before, the policy change was brought about following consultation between the Japanese and South Korean governments. In brief: the fingerprinting requirement was abolished, the threat of deportation only remains for crimes relating to 'vital national interests', and the visa regime has been made more user friendly. In reports to the UN Human Rights Committee, government commits itself to opening more occupations to qualified non-Japanese, i.e. to resident Koreans, but there has been little progress.

Unable to win political support, some Koreans turned to the legal system. A high-profile case against Hitachi in the 1970s, which alleged that discrimination had occurred in the recruitment of a Korean resident, resulted in a judgement that found the company in breach of both the Labour Standard Law and the Civil Code. Nevertheless, even now many companies will still not knowingly employ a Korean Japanese. An attempt by a Korean nurse to challenge a decision in 1996 by the Tokyo Metropolitan government to refuse to allow her to take an examination which would have led to a management position was turned down by a district court on the grounds that it was a 'natural principle of law' that those who do not hold Japanese nationality cannot be appointed to supervisory positions in local government. Such discrimination in the public sector legitimates discriminatory practices in private companies. On the other hand, some local authorities, Kanagawa prefecture for example, have opened up all but the most senior positions in its administration to permanent residents.

In the early 1990s some Koreans argued before the courts that it was unlawful for them to be prevented from voting in local elections despite the fact that they paid local taxes. The Supreme Court ruled on this in 1995, rejecting the plaintiffs' case but pointing out that it would not be unconstitutional for a law to be passed which did give permanent residents the right to participate in local elections. This passed the buck to the politicians, and for a while it seemed as though some might take up the issue. The topic is still aired from time to time, but one suspects that it will need pressure from outside Japan for there to be further progress.

The number of Koreans marrying Japanese exceeded 70 per cent in the 1990s, which is an indication of a reduction in mutual suspicion. The number of naturalizations increased from a meagre 2,000 per year in the 1950s to around 5,000 each year by 1990 and more than 10,000 after 1995, when the regulations were relaxed somewhat. There were 693,050 Koreans registered in 1991 and 197,479 who took Japanese nationality between 1952 and 1995. If we include the children of 'mixed marriages', the number of people who could claim to be Korean-Japanese must now exceed one million.

The 'myth of return' was powerful among the first and second generations, but most Korean-Japanese now regard Japan as home. Government policy, too, no longer seems to be premised on the notion that Koreans are essentially foreigners who will return home at some point, although it seems to be unable to accept them as a resident ethnic population. If there is a core to current policy, it is that they should acquire Japanese nationality. It is said that only 10–20 per cent of Korean residents use their Korean names, the majority preferring to try to pass as Japanese. There is still some way to go before government or people positively embrace the presence of Koreans within Japanese society and their contribution to the diversity of contemporary life.

Ainu

At the start of the Meiji era there were very few ethnic Japanese living in Hokkaido, even though it was regarded as part of Japan proper and, as such, to be defended from possible invasion by the Russians. Nineteenth-century policy was to treat it as an 'empty land' to be settled by migration and developed with scant regard for the interests of those already there. This required the effective dispossession of the resident Ainu, who, consistent with the social Darwinism of the times, were defined as a 'dying race'. Land on which the Ainu had hunted and fished for centuries was designated for agricultural settlement by Japanese immigrants. Some land was set aside for the Ainu in an attempt to turn them into farmers.

Historically, the Ainu population had never been large, probably at no point greater than 100,000, and they never generated robust socio-political institutions. When they came into contact with the Japanese during the Tokugawa period they were unable to resist the predation of the Japanese merchants, and diseases such as measles that killed a large proportion of their population. In the late nineteenth century the Japanese were able to impose a Hokkaido development policy with no resistance from the Ainu. Very soon they were a small minority group on an island across which they had previously roamed freely. The only concession to them was the 1899 Aboriginal People Protection Act, which gave them some small parcels of land but which bound them to that land in that they were not permitted to sell it without the express permission of the governor of Hokkaido.

In 1930 an Ainu association was set up under government control mainly to contain any dissent, but it did create an arena for the leaders of the isolated communities in which they managed to create a fragile sense of common heritage (Siddle 1997: 24–5). Even this disappeared after 1945. The notion of Ainu nationhood started to reappear in the 1970s as younger Ainu sought to revive their own culture and reassess their history. They were encouraged by support from the Buraku and Korean groups within Japan and contact with other indigenous groups such as the native peoples of the American Arctic. Japan's 1980 report to the UN, which denied their existence, angered both radical and moderate Ainu and prompted them to propose legislation to address the problems they faced in a way similar to the Basic Law on Buraku Liberation. Their demands included reserved seats in central and local government, funds to promote Ainu economy and culture and the creation of a standing council on Ainu issues. Developing this campaign has resulted in a new notion of an Ainu nation linked by language, history and culture, which defines itself as an indigenous people.

Slowly, central government has taken note of these points. In 1995 a Round Table on Policy for the Ainu People was formed, and its report urged legislation that would ensure respect for Ainu language and culture. This became the basis for the Ainu Culture Promotion Law of May 1997, which abolished the humiliating Aboriginal People Protection Law and gave formal recognition to the importance of the promotion of Ainu culture. While an important step forward, this Act contained nothing to improve the economic and social conditions within Ainu communities, and stopped short of recognizing Ainu as an indigenous minority. This would give them more extensive rights compared, for example, to immigrant groups, including the right to some degree of self-determination and to land and resources. This might give Ainu groups the power of veto over development policies, which, for example, sought to build dams in areas they considered sacred. Not surprisingly, Japanese policymakers resist these demands.

Ainu organizations have made significant advances over the last twenty years. Ainu are now recognized as minority residents in Japan who have a different language and culture. However, it remains to be seen how far they will be able to go to win recognition as an indigenous group. Given the small size of the Ainu community – no more than 24,000 – it would not be an expensive policy, and yet would still attract applause from the international community. In its second report to the UN under the ESCR, submitted in 1998, the Japanese government reported on its efforts 'for the realization of a society where the pride of the Ainu people as a race is respected and for the development of a multi-faceted culture in Japan' (United Nations 1998: par. 234). Such a culture is not much in evidence yet, but for the Japanese state to commit itself to such an objective is a significant advance.

Foreign workers

The rapid expansion of the economy of the 1980s created a demand for labour that could not be met domestically. Urbanization and industrialization since the 1950s had drained the rural areas of all their surplus labour. Overall,

Table 13.4 Foreigners resident in Japan

	1990	1993	1996	1999	Change from 1990 (%)
N and S Korea	687,940	682,276	657,159	636,548	−7.5
China	150,339	210,138	234,264	294,201	+95.7
Brazil	56,429	154,650	201,795	224,299	+297.5
Philippines	49,092	73,057	84,509	115,685	+135.6
USA	38,364	42,639	44,168	42,802	+11.6
Peru	10,279	33,169	37,099	42,773	+316.1
Other	82,874	124,819	156,142	199,805	+141.1
Total	1,075,317	1,320,748	1,415,136	1,556,113	+44.7

Source: Ministry of Justice, *The Nikkei Weekly*, Nihon Keizai Shimbun, Inc., 15 January 2001

the population was ceasing to grow and there were some jobs – dirty, dangerous and difficult – that young Japanese did not want to do. Meanwhile, the value of the yen was rising and Japan became the destination of choice for enterprising young workers in Asia and Latin America. The scale of the 'problem' can be exaggerated (and often is). For policy-makers the difficulty is to try to balance the need to ensure a steady flow of labour to meet the demands of domestic industry with the need to satisfy critics that the arrival of these immigrants will not threaten Japan's cultural homogeneity. However, before looking at the policy aspects of the issue, we need to try to make sense of the statistics and distinguish between different types of foreign worker.

Discussion of this issue often starts with reference to figures of the total number of foreigners in Japan – 1,556,113 in 1999, up from 1,075,317 in 1990 (see table 13.4). However, this figure also includes all permanent residents, most of them Koreans (626,000), wives of Japanese nationals (260,000), and students (25,000) (Ministry of Justice 1999). Secondly, there are among this number many white-collar foreign workers who have 'special or technical abilities and unique skills ... [who] ... will help Japan to become more vitalized and internationalized' (United Nations 1992: par. 52). These are mainly from the industrialized countries of Europe and North America and their presence in Japan is not regarded as a problem; indeed, they are seen as a positive contribution to Japanese society.

It is the unskilled workers, especially those who are not in possession of valid work visas, whose presence is regarded as, or likely to become, a problem. The number of unskilled workers, both legal and illegal, increased rapidly in the 1980s with the number of undocumented workers being around 200,000 by 1991. A fourth group of workers, who form a sub-group of the above, are the female immigrants who have arrived in Japan to work in the entertainment industry. About half of all the female workers, mostly from Thailand, the Philippines and Taiwan, are in this category and a large proportion of them end up in sex-related occupations. The most serious human rights violations are encountered by workers in these latter two categories.

Immigration law was changed in 1990 in four significant ways. First, it became somewhat easier for skilled foreign workers to gain entry. Secondly, Latin Americans of Japanese descent could get easy access to visas and were not limited to the kind of work they could do. Thirdly, employees were for the first time subject to sanctions if they were caught employing foreigners illegally. Finally, a system of on-the-job training was established that would permit small and medium-size factories to employ workers from developing countries in unskilled jobs as long as they could demonstrate there was some training element.

Parts two and four of this law require further explanation. During the first half of the twentieth century there had been a steady flow of migrants from Japan to Latin America, particularly to Brazil, where in 1990 there were 1,228,000 people of Japanese descent (Ferreira de Carvalho 2000: 38). Until 1988 very few of them returned to Japan, but migration increased rapidly over the next few years, encouraged by the 1990 legislation, such that by 1998 there were 224,299 Brazilians in Japan (up from 56,429 in 1990 despite the economic recession of the 1990s) and 41,317 Peruvians. Official policy is that immigrants of Japanese descent are likely to have knowledge of Japanese culture, even though few of them speak Japanese, and will therefore be more easily absorbed into Japanese society.

By the end of the 1980s it was clear that in some industries foreign workers were playing an indispensable role. In the construction and smelting sectors as many as a quarter of the employees were from overseas, many 'undocumented'. Meanwhile, government was placing increased emphasis on its ODA programme as an important dimension of foreign policy. In this context, the Keizai Dōyukai and Tokyo Chamber of Commerce and Industry suggested the creation of a 'work and learn' programme that would recruit foreigners to work in Japanese factories while being 'trained' (Shimada 1994: 56). Such a system was enabled by the 1990 immigration law and elaborated by guidelines issued in 1993 by MoJ which suggested how employers should provide return fares, accommodation and both 'initial' training and ongoing practical training.

This policy has so far managed to balance contradictory demands. The commitment not to allow free access to the Japanese job market has been maintained, while the relaxation of controls on Latin Americans of Japanese origin and the 'foreign trainee' scheme have enabled the continued flow of labour into sectors of industry that are unable to recruit Japanese workers. It is unclear whether it has reduced the flow of undocumented workers. Each year in the 1990s about 50,000 such workers were detected (one-third of them women) and it is estimated that there remain 250,000–300,000 who are overstaying their visas or who are in some other way illegal. To the extent that the flow of workers into Japan has been reduced, it is more likely to be due to the state of the Japanese economy than the impact of the migration policy.

Male foreign workers employed in manual occupations receive wages on average only 50–70 per cent of their Japanese peers. Moreover, where workers have been recruited by agents, some of whom have links with organized crime, they may find that a large portion of their earnings goes to others. Although all workers are covered by the minimum wage legislation and the laws on workplace accident compensation irrespective of nationality, illegal workers are not in a position to complain to the authorities, since this would reveal their illegal status and make them liable to immediate deportation (Japan Federation of Bar Associations (JFBA) 1993: 176–7). Similarly, although there is no nationality restriction in the national health insurance system, many foreign workers do not subscribe, either because they do not know about it or because the premiums seem too high. A liberal interpretation of the Livelihood Protection Law enabled local governments to provide emergency medical treatment to short-stay and undocumented foreign workers. However, MHW directed in 1990 that this should cease and over the next few years there was further tightening up of the regulations restricting access to both regular and emergency health care. In other words, there are significant infringements of the economic and social rights of foreign workers. Those on the trainee schemes have better legal protection, but there is evidence that companies provide little or no training and not much by way of a training allowance.

Female workers are even more vulnerable to exploitation. In 1990 MoJ estimated that 55.6 per cent of foreign female workers were employed as 'hostesses'. Mounting evidence suggests that agencies recruit Thai and Filipino women who arrive in Japan unaware that they will be asked or forced to work as prostitutes. The JFBA has documented many cases of women being imprisoned and kept as virtual slaves during their stay in Japan (Japan Federation of Bar Associations 1993: 178–80).

The mix of policies taken by Japan seems to have worked, but it will only be tested when the Japanese economy starts to grow once more and demand for labour increases. If the number of foreigners in Japan has increased over 40 per cent during an economic recession, how fast will it grow if and when the Japanese economy starts to grow again? Japan's population will peak in 2005 and thereafter decline, while the proportion of old people will increase until 2025. If the economy expands while the size of the working population declines, the demand for immigrant workers will certainly grow and the framework of the 1990s is unlikely to be adequate. Some estimates suggest that as the size of the population decreases, Japan will need 600,000 immigrants every year to maintain the nation's workforce and productivity (*Nikkei Weekly*, 15 January 2001).

Government may have to relax immigration control and abandon the notion of Japan as a monocultural society. While economics and demographics suggest this might be unavoidable, to do so would, in the words of the Japanese government, 'cause considerable effects on the Japanese economy and society', which will require careful consideration (United Nations 1997: par. 30). There is, to say the least, no consensus on this in Japan at the moment.

Given a total of 125 million, the immigrant worker population is tiny. They are, however, to be found mainly in urban areas of Tokyo where they are highly visible. At the same time there are now more than 100,000 'foreign spouses', mainly wives, of Japanese who are spread across the country. Rural depopulation in the 1970s and beyond meant many farmers arranged marriages with Chinese, Korean or Filipino women when they were unable to find Japanese women willing to be farmers' wives. The Japanese school system is facing considerable problems, unused as it is to children with a 'double' cultural background. As these children grow up, not only the educational systems but the whole of Japanese society will need to adapt to cope with these new citizens.

Japanese society has prided itself on its monoculture, but now has to confront a number of problems. Evidence from the Korean and Ainu cases suggests that there may be slow acceptance of the way Japan is developing a multifaceted culture. Can the country go further to accept that this diverse immigrant community may be able to add one or more new facets to its culture?

A human rights policy for the twenty-first century

Socialist Party prime minister Murayama Tomiichi may have caused his party to abandon many of its signature policies soon after he took office in June 1994, but he did bring with him a commitment to human rights policies. A high-profile committee was created in the PMO in 1995 to formulate Japan's plans for the UN Decade of Human Rights Education. During that year rapid progress was made on the ratification of the Convention on the Elimination of all forms of Racial Discrimination (CERD) – regarded as a lost cause by many human rights activists. It became effective in January 1996. Hashimoto Ryūtarō took office as prime minister that same month, but the government's commitment to human rights was sustained, and the following December a Law for the Promotion of Human Rights Protection was passed. This committed the state not only to the promotion of human rights education, but also to ensuring protection to those whose rights had been violated. A committee, nominally under the chairmanship of the prime minister, was set up to create within two years a plan on human rights education and within five years a report on ways to provide redress for human rights victims. The proposals for establishing human rights education in Japan, published in 1998, set out the aims of ensuring equality before the law and respect for the individual in nine named areas: women, children, old people, the disabled, Dōwa issues, Ainu, foreigners, HIV patients and former prisoners. This was followed in December 2000 by a law which committed central government to formulating a basic plan on human rights education and human rights consciousness-raising about which an annual report will have to be submitted to parliament.

At least part of the reason for this sudden interest in rights issues is that Japan is now openly campaigning for a permanent seat on the Security Council of the United Nations. At the same time, pressure groups such as the JFBA, the BLL and Korean groups started to demand that government take human rights seriously. Moreover, there are now a number of grassroot networks that promote interest in children's and patients' rights. It may be that the human rights movement in Japan has now achieved a critical mass.

More remains to be done. Ironically, the organization that looks increasingly superfluous is the one apparently most committed to human rights promotion. In the late 1940s a system of civil liberties commissioners was created with the twin aims of spreading awareness of the human rights listed in the constitution and providing an easily accessible means of redress for victims of human rights violations. Very similar to the *minseiiin* system, it uses volunteers under bureaucratic (MoJ) control. It has not been in the vanguard of the human rights movement and many activists are dismissive of its work (more detail in Neary 1997). In 1991 the UN devised a set of principles that set out guidelines for the creation of national human rights institutions, known as the Paris Principles. Since 1999 a committee has been studying ways in which the civil liberties commissioner system might be restructured so as to be compatible with these Paris Principles.

There is no regional human rights framework in Asia, the only region of the world not to have one. Such a structure is unlikely to emerge in the same way as in Europe, the Americas or Africa, but there is a possibility that one might develop based on a federation of national human rights institutions (NHRIs). Indeed, there already exists an Asia Pacific Forum of NHRIs with seven members. If a robust organization can be created within Japan, then it may be able to play a role in the development of an Asian transnational mechanism for human rights protection.

Japan was reluctant to adopt a human rights dimension to its domestic or foreign policy, despite its unequivocal constitutional commitment. Ratification of the UN covenants in the late 1970s and early 1980s provided some added protection for residents in Japan, but little progress was evident thereafter. The first optional protocol to the UN civil and political rights covenant is not likely to be ratified and Japan seems firmly committed to the use of the death penalty, the topic of the second optional protocol. However, significant changes in policy have been made in the 1990s as, for example, government seemed to accept the need for legal support for women in the workplace, that Koreans will remain in Japan, that Ainu have a right to a separate culture and that the Dōwa/Buraku problem is related to broader human rights issues. Attitudes to foreigners may prove more resistant to change, but even these are covered in the most recent legislation. If Japan is going to be able to contribute a distinct voice to regional and international affairs, human rights may well be a key theme.

Conclusion

In the Introduction to this book I suggested that my main aim was to outline the basic structure of Japanese politics and give a broad indication of where it is going. By way of a conclusion, I want to risk a few comments on the nature of the Japanese state and the likely future of party politics.

Many outside observers are impressed by the size and apparent power of the state in Japan. It is often perceived to be bigger and/or stronger than its equivalent elsewhere in the developed world. This view is also shared by some Japanese and, indeed, it was for this reason that reformers in the 1990s decided that the state needed to be restructured, slimmed down and decentralized. On the other hand, one can point to the empirical data that suggest it is quite small, a feature it shares with some other East Asian states. One explanation of the ability to combine small size with authoritative government might be that some aspect of Confucian tradition still active within the political culture makes non-political actors more likely to take account of the wishes of government than in non-Confucian states. While I would not want to dismiss political culture as a significant influence, there are other more proximate explanations.

Muramatsu and Krauss suggest that the reason for the integration of state and society is that one party has been in power for most of the time since 1955, and that party, the LDP, has been responsive to a wide variety of social interests (1987: 537). Calder (1988) goes further to suggest that the LDP has deliberately devised an electoral policy to take on new issues so as to develop new bases of electoral support. The LDP's prolonged dominance of party politics and its links with central and local government and national and local capital has obviously helped. However, there are also structural features of the state–society boundary that keep the state small but pervasive.

For example, in 1996 there were ninety-two public corporations with a total of 600,000 employees and 784 managing directors – which were supervised

220   CONCLUSION

by, but often not regarded as part of, central government. Top management
posts are filled by retired bureaucrats from the supervising ministry. Organizations such as JETRO and the JDB played a key role in the implementation of MITI industrial policy in the 1960s and 1970s. We might also note that
a slightly less grand form of *amakudari* also occurs at the local level, with
high-ranking prefectural and municipal officers retiring to take up posts in
semi-public bodies which serve the locality. The Japanese government would
look considerably bigger if we were to include the personnel and activity of
these bodies.

If these public corporations lie on the state side of the state–society boundary, there are a number just over on the society side that are routinely subject
to state influence. The Japan Pharmaceutical Manufacturers Association is a
pressure group funded by the major Japanese drug companies, with most of
the posts filled by workers seconded from them. However, the executive
manager is always a recently retired senior official from MHW who will serve
in the post for two years before moving on to an executive position in a pharmaceutical company (Howells and Neary 1995: 49). This is not just a way in
which the state extends its control over society, in this case the drug manufacturers. There is an important sense in which the industry is employing such
an official to ensure it has access to latest government thinking. As Johnson
says, when the developmental state is working well, 'neither the state nor the
civilian enterprise prevails over each other . . . each side *uses* the other in a
mutually beneficial relationship' (Johnson 1999: 60). While there are examples of MITI guidance being ignored or resisted by individual companies,
most of the time there is compliance with pre-agreed policy. One could find
examples of this in the way that most other ministries relate to organizations
outside the state, formally defined.

Also situated along this boundary are the advisory councils, *shingikai*.
While it would once again be unreasonable to regard these simply as ways
to project state power over non-state actors, there is growing evidence from
'micro'-policy studies that illustrates how *shingikai* function less to provide
outside input into the policy-making process than to serve to legitimate pre-
selected policies. To take just one example: in the process of devising a system
to fund long-term care for the elderly, MHW appointed a *shingikai* to make
suggestions on socialized care. However, this was not an independent body
engaged in objective study. 'The scholars and experts were assembled to lend
their authority and prestige to the bureaucrats' preferences.' And, unsurpris-
ingly, their report recommended just what the ministry wanted even if on this
occasion it took somewhat longer than expected (Etō-Murase 2000: 33).

Another strategy to keep the cost of government low but its influence
pervasive is to encourage the development of voluntary groups which are
nevertheless under the close control of the responsible ministry. In chapter
12, on social welfare, we noted the 190,000 *minseiiin* who supported the work
of 15,000 paid social workers. They are just one of a number of groups of reliable citizens who do good work at the behest of full-time central or local government workers. Not all these groups work in welfare; the MoJ created the
civil liberties commissioners in the 1940s to enable the ministry to promote,
monitor and control demands for greater human rights protection. There are

also road safety groups and crime prevention associations which liaise with the police. This apparently 'voluntary' sector of mostly elderly citizens acting under ministerial guidance extends the range of state authority at minimal cost. Beyond them there are also a number of genuinely independent voluntary groups, although even some of these are open to state influence.

A fourth tendency has been for the Japanese state to encourage the formation of groups to represent the interests of sectors of society that have been under its control, or incorporate into state structures those which were not. In her monumental study of Nōkyō (Farmers' Cooperatives), Mulgan shows how from the time of their formation they were always more of a top-down creation of government than a bottom-up farmers' movement (2000: 66). When the state was having difficulty controlling the Buraku Liberation League, it encouraged the formation of Dōwa groups which were more biddable. The administration of the Dōwa projects would often include representatives of the local BLL branches that was similar to the involvement of Nōkyō in MAFF schemes.

But are these structures changing? The structure of the state has been radically reformed since 1999. Fewer ministries exist. The number of *shingikai* has been drastically reduced. Parts of central government have already been 'agency-fied' and there are plans to privatize even more. Koizumi's reforms may disrupt the system described above. He has spoken of the need to strengthen regulation of the *amakudari* process and seems determined to carry through the process of reform of central government started in January 2001.

It remains to be seen whether this will interrupt the patterns of authority that have been developed since the end of the Second World War. If the flow of personnel between public and private bodies and between the bureaucracy and politics continues, then it may be that the change in the formal structures will not disrupt the informal linkages that are important in the policy-making process. Despite reform, we may need to take heed of a Chinese observer who remarked:

> In East Asia, the pattern of state society relations historically differs from the modern western pattern and the distinctive features of the East Asian pattern do not simply disappear after industrialisation or democratisation. In East Asia the states are organisationally pervasive, without clear cut boundaries. . . . Consequently, the lines between public and private, political and personal, formal and informal, official and non-official, government and market, legal and customary and between procedural and substantial are all blurred. This is the case in pre-communist China, semi-authoritarian Taiwan as well as democratic Japan. (Ding 1994: 317)

How resilient will the contours of this East Asian pattern be to the reforms? One doubts whether reform will do much to define the state–society boundary clearly. To subscribe to this view is not an attempt to exoticize or orientalize Japanese political activity, setting it apart from 'normal' western practice. It is a conclusion no different from pointing out the common features of the Nordic countries of Europe that set them apart from their neighbours.

Reformers in the 1990s looked to western governments, particularly Britain, as a source of inspiration for reform both of the administrative structures and of electoral arrangements. The aim was to create a stable two-party system, preferably composed of two conservative parties. What is the likelihood of this?

Koizumi not only supported administrative reform; he has also argued for reform of the LDP. His selection of cabinet colleagues in spring 2001 took little or no account of faction allegiance. Although he has massive popular support (at the time of writing), he is not liked within the LDP. Some suggest that he might risk splitting the party if they oppose his reform strategy. Meanwhile, observation of the DPJ shows it to be composed of at least four factions and deeply divided on fundamental issues such as constitutional reform. Dramatic action by Koizumi which split both the LDP and DPJ and created a new party around him and his policies is not inconceivable. However, the Japanese political system has never favoured charismatic leaders for long. Would there be a basis for a political organization that could survive Koizumi's fall from power? It seems unlikely. Moreover, the list system in both house election systems and state subsidies for party finance give support to existing parties and would penalize party breakdown.

The party system seems complex, but a broad pattern is emerging in which only the LDP, DPJ and JCP can offer a future to those who want to enter Japanese politics or who are already in it and want to have greater influence. The New Conservative Party has no independent appeal or base, the Liberal Party is dependent on one man, Ozawa Ichirō, the SDP only slightly less dependent on one woman, Doi Takako. The Kōmeitō future is assured but only as the political wing of Sōka Gakkai. The JCP has integrity and serious policies that offer a genuine alternative to those of the government. It may never be the party of government, but it has a hierarchy that offers prospects for recruits and permits just enough internal debate to keep the elite attentive to policy innovation. The DPJ is able to attract ambitious young people, established politicians who want to end the LDP domination of power and support groups who fear being isolated from policy processes through their identification with the SDP. While it stays together, it can entertain the realistic ambition of replacing the LDP in power. Divided, its members have no permanent home. The LDP, while lacking principle and policy, has the massive advantage of being in power with all the rewards that can bring to its members. Tensions threaten the stability of each of these three parties, but the reasons for staying together far outweigh the temptations of breaking up.

There is little prospect for a stable two-party system in the foreseeable future. What seems most likely is two major parties, the LDP and the DPJ, with two smaller parties, Kōmeitō and the JCP, existing in the margins and kept in business by their loyal supporters. As Pempel (1998) concludes, neither the LDP nor any other party will be able to recreate the unchallenged hegemony of the 1950s and 1960s any more than the economy will reproduce the unchallenged success of that time. Both political and economic systems are entering an era of uncertainty.

References

Ackroyd, J. A. 1959: Women in Feudal Japan. *Transactions of the Asiatic Society of Japan*, 7: 31–68.

Akiba, F. 1998: Women at Work. *Look Japan*, 43 (504): 4–11.

Akizuki, K. 1995: Institutionalising the Local System: The Ministry of Home Affairs and Intergovernmental Relations in Japan. In H.-K. Kim, M. Muramatsu, T. J. Pempel and K. Yamamura (eds), *The Japanese Civil Service and Economic Development* (Oxford: Clarendon Press), pp. 337–66.

Baerwald, H. H. 1974: *Japan's Parliament: An Introduction* (Cambridge: Cambridge University Press).

Bailey, P. J. 1996: *Postwar Japan 1945 to the Present* (Oxford: Blackwell).

Beasley, W. 1989: Meiji Political Institutions. In M. B. Jansen (ed.), *Cambridge History of Japan. Vol. 5, The Nineteenth Century* (Cambridge: Cambridge University Press), pp. 618–73.

Benson, J. and Matsumura, T. 2001: *Japan 1868–1945* (Harlow: Pearson Educational).

Berger, G. M. 1988: Politics and Mobilisation in Japan 1931–1945. In P. Duus (ed.), *Cambridge History of Japan. Vol. 6, The Twentieth Century* (Cambridge: Cambridge University Press), pp. 97–153.

Broadbent, J. 1998: *Environmental Politics in Japan* (Cambridge: Cambridge University Press).

Calder, K. E. 1988: *Crisis and Compensation: Public Policy and Political Stability in Japan 1949–1986* (Princeton: Princeton University Press).

Callon, S. 1995: *Divided Sun: MITI and the Breakdown of Japanese High Technology Policy, 1975–1993* (Stanford: Stanford University Press).

Campbell, J. C. and Ikegami, N. 1998: *The Art of Balance in Health Policy: Maintaining Japan's Low Cost Egalitarian System* (Cambridge: Cambridge University Press).

Chōchiku Kōhō Chūō Iinkai (Central Council for Savings Information) 1997: *Seikatsu to Chōchiku Kanren Tōkei* (Statistics on Life and Savings) (Tokyo: Nihon Ginko Service Kyoku).

Cohen, T. 1987: *Remaking Japan: The American Occupation as New Deal* (New York: The Free Press).

Day, S. 1999: Understanding the World of the Japanese Communist Party. Unpublished paper presented at the Japanese Politics Colloquium, Birmingham University.

Ding, X. L. 1994: Institutional Amphibiousness. *British Journal of Political Science*, 24 (3): 293–318.

Dower, J. 1993: Peace and Democracy in Two Systems. In A. Gordon (ed.), *Postwar Japan as History* (Berkeley: California University Press), pp. 3–33.

Dower, J. 1999: *Embracing Defeat* (London: Allen Lane).

Drifte, R. 1996: *Japan's Foreign Policy in the 1990s* (London: Macmillan).

Duus, P. 1988: Introduction. In P. Duus (ed.), *Cambridge History of Japan. Vol. 6, The Twentieth Century* (Cambridge: Cambridge University Press), pp. 1–52.

Duus, P. and Scheiner, I. 1988: Liberalism and Marxism, 1901–1931. In P. Duus (ed.), *Cambridge History of Japan. Vol. 6, The Twentieth Century* (Cambridge: Cambridge University Press), pp. 654–710.

Etō-Murase, M. 2000: The Establishment of Long Term Care Insurance. In H. Otake (ed.), *Power Shuffles and Policy Processes* (Tokyo: JCIE), pp. 21–50.

Ferreira de Carvalho, D. 2000: Nikkeijin Lineage and Identity, PhD thesis, Sheffield University.

Francks, P. 1999: *Japanese Economic Development: Theory and Practice* (London: Routledge).

Fransman, M. 1990: *The Market and Beyond* (Cambridge: Cambridge University Press).

Friedman, D. 1988: *The Misunderstood Miracle* (Ithaca and London: Cornell University Press).

Fujioka, A. 1997: *Gyōsei no Shikumi ga Wakaru hon* (A Book to Understand the Administrative Structure) (Tokyo: Daiyamondosha).

Fukuoka, M. 1993: *Seiji no Koto ga Wakaru hon* (A Book to Understand Politics) (Tokyo: Kamki Shuppan).

Fukuoka, M. 2001: *Seiji no Shikumi* (The Political System and How it Works) (Tokyo: Daiyamondosha).

Garon, S. 1997: *Molding Japanese Minds: The State in Everyday Life* (Princeton: Princeton University Press).

Goodman, R. 1998: The 'Japanese Style Welfare State' and the Delivery of Personal Social Services. In R. Goodman, G. White and Huck-ju Kwon (eds), *The East Asian Welfare Model* (London: Routledge), pp. 139–58.

Gotoda, M. 1994: *Sei to Kan* (Politics and Bureaucracy) (Tokyo: Kōdansha).

Haley, J. O. 1995: Japan's Postwar Civil Service. In H.-K. Kim, M. Muramatsu, T. J. Pempel and K. Yamamura (eds), *The Japanese Civil Service and Economic Development* (Oxford: Clarendon Press), pp. 77–101.

Halliday, J. 1975: *A Political History of Japanese Capitalism* (New York and London: Monthly Review Press).

Hanneman, M. L. 2001: *Japan Faces the World 1925–1952* (Harlow: Pearson Education).

Hata, I. 1988: Continental Expansion 1905–1941. In P. Duus (ed.), *Cambridge History of Japan. Vol. 6, The Twentieth Century* (Cambridge: Cambridge University Press), pp. 271–314.

Hemmert, M. and Oberlander, C. 1998: The Japanese System of Technology and Innovation. In M. Hemmert and C. Oberlander, *Technology and Innovation in Japan* (London: Routledge), pp. 1–19.

Horie, K. 1989: Senkyo Seido Kaikaku no Shimureeshon (Simulating Reform of the Electoral System). *Ekonomisuto*, 67 (27): 138–44.

Howells, J. and Neary, I. 1995: *Intervention and Technological Innovation: Government and the Pharmaceutical Industry in the UK and Japan* (London: Macmillan).

Hoye, T. 1998: *Japanese Politics: Fixed and Floating Worlds* (New Jersey: Prentice Hall).

Huffman, J. L. 1998: *Modern Japan: An Encyclopedia of History, Culture and Nationalism* (New York: Garland).

Hunter, J. 1984: *Concise Dictionary of Modern Japanese History* (Berkeley: University of California Press).

Ijichi, T. and Goto, A. 1998: Restructuring Basic, Applied and Developmental Research. In M. Hemmert and C. Oberlander, *Technology and Innovation in Japan* (London: Routledge), pp. 23–36.

Industrial Structure Council 2000: *Economic and Industrial Policy in the 21st Century* (Tokyo: METI).

International Institute for Strategic Studies 1999: *The Military Balance 1998/9* (London: Oxford University Press).

Inoguchi, T. 1988: The Ideas and Structure of Foreign Policy. In T. Inoguchi and D. I. Okimoto (eds), *Political Economy of Japan. Vol. 2, The Changing International Context* (Stanford: Stanford University Press), pp. 23–63.

Inoguchi, T. 1997: Japanese Bureaucracy: Coping with the New Challenge. In P. Jain and T. Inoguchi (eds), *Japanese Politics Today* (Melbourne: Macmillan), pp. 92–107.

Inoguchi, T. and Iwai, T. 1987: *Zoku Giin no Kenkyū* (Research on Zoku Members of Parliament) (Tokyo: Nihon Keizai Shimbunsha).

Inoki, T. 1995: Japanese Bureaucrats at Retirement: The Mobility of Human Resources from Central Government Public Corporations. In H.-K. Kim, M. Muramatsu, T. J. Pempel and K. Yamamura (eds), *The Japanese Civil Services and Economic Development* (Oxford: Clarendon Press), pp. 213–34.

Institute of Administrative Management 1997: *Organisation of the Government of Japan* (Tokyo: Administrative Management Bureau, PMO).

Japan Federation of Bar Associations (ed.) 1993: *A Report on the Application and Practice in Japan of the ICCPR* (Tokyo: JFBA).

Jiji Tsushinsha (ed.) 1997: *Seikan Handobukku* (A Handbook of Politics and Administration) (Tokyo: Jiji Tsushinsha).

Johnson, C. 1982: *MITI and the Japanese Miracle, 1925–1975* (Tokyo: Charles E. Tuttle).

Johnson, C. 1999: The Developmental State: Odyssey of a Concept. In M. Woo-Cumings (ed.), *The Developmental State* (Ithaca: Cornell University Press), pp. 32–60.

Johnson, S. 2000: *Opposition Parties in Japan* (London: Nissan Institute/Routledge).

Kabashima, I. 1998: The Upper House Election: How the LDP Went Down to Defeat. *Japan Echo*, 25 (5): 10.

Kabashima, I. 1999: An Ideological Survey of Japan's National Legislators. *Japan Echo*, 26 (4): 9–16.

Kabashima, I. 2000: The LDP's 'Kingdom of the Regions' and the Revolt of the Cities. *Japan Echo*, 27 (3): 22–32.

Kaneko, M. 2001: An Analysis of the 2000 General Election in Japan. *East Asian Review*, 5: 3–28.

Kataoka, T. 1991: *The Price of a Constitution* (New York and London: Crane Russak).

Kato, T. 2000: From a Class Party to a National Party. *AMPO: Japan Asia Quarterly Review*, 29 (2): 38–40.

Kawai, N. and Suzuki, Y. (eds) 2000: *Japan Almanac 2001* (Tokyo: Asahi Shimbun).

Keizai Kōhō Center (ed.) 1998: *Japan: An International Comparison* (Tokyo: Keizai Kōhō Center).

Koh, B. C. 1989: *Japan's Administrative Elite* (Berkeley: California University Press).

Komiya, R. and Itoh, M. 1988: Japan's International Trade and Trade Policy. In T. Inoguchi and D. I. Okimoto (eds), *Political Economy of Japan. Vol. 2, The Changing International Context* (Stanford: Stanford University Press), pp. 173–224.

Kosai, Y. 1988: The Postwar Japanese Economy, 1945–73. In P. Duus (ed.), *Cambridge History of Japan. Vol. 6, The Twentieth Century* (Cambridge: Cambridge University Press), pp. 494–537.

Kwon, H.-J. 1998: Democracy and the Politics of Social Welfare: A Comparative Analysis of Welfare Systems in East Asia. In R. Goodman, G. White and Huck-ju Kwon (eds), *The East Asian Welfare Model* (London: Routledge), pp. 27–74.

Lam Peng Er 1996: The JCP Organisation and Resilience in the Midst of Adversity. *Pacific Affair,* 69 (3): 361–79.

Lee Chang-soo 1971: The Politics of the Korean Minority in Japan. PhD thesis, University of Maryland.

Leichter, R. M. 1979: *A Comparative Approach to Policy Analysis: Health Care Policy in Four Nations* (Cambridge: Cambridge University Press).

Livingston, J., Moore, J. and Oldfather, F. (eds) 1976: *The Japan Reader 2* (London: Pelican Books).

Mabuchi, M., Kume, I. and Kitayama, T. (eds) 1997: *Seijigaku* (The Study of Politics) (Tokyo: Yuhikaku).

McKean, M. and Scheiner, E. 2000: Japan's New Electoral System. *Electoral Studies,* 19: 447–77.

Ministry of Justice, Immigration Bureau, 1999: *Statistics on Foreign Residents* (Tokyo: Ministry of Justice).

Mitani, T. 1988: The Establishment of Party Cabinets. In P. Duus (ed.), *Cambridge History of Japan. Vol. 6, The Twentieth Century* (Cambridge: Cambridge University Press), pp. 55–96.

Mitchell, R. H. 1996: *Political Bribery in Japan* (Honolulu: University of Hawaii Press).

MITI Industrial Structure Council, 1991: *International Trade and Industrial Policy in the 1990s* (Tokyo: MITI).

Miyawaki, A. 1993: The Fiscal Investment and Loan System Towards the 21st Century. *Japan Research Quarterly,* 2 (2): 15–66.

Mulgan, A. G. 2000: *The Politics of Agriculture in Japan* (London: Routledge).

Muramatsu, M. 1994: *Nihon no Gyōsei* (Japan's Administration) (Tokyo: Chūōkōronsha).

Muramatsu, M. 1997: *Local Power in the Japanese State* (London: California University Press).

Mutoh, H. 1988: The Automotive Industry. In R. Komiya, M. Okuno and K. Suzumura (eds), *Industrial Policy of Japan* (Tokyo: Academic Press Japan), pp. 307–31.

Nakano, M. 1997: *The Policy-Making Process in Contemporary Japan* (London: Macmillan).

Namikawa, S. 1997: *Gyōsei Kaikaku no Shikumi* (The Structure of Administrative Reform) (Tokyo: Tōyōkeizai Shimbunsha).

Neary, I. J. 1989: *Political Protest and Social Control in Pre-War Japan: The Origins of Buraku Liberation* (Manchester: Manchester University Press).

Neary, I. 1997: The Civil Liberties Commissioners System and the Protection of Human Rights in Japan. *Japan Forum,* 9 (2): 217–32.

Neary, I. 2000: Serving the Japanese Prime Minister. In B. G. Peters, R. A. W. Rhodes and V. Wright (eds), *Administering the Summit* (London: Macmillan), pp. 196–222.

Noguchi, Y. 1995: The Role of the Fiscal Investment and Loan Program in Postwar Japanese Economic Growth. In H.-K. Kim, M. Muramatsu, T. J. Pempel and K.

Yamamura (eds), *The Japanese Civil Service and Economic Development* (Oxford: Clarendon Press), pp. 261–87.

Oinas-Kukkonen, H. 1996: The Principal Japanese Communist Leaders in the View of US Officials 1944–6. In I. J. Neary (ed.), *Leaders and Leadership in Japan* (London: Japan Library), pp. 206–16.

Okimoto, D. I. 1989: *Between MITI and the Market: Japanese industrial policy for high technology* (Stanford: Stanford University Press).

Otake, H. 1998: Overview. In H. Otake (ed.), *How Electoral Reform Boomeranged* (Tokyo and New York: Japan Center for International Exchange), pp. ix–xxi.

Otake, H. 1999: Developments in the Japanese Political Economy. *Government and Opposition*, 34 (3): 372–96.

Ozawa, I. 1994: *Blueprint for a New Japan* (Tokyo: Kodansha).

Patrick, H. 1986: *Japan's High Technology Industries* (Seattle: University of Washington Press).

Pempel, T. J. 1998: *Regime Shift: Comparative Dynamics of the Japanese Political Economy* (Ithaca: Cornell University Press).

Pempel, T. J. and Muramatsu, M. 1995: Starting a Pro-active Civil Service. In H.-K. Kim, M. Muramatsu, T. J. Pempel and K. Yamamura (eds), *The Japanese Civil Service and Economic Development* (Oxford: Clarendon Press), pp. 19–76.

Preston, P. W. 1998: *Pacific Asia in the Global System* (London: Blackwell).

Preston, P. W. 2000: *Understanding Modern Japan* (London: Sage).

Pyle, K. B. 1988: Japan, the World and the Twenty-first Century. In T. Inoguchi and D. I. Okimoto (eds), *Political Economy of Japan. Vol. 2, The Changing International Context* (Stanford: Stanford University Press), pp. 446–86.

Ramsdell, D. B. 1992: *The Japanese Diet: Stability and Change in the House of Representatives, 1890–1990* (Lanham: University Press of America).

Rose, R. 1986: The State's Contribution to the Welfare Mix. In R. Rose and R. Shiratori, *The Welfare State East and West* (New York and Oxford: Oxford University Press), pp. 64–79.

Reed, S. R. 1999: The 2000 General Election. *Japanese Journal of Political Science*, 2: 337–9.

Richardson, B. 1997: *Japanese Democracy* (New Haven and London: Yale University Press).

Sasaki, T. 2000: Assessing the Obuchi Administration. *Japan Echo*, 27 (4): 21–5.

Schonberger, H. B. 1989: *Aftermath of War: Americans and the Remaking of Japan 1945–1952* (Kent, Ohio: Kent State University Press).

Schwartz, F. J. 1998: *Advice and Consent: The Politics of Consultation in Japan* (Cambridge: Cambridge University Press).

Shillony, B. A. 1991: *Politics and Culture in Wartime Japan* (Oxford: Clarendon Press).

Shimada, H. 1994: *Japan's 'Guest Workers'* (Tokyo: University of Tokyo Press).

Siddle, R. 1997: Ainu: Japan's Indigenous People. In M. Weiner (ed.), *Japan's Minorities* (London: Routledge), pp. 17–49.

Smethurst, R. J. 1972: The Creation of the Imperial Military Reserve Association in Japan. *Journal of Asian Studies*, XXX: 815–28.

Smethurst, R. J. 1974: *A Social Basis for Pre-war Japanese Militarism* (Berkeley: University of California Press).

Smith, R. J. 1996: The Japanese (Confucian) Family. In Tu Wei-ming (ed.), *Confucian Traditions in East Asian Modernity* (Cambridge, Mass.: Harvard University Press), pp. 155–74.

Stockwin, J. A. A. 1991: Japan's Opposition Parties and the Prospects for Political Change. *Japan Foundation Newsletter*, XIX (2): 1–6.

Stockwin, J. A. A. 1999: *Governing Japan* (Oxford: Blackwell).

Stockwin, J. A. A., Rix, A., George, A., Horne, J., Ito, D. and Collick, M. (eds) 1988: *Dynamic and Immobilist Politics in Japan* (London: Macmillan).

Takizawa, A. 2001: *Seiji Nyusu ga Omoshiroi hodo Wakaru Hon* (Tokyo: Chukei Shuppan).

Tsuneoka, S. (ed.) 1993: *The Constitution of Japan* (Tokyo: Kashiwashobo).

Tsuzuki, C. 2000: *The Pursuit of Power in Modern Japan 1825–1995* (Oxford: Oxford University Press).

United Nations, 1992: *Third Periodic Report of Japan Under the CCPR* (CCPR/C/70/Add.1).

United Nations, 1997: *Fourth Periodic Report of Japan Under the CCPR* (CCPR/C/115/Add.3).

United Nations, 1998: *Second Periodic Report, Japan, Implementation of the ICESCR* (E/1990/6/Add.21).

Vasishth, A. 1997: The Chinese Community: A Model Minority. In M. Weiner (ed.), *Japan's Minorities* (London: Routledge), pp. 108–39.

Vestal, J. E. 1993: *Planning for Change* (Oxford: Clarendon Press).

Wada, S. 1998: The Electoral System and Political Reform. In H. Otake (ed.), *How Electoral Reform Boomeranged* (Tokyo and New York: Japan Center for International Exchange), pp. 173–7.

Waswo, A. 1996: *Modern Japanese Society* (Oxford: Opus).

Watabe-Dawson, M. 1995: An Overview: Status of Working Women in Japan under the EEOL of 1985. *Waseda Journal of Asian Studies*, 19: 41–63.

Weir, T. 1999: Tanaka Kakuei and the Politics of Post-war Japan. PhD thesis, University of Ulster.

Weiss, L. 1998: *The Myth of the Powerless State* (Ithaca: Cornell University Press).

Woo-Cumings, M. 1995: Developmental Bureaucracy in Comparative Perspective: The Evolution of the Korean Civil Service. In H.-K. Kim, M. Muramatsu, T. J. Pempel and K. Yamamura (eds), *The Japanese Civil Service and Economic Development* (Oxford: Clarendon Press), pp. 431–58.

Wright, M. 1999: Who Governs Japan? Politicians and Bureaucrats in the Policy Making Process. *Political Studies*, XLVII: 939–54.

Zenkoku Jinken Yōgo Iin Rengōkai, 1988: *Jinken Yōgo Iin no Tebiki* (A Civil Liberties Commissioner's Handbook) (Tokyo: Ministry of Justice).

Journals referred to in the text

AMPO
Buraku Liberation News
Daily Yomiuri
Economic Eye
Japan Echo
Japan Times International
Jurisuto
Law in Japan
Nikkei Weekly

Index